I BELIEVE
I'LL GO
BACK HOME

CW00504436

OTHER BOOKS FROM BRIGHT LEAF

House Stories
The Meanings of Home in a New England Town
BETH LUEY

Bricklayer Bill
The Untold Story of the Workingman's Boston Marathon
PATRICK L. KENNEDY AND LAWRENCE W. KENNEDY

Concrete Changes
Architecture, Politics, and the Design of Boston City Hall
BRIAN M. SIRMAN

Williamstown and Williams College
Explorations in Local History
DUSTIN GRIFFIN

Massachusetts Treasures
A Guide to Marvelous, Must-See Museums
CHUCK D'IMPERIO

Boston's Twentieth-Century Bicycling Renaissance
Cultural Change on Two Wheels
LORENZ J. FINISON

Went to the Devil
A Yankee Whaler in the Slave Trade
ANTHONY J. CONNORS

At Home
Historic Houses of Eastern Massachusetts
BETH LUEY

Black Lives, Native Lands, White Worlds
A History of Slavery in New England
JARED ROSS HARDESTY

At Home
Historic Houses of Central and Western Massachusetts
BETH LUEY

Flight Calls
Exploring Massachusetts through Birds
JOHN R. NELSON

Lost Wonderland
The Brief and Brilliant Life of Boston's Million Dollar Amusement Park
STEPHEN R. WILK

Legends of the Common Stream
JOHN HANSON MITCHELL

I BELIEVE
I'LL GO
BACK HOME

ROOTS AND REVIVAL IN
NEW ENGLAND FOLK MUSIC

THOMAS S. CURREN

BRIGHT LEAF
Amherst and Boston
An imprint of University of Massachusetts Press

I Believe I'll Go Back Home has been supported by the Regional Books Fund, established by donors in 2019 to support the University of Massachusetts Press's Bright Leaf imprint.

Bright Leaf, an imprint of the University of Massachusetts Press, publishes accessible and entertaining books about New England. Highlighting the history, culture, diversity, and environment of the region, Bright Leaf offers readers the tools and inspiration to explore its landmarks and traditions, famous personalities, and distinctive flora and fauna.

Copyright © 2021 by University of Massachusetts Press
All rights reserved
Printed in the United States of America

ISBN 978-1-62534-565-3 (paper); 566-0 (hardcover)

Designed by Deste Roosa
Set in Anodyne and Minion Pro Condensed
Printed and bound by Books International, Inc.

Cover design by 4 Eyes Design
Cover art by Iraid Bearlala, "Musical instruments." Shutterstock.com.

Library of Congress Cataloging-in-Publication Data
Names: Curren, Thomas S., author.
Title: I believe I'll go back home : roots and revival in New England folk music / Thomas S. Curren.
Description: Amherst : Bright Leaf, an imprint of University of Massachusetts Press, 2021. | Includes bibliographical references and index.
Identifiers: LCCN 2020053165 (print) | LCCN 2020053166 (ebook) | ISBN 9781625345653 (paperback) | ISBN 9781625345660 (hardcover) | ISBN 9781613768181 (ebook) | ISBN 9781613768198 (ebook)
Subjects: LCSH: Folk music—New England—History and criticism.
Classification: LCC ML3551 C87 2021 (print) | LCC ML3551 (ebook) | DDC 782.42162/13074—dc23
LC record available at https://lccn.loc.gov/2020053165
LC ebook record available at https://lccn.loc.gov/2020053166

British Library Cataloguing-in-Publication Data
A catalog record for this book is available from the British Library.

For Declan, Hattie, and Lila

Remembering
the place out in the ocean
off of Kittery Point
where all the winds are laughing
and where you can still find
magic dragons,
mean pirates,
and whiskey in the jar.

The prodigal son
left home, strange land,
and he became destitute,
and hungry, and weary.
And then he came to his self:

"I believe I'll go back home."

—REVEREND ROBERT WILKINS,
introducing his song "The Prodigal Son"
at the Newport Folk Festival, 1964

CONTENTS

CONTENTS

PREFACE

Washington Irving began the first edition of his *Sketch Book* with a piece he titled "The Author's Explanation of Himself," which has always struck me as a fine way to begin a literary relationship. The book that I am honored to place in your good hands is about music and history in the context of the culture and character of New England. My experience has been that writing about traditional music is more like improvising from an old recipe than following a formula; it's a lot more like making a chowder than filling a prescription. You can learn to make a pretty good chowder with a variety of ingredients as long as you avoid tomatoes. Over the course of six years, I've spent a lot of time putting this kettle together and hope that along with good fresh local codfish, I've gotten the right amount of sage, salt, pepper, potatoes, top milk, butter, and onion into the mix.

This work comes out of a combination of music, memory, experience, and conversation, coupled with the reading and research that I've done over fifty years, out of my love of both traditional music and the New England region. Anyone who reads this book will quickly see that I am not a scholar, but I've endeavored to cite and footnote published resources that I heartily recommend to the reader as worthy of further attention. I urge you, as well, to seek out the sound of a ticking clock that, these days, can often be encountered only near an easy chair in the reading room of a local library. Significant amounts of critical literary, musical, and historical resources are not "making the cut" to digitization (indeed, like some of the best of the old music), but these vintage volumes and pamphlets are well worth discovery by anyone who wishes to arrive at an understanding of human events as they were remembered by their participants.

I have been fortunate to know some wonderful people in the world of folk music; I am deeply indebted to them, and grateful to have been entrusted with their thoughts, their impressions, and their stories. As points of memory and recollection included here, they are accurate, yet they may not be exact. Of course, everyone is free to have their own tastes and opinions, as the written record of *Broadside* and *Sing Out!*

and much of the character and course of traditional, folk, and popular music history demonstrates.

I'll begin by giving special thanks to my wife, Kathy Neustadt. She is not only a faithful and loving partner, but she has also been a tolerant and attentive listener to countless stories that by now she could probably recite better than I can. More to the point here, she has been a skilled and extremely patient editor for an unschooled and, at times, obstinate writer. Kathy's own book, *Clambake,* is a prime example of what a serious cultural inquiry should be, and if this piece, one way or another, has fallen short of that high mark, the responsibility is mine. Thank you, sweetheart.

I want to thank Glynn Talley for fifty years of friendship and for the character and clarity of his vision over the decades. We have shared a love of music and continue to rejoice in harmony of all kinds. Over the years, after our hunting, fishing, and antiquing expeditions, we have spent long nights sharing home brew and peanuts and swapping our perspectives. In all that time, I've never managed to adequately define or explain the term "folk music" to Glynn, which probably has a lot to do with the fact that I grew up in the green pastures of suburbia and he was raised on a cotton farm in West Texas. I hope that these stories help.

This work reflects conversations that I've had with Fred Barzyk, Art Bryan, Peter Childs, John Cohen, Rob Cox, Bonnie Dobson, Ed Freeman (who taught me how to play the guitar), Carl Hultberg, Jim Kweskin, Jack Landrón, Dudley Laufman, Catherine Linardos, Michael Melford, Sylvia Miskoe, Alan McIntyre, Geoff Muldaur, Carolyn Paton, Gerry Putnam, Tom Rush, Jim Rooney, Betsy Minot Siggins, Felice Linardos Silverman, Jack Sloanaker, Dayle Stanley, Rick Sullo, Nancy Sweezy, Caitlin von Schmidt, Helen von Schmidt, Don West, David Wilson, and others. My inspiration has been accelerated and illuminated by the photographic work of Rick Sullo, Ed Freeman, and Roland Schermann, and through Peter Guralnick's books. My thanks go to all of these good folks who have invited me into their lives and who have shared remembrances of the music they love.

My heartfelt gratitude goes to those who have read parts or all of this manuscript and made helpful suggestions: Molly Curren Rowles, Becca Curren Kronenbitter, Susanna Witt, Sydney Lea, Margaret Baker-Salmon, Tom Bocci, Jane Nylander, Carolyn Rudy, and Daniel Sussman. For their support, enthusiasm, and inspiration, past and present, I would also like to thank Ada Felch Allen, Chance Anderson, Rachel

Armstrong, Janet Baker-Carr, Forrest Berkley, Martin Berman, Don Berry, Kitty Boyle, Joe Breiteneicher, Alan Brownell, Elizabeth Butters, Ron Cameron, Randolph Carter, David Coburn, Michael Cohen, Dale and Twyla Cook, Nick Cross, Elisabeth and George Curren, Chris Curren, Mike Curren, Kurt Davis, Steve Davis, Chris Dellea, Nestor Deshaies, Don and Martha Dolben, Sue Drouin, Jay Espy, Lou Ferland, Andy Fussner, Joan Gilmour, Phil Ginsburg, Frank Griswold, Donald Hall, Ralph Heyward, Mark Humpal, Donna Sprague Huntoon, Roy Hutchinson, Heather Keene, Jane Kenyon, Russell Lary, Jacqueline Laufman, Billy Lawrence, James Livermore, Mary McGowan, Kim Moburg, Bud Moore, Bob and Betty Moulton, Willard Murray, Becky and Ted Neustadt, Mary Jane Ogmundson, Alice Parker, Peter Peirce, Myrl Phelps, Jr., Don Pingree, Brian Quinn, Chris Ramsey, Peggy Randol, Mary Lyn Ray, Warren and Rachel Remick, Dustin Rowles, Fred Rozelle, Aaron Rubinstein, Mary Lynn Sabourin, Taylor Seidler, Dick and Nan Smart, Todd Smith, George Sugai, Casey Cross Sussman, Homer Tarr, Jeffrey Taylor, Bud Thompson, Kate Thompson, Amy Townsend, Nancy Vasilis, Carl Vigeland, Lisa Wenner, Dan and Linda Wentworth, Sam Worthen, and Phil Zea. And special thanks to the Bright Leaf / University of Massachusetts Press staff: Rachael DeShano, Ivo Fravashi, Brian Halley, and Sally Nichols, for their encouragement and the exercise of their craft.

For joyful enrichments to my own cultural life, I am grateful to the Allen's Neck Clambake (and Bean Hole Beans), Bridgewater Old Home Day, Bridgewater Vespers, Canterbury Shaker Village, the Danbury Grange and its fair, Historic Deerfield, Old Sturbridge Village, and my fellow members of the Good Old Plough, Fred Ogmundson and Don Towle. I want to give special thanks to the Danbury Country Store for its Midnight Oil Coffee and for the French Roast at Mocha Maya's in Shelburne Falls, Massachusetts: both have been good to the last drop, as well as to the last keystroke.

As I trust will become evident in these pages, this book has been conceived and written in the belief that the Boston-Cambridge Folk Revival is an example of the transformative and redemptive power of regional folk culture. The stories that I tell here originate from the intersections of history, ideals, culture, and music and grow into what is possible in the present. I see the decade of the Folk Revival as a critical hinge that connects the lives and events of our region's rich past with an increasingly challenging future. The cultural excesses and deficits that the Revival sought to address are still apparent in our present circumstances; I believe that the ideals, strengths, and experiences of New England's unique culture and heritage are, and by all rights ought to be, healing resources of first resort. I can see the magic that still remains in all of these things, awaiting only our understanding, our embrace, and our commitment.

The reader is encouraged to make the journey into these stories without the expectation that they are either an exposé or an homage to famous people. Some of the cast members in these pages will be recognizable, but most will not be, and nearly all make their entrance onto the stage of the Folk Revival in Boston and Cambridge as "complete unknowns." The moral of the story here lives in a love of music and of heritage, both of which I hope to have rekindled or inspired in the good people who take the time to read these pages.

About sixty years ago, a handmade musical renaissance bloomed in the bulrushes along both banks of the Charles River. A generation took it upon itself to "light out for the territories" on a raft cobbled together out of banjoes, old records, borrowed cultures, and an inherited sense of purpose. Our hopes have not yet been fulfilled, but our dreams have never failed us. I hear a rooster crowing right now, just like the ones in the folk songs that I listened to back in coffeehouse days, and I think I better charge up the percolator and go collect the morning's eggs. There is a lot of work to be done, and that's a good thing.

Tom Curren
The Hope Farm
South Danbury, New Hampshire

I BELIEVE
I'LL GO
BACK HOME

FIGURE 1.
Dayle Stanley on *Folk Music USA*, c. 1964. Photograph © 2020 by Rick Sullo.
All rights reserved. Used by permission.

CHAPTER ONE

TO MAKE A BETTER WORLD

We Came Here for to Sing

THIS BOOK TELLS THE story of the Boston-Cambridge Folk Revival of the early 1960s, which set about to rekindle the fires of traditional music while doing its part to tend to the unfinished pursuit of liberty and justice for all in America. The Folk Revival, which deployed the integrity of our enduring national music as counterbalance to a toxic and heedless modern consumer culture, lasted roughly from 1959 to 1968. It is my belief that the Revival was an extension of the vigor of the eastern frontier, a renewal of the vows of the American Revolution, a restatement of the visions of transcendentalists, a reprise of the fervor of the abolitionists, and a reincarnation of the convictions of the Progressive Era in New England history.

In the beginning, the Folk Revival was meant to be not about celebrities but rather about art and ideals, regional culture, and youthful community. Its young participants sought to marshal the power of tradition, relationships, and creativity as an alternative to a civilization dominated by technology, materialism, and competition. Many of the people who were touched by folk music in their youth are still living among us. As both Club 47 and the Newport Folk Festival have marked the sixtieth anniversary of their founding, this seems to be a good time to take stock of the long musical inheritance and the growing legacy of the Folk Revival of New England.

I WAS DRIVING NORTH on Route 6 toward Provincetown, Massachusetts, in the spring of 2017, across a Cape Cod landscape that was just losing the last of its snow cover. In a few months, these lanes would be choked with summer traffic, but under the lemony light of an early April morning, the road was nearly deserted. In the truck with me was Betsy Siggins, who at one time or another had been Joan Baez's college roommate at Boston University, comanager of Club 47 in Cambridge, and founder of the musical archive Folk New England. We were due to arrive at radio station WOMR to join disc jockey Bob Weiser at an on-air meeting with folk singer Dayle Stanley, whom neither Betsy nor I had seen since 1965.

In the early 1960s, dozens of young women musicians had followed in the musical footsteps of Odetta and Joan Baez, singing repertoires of traditional English ballads, African American blues, Appalachian tunes, and love songs to the accompaniment of acoustic guitars. Dayle Stanley stood out because she had begun to compose her own words and melodies, and because her work ventured beyond the conventional ideas of "folk music" and into the creative realm of what might have been called "art songs." Her writing stood on its own as poetry, and her music blended traditional forms and classical influences. Later in the decade, Joni Mitchell would come on the scene, followed, over time, by Carly Simon, Tracy Chapman, the Indigo Girls, and a host of other singer-songwriters who became leading forces in American music. But back in a time when women singers in the folk scene were far more likely to be described as "interpreters" than as "creators," Dayle and her contemporaries Buffy Sainte-Marie and Bonnie Dobson had been among the earliest composers of the Folk Revival.

In 1963, Dayle was voted Boston's "Most Popular Female Folk Artist" in a poll conducted by *Broadside* magazine. Growing up in Weymouth, Massachusetts, she had trained for opera and honed skills that she began to apply to folk music around the time that John F. Kennedy was inaugurated president. Dayle became an integral part of the new wave of about a dozen young Cambridge folk singers who gravitated around a coffeehouse called Club 47 Mount Auburn, located a bit south of Harvard Yard. There, an espresso-drinking, chess-playing clientele could hear her sing from a small stage that she shared with Tom Rush, Jackie Washington (whose given name is Jack Landrón), Geoff Muldaur, Sylvia Mars, Keith & Rooney, Jim Kweskin, the Charles River Valley Boys, and, most notably, Joan Baez.

The Folk Revival gained momentum at nearly three dozen venues throughout Massachusetts, and many of the first performers started releasing recordings on small labels. Dayle's first album, *Child of Hollow Times,* came out in 1963, a collection of love ballads, civil rights anthems, peace songs, and her own compositions. On the strength of that first record, Dayle won her *Broadside* "election"; her songs were featured on radio station WBZ, and that September she appeared on WGBH's televised program *Folk Music USA.* Her pure voice, choice of material, and riveting beauty drew a loyal audience, and in 1964 she released a second album, *After the Snow.* About a year later, she disappeared from public view, suddenly and completely. The Folk Revival would come to an end by 1968, and youthful attention moved on to rock music, adulthood, and the decades that followed, but at folk music gatherings and, later, on related websites, the question was often raised, Whatever happened to Dayle Stanley?

By 2014, I had become friends with David Wilson, former editor of the *Broadside,* and soon afterward I started volunteering with Betsy Siggins to collect recordings and publications from the 1960s for the Folk New England archive, which at that point resided in a number of personal residences and, in part, at the Cambridge Historical Society. Through David, I heard that Dayle might be living on the North Shore under a new name, and we sent word around folk music circles that we were interested in talking with her. Eventually, she got in touch, and it was arranged that Dayle, Betsy, and I would meet for an interview at the radio station in Provincetown.

We arrived early and walked up to the second-floor reception area. We sat for a bit, drinking coffee, then Betsy went down the hall for a moment. While she was gone, the elevator door across the way opened, and a short-haired woman in her seventies in a wheelchair was helped into the lobby by the gentleman who accompanied her. Dayle looked at me and asked, "Should I know you?" "No," I answered, "I was a fifteen-year-old kid watching you play at Club 47 ... but you might remember *her,*" and I pointed to Betsy, who was just walking back toward us. Dayle's face lit up, and she took Betsy's hand in hers. "Oh, *Betsy!*" she cried, "You were *so* good to me!"

The two friends talked, exchanging stories of times together and the fifty years that had passed since last they had spoken. The decades of marriages, children, moves, and jobs were covered in a matter of minutes. The story emerged of Dayle's abrupt retreat from performing; in reaction to personal crisis, she had felt compelled to leave her music behind and to begin a new life as "Ramona Murray" in a nearby seaport town. She had raised a family, but challenges and serious physical illnesses had taken years, and then the love of a new husband, to heal. With the passage of time, she felt ready to come forward and talk with us at the studio and to hear songs that she had not listened to for five decades.

"What would you like us to play?" our announcer asked, and Dayle turned to me and said firmly, "You choose." I picked a civil rights song she had written titled "Nobody Knows That I Have a Name." As the record spun on the turntable, a compelling song issued forth from a youthful voice, and, in no time, radio host Bob Weiser was looking at me as if to say, Where has *this* been? After the piece came to a close, I turned to ask about its creation.

"Dayle, you grew up in Massachusetts, in a comfortable suburban town, and yet you wrote one of the most powerful songs to come out of the Civil Rights Movement. How did you do that? How did you manage to put yourself so firmly in the circumstances of a Black man about to be murdered for stealing a bag of groceries?"

I watched her reflect for a moment, put her hand to her chin, and then she spoke, emphatically and clearly. Fifty years fell away, her physical challenges with them, and her eyes flashed as she said, "It just wasn't *fair,*" she said, pronouncing the last word as if, in two Massachusetts syllables, it rhymed with *day-uh.* "It was about the way they were treating Black people back then, not just in the South, but everywhere." And then, turning in affectionate remembrance to her old friend, she repeated, "It just wasn't *fay-uh,* Betsy! We had to do something!"

BETWEEN ROUGHLY 1959 AND 1968, Dayle Stanley, Betsy Siggins, thousands of other young people in New England, and eventually millions of them throughout the country were resolving that they should "do something" about race relations, about ending war as a method of handling political conflict, and about America's abandonment of its cultural roots and its soul. We found ourselves drawn to music and, in particular, to traditional music, in an attempt to find a source of hope and stability in the throes of a chaotic world. Some of us marched, some of us organized, and some of us joined the Peace Corps. We were drawn together by the sudden, daunting, and exhilarating conviction that we all needed to set about to "make a better world."

There is much to remember from those times. Envisioning a better world was easy, but actually venturing forth to make it happen involved turning our backs on much of what we had been raised with in modern American culture. At fourteen years of age, it was easy for me to read *Mad* magazine and to mock the adult world of careers and conformity; at sixteen, the stories I was seeing on television about the Civil Rights Movement were no laughing matter. By the time I was eighteen, my older friends were coming back from Vietnam more profoundly disturbed than inspired by their service to their country, and the draft card in my wallet felt like a mortgage on both my integrity and my future. America seemed to be riddled with fault lines, and the comforts of suburbia felt walled in by a cocoon of denial and hypocrisy. Our youthful lives were shadowed by the realization that the world was a very troubled and a very hostile place.

Music appeared like a guardian angel. Rock 'n' roll had served to set my generation free, and then folk music gave us inspiration. By its nature, it seemed to be an exercise in bravery: solo, acoustic performances of honest, heartfelt songs by vulnerable souls who were barely beyond adolescence. The music seemed to allow us room to discover ourselves. The beguiling power of melodies and stories were wrapped in the mantle of the past, legacies that had been hidden away until we were old enough to grasp them. If the world was haunted by dragons of bigotry and hatred, we would be ready for them. Folk music was the sword that we could pull from a stone with our youthful and untested arms.

A tide had turned; all we had to do was switch on a radio to hear songs that resonated on college campuses from California to New York: young, vibrant voices singing about green fields, new frontiers, and cabins in the hills. A national folk revival had sprung up in the wake of decades of war and depression. The music sang to us in the swagger of voices from the wild American West and in the syncopated drawls that drifted up our way from the fertile river lands of the South. Songs about Mississippi cotton fields were being sung in a part of the country where the farmland had long since grown up to forest or had been paved into parking lots. Yet, soon enough, we began to realize that, along with the magic that came from the prairies and along the levees, there were old voices, old stories, and old cadences aplenty to be revived right here in New England—from the country's oldest frontier.

I was very lucky to be living in New England, partly because of my proximity to the coffeehouses of Boston and Cambridge, but, underlying that, because I was growing up in a part of the country where the past *mattered,* where both the landscape and an invisible but persistent sense of ethic seemed to keep an ancient eye on things. I felt this dimension very deeply as a boy, and I read as much local and regional history as I could lay my hands on, using adult library cards borrowed from my dad and from my third-grade teacher. Out in the woods, in the days before the trees were all bulldozed, you could still discover cellar holes and old mill foundations throughout Middlesex County. Once in a great while, you might dig up an arrowhead or an Indian penny, which my young friends and I decided must have been what the Native Peoples had used for money.

On my bicycle, I could visit old house museums with diamond-paned windows and enormous hearths that had been spared the civilized barbarity of Victorian "improvement" and, later, the terminal blight of suburban development. Treading on floor planks that were as wide as half a tabletop, peering through wavy glass set in leaded mullions, smelling the summer tang of pine attic boards that remained sturdy, three centuries removed from the forest, I was drawn to look at the world through something other than ten-year-old eyes. I discovered that, right where I lived, the patriot-farmers of the Revolution had been succeeded by the poets, reformers, and back-to-the-landers of transcendentalism. I learned that Henry David Thoreau had not just been a hermit, but that he had also been part of a movement of artists and reformers who had borne witness against the injustices of slavery and the slavery-expanding Mexican War.

Dressed in the vests or crinoline of their days, these people had called for America to turn back from the selfish and self-destructive urges of the Industrial Age. Women should have the right to vote, they said; African Americans should be emancipated; Native Americans should be treated with whatever justice was still possible; and people should not be living lives of "quiet desperation." There were higher and better callings than being clerks or cogs in the machinery of commerce, and there was redemption to be had in the simplicity of the countryside. Witness had been made to all these truths, two decades before the Civil War, on my own home turf, which was now rapidly filling up with shopping centers, gas stations, and golf courses.

When I first saw Dayle Stanley wearing a jumper and leotards, Peter Childs in a beard and blue jeans, and Bob Dylan in dusty, thirdhand trousers that looked at least three inches wider at the waist than he was, I saw that they were more than "beatniks" and "weirdos." As outlandish as their appearance seemed to my young suburban eyes, the songs they were singing and the manner in which they were singing them rang a whole set of much older bells than I was accustomed to hearing out loud. Begun in the late 1950s, this was a spontaneous creation of a handful of college dropouts, young bohemians, and lovers of traditional music that served to renew the work of New England's revolutionaries, transcendental artists, abolitionists, pacifists, and reformers. In the very same streets of Cambridge that had been trodden by Alcotts and Emersons a hundred years before, young people were now lining up to listen to Joan Baez, Jack Landrón, Tom Rush, and Jim Kweskin and the Jug Band. The Boston-Cambridge Folk Revival was what the era came to be called, and this book is a remembrance of those times and the lives of those who lived them.

THIS FLOWERING OF TRADITIONAL music in New England would last for only about a decade, but its momentum continued to influence events for years. By 1968, many local musicians were leaving for Manhattan, Woodstock, Nashville, San Francisco, and Los Angeles. Boston folk singer Ed Freeman, who once described himself as "neck deep in good luck," went from being a coffeehouse performer of British ballads to being road manager for the Beatles' final tour. He also talked his way into New York recording studio work, where he produced albums for Tom Rush, Gregg Allman, Tim Hardin, and Carly Simon. In 1971, Ed arranged and produced Don McLean's popular saga "American Pie," closing the song with a final chorus sung in rousing old ale house fashion by James Taylor, Carly Simon, Livingston Taylor, and Pete Seeger.

A few years later, Maria Muldaur topped the national charts with "Midnight at the Oasis." Fritz Richmond, her fellow Kweskin Jug Band member, became a recording engineer, working on the creation of albums by Bonnie Raitt and Jackson Browne. Ragtime piano player Jeff Gutcheon became the original musical director of the New York production *Ain't Misbehavin'.* Out in California, Mitch Greenhill took over the management group of Folklore Productions from his father, Manny, and would eventually pass the worldwide business on to his own son, Matthew. The hit song "Up Where We Belong," cowritten by Buffy Sainte-Marie, won her an Academy Award in 1983.

Geoff Muldaur went west, continuing to apply his incredible vocal talents to traditional music, paying homage to the works of Bix Beiderbecke, Hoagy Carmichael, Frank Stokes, and Gus Cannon, and eventually venturing into classical music composition. Geoff continues to sing solo, and he regularly teams up with Jim Kweskin in this new century. Betsy Siggins founded an archive of recordings, photographs, and publications that became known as Folk New England. Jim Rooney became one of the most respected figures in Nashville, working with Sun Records guru Jack Clement and producing records by Iris DeMent, Nanci Griffith, John Prine, and old friend Tom Rush, among many others.

Soon after the Folk Revival generation left the Boston area, their places were taken by newcomers Joni Mitchell, Bonnie Raitt, James Taylor, and Carly Simon, all of whom had played the New England coffeehouses as young unknowns in the mid-1960s. These and other artists expanded the field of acoustic music, using folk idioms to create a new singer-songwriter tradition. Tufts student Tracy Chapman began singing in the Harvard Square T station in Cambridge in the late '80s, then went on to play Club Passim, a vibrant venue that opened in the mid-1990s on the second site of Club 47. The branches of the larger folk revival have continued to bear fruit, from the Indigo Girls and Nanci Griffith up to the new century and the music of the Carolina Chocolate Drops and the Old Crow Medicine Show, among hundreds of musicians now active in the thriving field of "American roots music."

In its day, the Boston-Cambridge Folk Revival had followed a recurring pattern of celebration and reconnection to folkways that has been a persistent theme and benchmark in the history of the region and the country as a whole. Forefathers' Days, Old Home Days, country fairs, fish fries, clambakes, bluegrass festivals, dances, and camp meetings have all been part of the American scene over the course of hundreds of years. Music, with its portability and its capacity to engage both body and soul, has been a vital coin that has circulated freely throughout this realm. Sometimes, these events are just comforting annual rites of our passage through life, and sometimes, and in some places, they erupt with a power that rocks the souls of everyone who comes within earshot and tends to put the *unum* back into our national *pluribus*.

From time to time, in both urban and rural settings, art explodes in an alchemical chain reaction of creativity, as if a community suddenly starts to recall its dreams, begins to share them, and then an entire region finds itself transformed by inspiration. This sort of creative process can express itself in any number of different art forms. The Hudson River school of artists, the New England transcendentalists, and the Harlem Renaissance are all examples of this sort of flowering, as was the transformative music that came out of both the Sun and Stax Studios of Memphis and the kind of magic that played out in the valley of the Charles River in the early 1960s.[1]

This phenomenon seems to fill an important need in all times and locations, particularly in America, a nation made up of people who either left their native culture behind when they came here or who were already at home here on tribal lands until they were displaced by the press of immigrants in search of easily available real estate and a self-made future. Isolated, and often feeling unconnected in our "other-ness," we share the need to establish, or to reestablish, a home in a place of faith and promise. We are all thrown-together Americans who set out to invent a new definition and a new direction for ourselves. Although this country embarked on its national journey in the 1770s with a set of brilliant plans and a lot of spirited gumption, it seems clear now that, in the haste of inspiration, we left town without a map. For generations, we have been accustomed to think of ourselves as the land of unlimited possibilities, but we are just beginning to realize that we are also living in the land of a whole lot of unfinished business.

I have written this book because I believe that its subject, the Boston-Cambridge Folk Revival of the 1960s, is a crucial hinge that connects the roots, revolution, and reform movements of eighteenth- and nineteenth-century New England with the deficits, possibilities, and perils of the present day. America seems, at this writing, to be immobilized in a period of cultural, moral, and political stagflation, much as it was after World War II, just before the national folk revival began. Despite our seemingly endless technical acceleration, we see strong evidence that we are in the process of losing much of the high ground that we had gained at great cost in the past.

We have fallen by the wayside of the pilgrimage to establish healthy relations between the races and the sexes, to increase our capacity to deal constructively with conflict, and to develop the ability to live without sickening ourselves by sickening the land that we live on. At times, the best that we can say for ourselves today is that we now have the capacity to monitor this disintegration on a second-by-second basis instead of having to wait for the daily newspaper or the six o'clock news. Instantaneous communications hover over us like a cloud of twittering buzzards, wheeling above an unhorsed cowboy in an old western movie: "Hand me those fancy digital binoculars. Oh, look up there: we're screwed!"

But we have been here before. Cynics love to say, smugly, that it will do no good for us to sit in a circle, hold hands, and sing "Kumbaya" together in the hope of salvation. But singing folk songs cannot be any worse than building walls around ourselves and shouting insults and threats over the ramparts. There is a magic in music that can melt the iron chains of greed and fear.

Up in the vast expanses of the New England North Woods, a hunting guide will tell you that if you get lost, the best way to proceed is to stop moving forward, to find a quiet place where your pulse can return to a normal rhythm, and then to carefully retrace your steps until you see a landmark that you remember, the last place you knew where you were; you can make your way back from there. These days, we find ourselves wandering around in a self-made cultural wilderness whose artificiality makes it all the more bewildering. Since, in many cases, we now lack the landmarks of trees or mountains to guide us, we may well discover that our way home depends, once again, on establishing an intuitive connection to our complicated cultural roots. If we take the time to listen, we can hear voices coming from old hearts and old settlements that can lead us back to the place where we belong.

FIGURE 2.
Engraving of a sailing ship, from Clarence P. Hornung,
2,000 Early Advertising Cuts (New York: Dover Publications, 1995).

WHEN FIRST UNTO THIS COUNTRY

Settlement and Song in New England, 1600–1820

DURING THE SUMMER OF 2014, author Barry Lopez traveled to eastern equatorial Africa in order to view a collection of ancient fossils. Archaeologists there were focusing on the pivotal point when hominids began to make noises that served to express emotion, the first moment when humans developed the ability to communicate. Lopez recounted a conversation he had with one of the scholars: "With his fingertips on the cranium of an australopithecine skull not much larger than a grapefruit, on the forward part of the vault where one day frontal lobes would rise up in *Homo* [*sapiens*], he says, 'Barry, I can't prove this, but I believe we sang before we spoke.'"[1]

We have no way of knowing exactly where the course of New England folk music begins. If we want to go back to our region's cultural genesis, we could start by following the footprints of the first great cross-continental American migration: the one that set out from Siberia and, over thousands of years, came southward to inlets, cornfields, and pueblos, then eastward ho! across the unstaked plains to the mounds and forests of Oheyo country. As the glaciers receded, some of the First People moved northward and eastward, arriving in the salmon-rich currents and the tidewater clam flats off the Penobscot, the Piscataqua, and the Passamaquoddy Rivers, at what would eventually become known as the Maine coast.

By custom, by culture, and because history tends to be written by the victors instead of the vanquished, the later European arrivals devoted very little time to seeking out the cultural roots of the ancient Native place that came to be called "New England." We can never really know those oldest elders, but we can attempt to try to understand their lives and resolve to respect their legacies. Over the course of thousands of years and hundreds of generations, millions of souls have lived in this place, learned to walk, to grow, to work and hunt, to fall in love, to sing, to dance, to be part of families and clans, and to seek wisdom and peace before "white people" ever got here. In ways that we have yet to learn, they knew how to live in balance in this fragile place that we now know as home.

When sometime in the dim past the wooden keel of a rowboat first grated on the gravelly wash of the New England coast, a groggy-legged crew from a sailing vessel anchored nearby stashed their ash oars and sloshed their way ashore, watched closely by Native eyes hidden in nearby forests. "What have we here?" the members of both groups may well have asked themselves, and we have all been attempting to answer that question, more and less successfully, ever since. Long before the formal exploration and settlement of the Pilgrim era, Native Americans and European fishermen were blending old cultures together at fishing camps located just off the northeast coasts.

The Natives solidly outnumbered the newcomers at first contact, when European fishermen began to occupy their summers in the rich fishing banks off the shores of "the main." Probably in the late 1500s, and certainly by the dawn of the following century, a few hardy fisherfolk began "wintering over" on coastal or island camps, partly to secure the wooden racks constructed the previous summer to dry salted codfish and partly to be on-site and catching fish as the early as possible the following spring.[2]

Eventually, Europeans moved in on the lands of the First Nations, and what we know as American cultural history began to make its way forward and backward and forward again, much like the tides it came in on. The oral traditions that were the foundations of Native American culture and music would be wiped out by the European settlers as thoroughly as civilization would later eradicate the woodland buffalo and the passenger pigeon. A few accounts of drumming, chanting, flute playing, and dancing were written by French and English explorers, but the Native Peoples were commonly denigrated as "savages," and tribal distinctions and cultures seem to have been reduced to the category of "they all look alike."

The first wary encounters between Natives and Europeans may well have engendered the idea of trade, since the men on the beach were dressed in rich furs and pelts and those in the boats were prominently outfitted with gleaming metal knives and hatchets. For a time, possibly for more than a half century on the eastern frontier, coexistence and mutually agreed-on barter were the order of the day. For example, the ships *Speedwell* and *Discoverer,* which set sail from England on April 10, 1603 (within weeks of the death of Queen Elizabeth I and just before the thirty-ninth birthday of William Shakespeare), were loaded with cargo to barter with the Natives of New England: saws, pickaxes, hatchets, brass fish hooks, "sizzers," looking glasses, thimbles, and thread. After cruising what is now the long coast between the Penobscot and Marblehead, they anchored off present-day Plymouth and began trading and harvesting wild plants. As many as sixty Natives joined with them, eating a meal of fish, beans, and peas. The sailors produced a "Gitterne" and began playing, and an impromptu dance ensued.[3]

The sailors' old English folk music originated in a dim European past when the common people's universe would have been bounded by a nobleman's farm, an ancient abbey, and a thatch-roofed village with a common stream running through it. The peasant culture of old "Albion" was shaped by the seasons and by farm chores that remained constant through shifting economic and political episodes. As was the case with other European traditions, communal time was marked not only by regular market days but also by dozens of feasts, saints' days, seasonal observances, and other remnants of pagan influence that mixed together to form a body of pious folkways.[4] In rural England, for example, the folk celebrated Candlemas, Valentine's Day, All Fools' Day, Easter, Whitsuntide, Hocktide, May Day, Rogation Days, Lammas, Midsummer, Saint Swithin's Day, Beltane, All Hallows' Day, Michaelmas, Saint Crispin's Day, and the twelve days of Christmas, which stretched from Christmas Eve to the Feast of the Epiphany.

These holidays tended to be ceremonial at the start of the celebration and more raucous later in the proceedings, when ale, wine, and mead flowed, the singing began, and couples broke into dance. The evolution of folk music found fertile ground in larger towns, where people mixed traditions, stories, melodies, and, in time, instrumentation. A particularly touching, ribald, or clever song would draw an appreciative response, and, memory and invention being what they are, variations would occur almost immediately. In time, a broadening quilt of musical heritage brought together traditions of songs and folk dance that were as rich and varied as the medieval landscape that fostered them.

Songs were the most memorable way to perpetuate stories in this oral tradition. In England, a singer's narrative verses were often interspersed with a chorus such as "Hey down, derry-derry-down" that the audience could join in enthusiastically without having to memorize (or improvise) a story line that might run a few dozen verses. Folk music was inseparable from folk dance, and both the market square and new-mown fields served as dance halls. The songs that would someday make landfall in New England came from a time when the village people of the British countryside looked a lot like the characters in a Brueghel painting.

What came to be called the British Isles had been gathered from a loose collection of tribes, clans, septs, and regional cultures that took their identities from ancient tradition and local custom. The folkways of maritime Ireland were far different from those of inland pasture, the Highlands of Scotland varied greatly from the Lowlands, and the mountainous villages of Wales developed their own distinct customs and characteristics. By the Age of Exploration, the cities of Dublin, Edinburgh, and London had begun to gather, popularize, and print up songs that playwrights such as Shakespeare sprinkled throughout their theatrical productions. Rough-hewn folk tunes were set to the lute and embellished with the flourishes that we now associate with Elizabethan music. Nowhere did all these disparate influences mix together as richly as they did along the teeming wharves and taverns of the seaport towns that stretched between Edinburgh and Essex and around Cornwall and Dublin. Thus the wet-legged English fishermen who first traded grunts and hand gestures with American tribesmen were carrying long and broad song traditions ashore with them.

The two cultures were divided at many points, but they shared traditions that were mostly oral in nature: the telling of tales, the singing of ballads and sagas, as well as the rough-and-tumble art of the dance. Island and shorefront fishing settlements became notorious as the scenes of rowdy parties, and eventually at least one Abenaki man was said to have picked up the fiddle and mastered it sufficiently to preside at fishermen's shindigs.[5] Through long winter nights in crude fish camps and meager hovels, by the sputtering light of driftwood fires, English fishermen spent their time "gulping down their home-brewed beer, repeating endlessly the same repertory of bawdy songs and stories, and intensifying the constant battle of wits until a session of rough raillery ended in a fist-fight."[6]

For decades, the early settlers lived in peace and friendship with the Natives. Along the mouth of the Piscataqua, near what is now Portsmouth, New Hampshire, a Native American named Sagamore Rowles perceived the increasing value of real estate around Kittery Point and began negotiating the sale of inland lots, shorefront wharfages, and upriver water power sites. He is variously described as "a man of sense" and as someone who the English "courteously and kindly regarded." He was fortunate to live out his life at a time when rugged fishermen were willing to negotiate an agreeable asking price for land, before the English felt themselves to be in a position to simply take whatever they wanted by force.[7]

Around 1616, fatal viruses from Europe had begun to sweep across the landscape, and the indigenous people had no resistance to these imported microbes. Thousands of Native New Englanders perished in the course of a few plague years, with some tribes reduced to just a small fraction of their strength in a matter of a few months. While impossible to know how history would have played out in the absence of this epidemic, it is clear that it made a major difference in the balance of power, since European settlers were able to move more or less freely onto a largely vacated landscape. In the 1630s, when two Natives were kidnapped on the Lower Connecticut River by an English smuggler, aggrieved tribesmen attacked his ship, and the resulting Pequot War ignited a pattern of racial conflict that lasted for centuries.

Slaughter begat slaughter. Before the 1600s ran their bloody course, 10 percent of the combined human population of all races in pioneer and tribal New England had been murdered. Fifty towns and dozens of Native villages were burned to the ground, and colonial officials resorted to paroling imprisoned pirates and arming them for combat.[8] The Native Peoples were eventually all but eradicated, driven from their lands to a cold northern outpost along the banks of the Saint Lawrence or captured and sent off in chains by Puritan Christians to lives of slavery in the islands of the Caribbean. There, Abenaki and Wampanoag exiles labored in cane fields alongside Africans who had been kidnapped by slave traders and crammed into the holds of crowded ships headed for the New World. Under blistering sun and in unrelieved bondage, generations of these people sustained themselves with the only things they still owned: their souls and their songs.

The young culture of New England was indelibly shaped by the folk-ways of the displaced Native tribes who had lived for centuries between the Housatonic and the Saint Lawrence Rivers. Yankee fishermen, farmers, and trappers all learned their trades from the Natives, and when timber cruisers and pioneers wound their way into the forested interior on birch-bark canoes, they retained the old names of waterways and landscapes: Presumpscot, Merrimack, Winnipesaukee, Nashua, Coos, Connecticut, and Massachusetts. Every May and June saw the settlers planting the "Three Sisters" of corn, squash, and beans, the staples of the indigenous horticulture. Although the Abenaki and the Wampanoag were largely exiled from their land, they left behind a cultural iconography of camp and lakeside, forest trail and pumpkin-studded cornfield that still resonates across the generations. Through the course of the seasons in New England, we still feel deeply drawn to do things "that fit here," things that were done on the land long ago.

Prior to the American Revolution, as many as three-quarters of the colonists arrived in America in some state of unfreedom, either as African slaves or as poor white indentured servants. Indenture was essentially slavery-for-a-term, whereby an impoverished young person was bound to perform labor and to take orders from the person who owned them. Common in the North, indenture became an almost universal reality in the South, where the large-scale plantation model of agriculture was imported from Barbados. Using these practices developed in profitable sugar cane production in the burgeoning West Indies, a small number of wealthy British landowners applied the labor of white indentured servants, convicts removed from overcrowded English and Irish jails, and African slaves who had been kidnapped and brought over in chains to the American South and the growing of tobacco, indigo, and, ultimately, cotton.[9]

We have suffered as a people for hundreds of years with the burden of these "old times there, not forgotten," and we are unlikely to be unshackled from them as long as Americans continue to "look away" from the chronic cause-and-effect influence of slavery in our family story. Rhode Island sea captains became major participants in the triangle trade between New England, Barbados, and Africa, and thousands of slaves labored in plantations just south of Providence. While many poor white youths were bound to indentured servitude for a defined period, Africans who functioned even as "house servants" to their wealthy owners were slaves for life, except in the few cases where they were freed out of conscience or in reward for military service.[10]

There was scanty record kept of the lives of any common folk, especially those who left little in the way of probate records. Many held on to what they could of the ways of their "old country," and for Yankee slaves this primarily meant the telling of tales, the singing of songs, and the growing of herbs and vegetables and foodstuffs from their home cultures of Africa or the islands of the West Indies. Eventually, however, a few were powerful enough personalities to break through the anonymity of race and gender to leave their marks on the larger communities that they lived in, among these, a woman named Lucy Terry of Deerfield, Massachusetts, who was an African past keeper of the first order. In addition to being a community leader and a fierce self-advocate, Terry became the first published African American poet when she composed a long ballad about a French and Indian raid on her town that occurred in August 1746.[11]

The century and a half that followed the Pilgrim landing in 1620 saw an explosive growth of maritime New England culture, since most trade and transportation through the region was conducted by canoe, rowboat, and ship in the days before dependable inland roads. But even as the tidewater settlements swelled with new residents during this period, New Englanders never amounted to more than a small fraction of the English population that settled the wealthy plantations of the West Indies: the first real boom towns in the New World were in the Caribbean. So, out of timber ports such as Portsmouth and Falmouth (now Portland), in hundreds of locally built Yankee ships, captains filled their holds with fresh pine lumber and barrel staves and set sail for treeless Barbados or Jamaica, assured that their hand-hewn cargoes would sell for ten times the amount they would bring in New England.

Once on the islands, some Yankee crew members inevitably would have been swallowed up in seaport taverns and brothels, and the missing hands would have to be replaced before a ship chock full of molasses, dyes, and spices could venture back north. The labor force available at a Caribbean wharfside in those times would have been overwhelmingly African and undoubtedly in bondage, and the necessity of a quick homeward voyage could readily have become the mother of bootleg emancipation. A few gold coins might have changed hands in the dark, and soon a new mixed-race crew could have been running its course northeast. We can speculate that the first free Africans in New England were quite possibly not slaves but just such "black jack" sailors on coastal ships, who brought the beginnings of an emancipating mixture of culture and music up and into the teeming streets of Yankee ports.[12] Over the course of the next century and a half, prior to the Revolution, the New England countryside echoed with sea shanties, ballads, lullabies, lumber camp songs, hymns, and ancient dance tunes that had come over from Europe and Africa and up from the West Indies.

In the long span of time before the invention of mass media, music and speech at the personal level seem to have been far more powerful than they are today. People spoke in colorful declarations; the querulous modern usage of "you know?" at the end of sentences was unknown. A dance, a banjo tune, or a clever turn of phrase that struck a person as memorable was very likely to be copied and repeated, particularly across cultures. It took little time for there to be "white versions" of Black tunes and "Black versions" of white ones, and it wasn't long before everyone was singing mixed variations of all the old ballads and songs. African syncopation and diction had enormous influence on the development of vernacular American music. The races came together on something like more equal footing on market days, on slave holidays, and in the celebration of festivals such as springtime's "Pinkster,"[13] which took place in parts of New England and New York.

Slaves were rarely paid for their labor, but by the 1700s, on special occasions, a banjo player, a fiddler, or a dancer could earn pocket money in performance, and musical skills quickly became a ticket to a minor sort of income, particularly in the seaport towns. During the 1790s, at the Assembly House ballroom in Portsmouth, New Hampshire, African American fiddler Cuffee Whipple presided over dozens of whirling couples as they engaged in "mazy dances." Whipple had been given his freedom by his master, and from time to time, he was joined on "second fiddle" by Colonel Wentworth, scion of an elite family that had been wealthy colonial merchants since the 1630s. Music provided a redeeming opportunity to slacken the ligatures of race and of social class and to begin a connection between "bond and free" in a land that would increasingly attempt to define itself in terms of a new American liberty.[14]

In the New World, during the century and a half that America would later remember as "the good old colony days," the polyglot immigrant base of tidewater musical stock was enriched by three new and distinctive Yankee creations. First, popular ballads were being printed up in long "broadside" sheets of paper and hawked on the bustling streets of Boston by the early 1700s. Then, a few decades later, in wayside churches, parlors, and taverns, "singing schools" began teaching "by note and by rule," and the first formal American musical composers started to create "fuguing tunes," hymns set to an interplay of four-part harmony. In addition, around the same time, a popular wave of contra dances swept its way across the rolling northern landscape. These influences all combined to give a robust and enduring musical voice to the period known as the Village era, which flourished throughout the 1700s in New England.[15]

> In good old colony days,
> When we lived under the King,
> Lived a miller and a weaver and a little tailor,
> Three jolly rogues of Lynn.
>
> Oh, the miller, he stole corn,
> And the weaver, he stole yarn,
> But the little tailor, he stole broadcloth,
> For to keep those three rogues warm.
>
> Oh, the miller drowned in the dam,
> And the weaver hanged in the yarn.
> But the Devil got his claw on the little tailor,
> With the broadcloth under his arm.
>
> Well, the miller still floats in the dam,
> And the weaver still hangs in the yarn.
> But the little tailor, he skips through Hell,
> With the broadcloth under his arm![16]

Broadside ballads like "Three Jolly Rogues of Lynn" were largely the work of amateur composers in the new land. Often written in and under the influence of taverns and coffeehouses, they were laid out in small print shops on long sheets of paper strung onto dowels, and hundreds of them were sold by singing peddlers on cobbled city streets. The subjects of these broadsides could be crimes, politics, or any newsworthy items of the day, most of them set to tunes borrowed from Anglo-Irish tradition. Young Benjamin Franklin composed at least two such ballads while still in his early teens, and his brother helped him print them up for sale in the crooked alleys of their native Boston. Those verses, like the ones in "Captain Kidd," "Brave Wolfe," "The Golden Vanity," and "Barbara Allen," competed with the cries of sea gulls in bustling markets, ale houses, and wharfside walkways, forming the basis for many of the folk songs that found their way a century later into the vast interior regions of the American continent.

During the colonial period, the Massachusetts Bay experiment with the merger of Church and State had led to tragedy and disgrace in the witch trial hysteria of the 1690s. As a result, reasonable people concluded that there was a limit to the amount of trust that could be left in the hands of a cadre of "worthy divines" whose superstitions and pride had overridden both their humanity and their capacity for common sense. Over the course of time, a hybrid blend of conventional devotion and more freethinking creativity came to replace the iron hands of Puritan oligarchy. As the old order was weakening, immigrant Huguenot craftsmen arriving in Massachusetts from France began to occupy a social position between the acculturated British extremes of haughty "elect" and struggling serf. For the poor, this new middle class was something to aspire to; for the rich, these craftsmen and farmers were the sort of people who could, and did, actually get things done, albeit mostly on their own terms.

The glacial crust of harsh clerical rule thawed further in the early 1700s when itinerant song masters began to thread their way on horseback throughout the villages of New England. The singing schools they established were encouraged by the more open-minded clergy of the day, who wanted to see the old drone of call-and-response in *The Bay Psalm Book* supplanted by the magic of inspired harmony. These classes were attended by young people of both sexes eager to learn their parts, and the gatherings became a wildly popular confluence of music, scripture, and youthful hormones.

> While others may seek for vain and foolish pleasures,
> The Sabbath school shall be my choice; O come, come away!
> How dear we hear the plaintive strain,
> From youthful voices rise amain,
> With sweetest tones again! O come, come away![17]

The work of the singing schools spread quickly throughout the region, making strong and life-long impressions on the students in attendance. A number of young people began serious composing very soon after they enrolled in singing schools. Timothy Swan of Worcester, Massachusetts, entered such a school at age sixteen; within a year, he had written the hymn "Montague," which would become the most popular musical creation of a productive life that spanned from 1758 to 1842. Oliver Holden of Boston began composing hymns about a month after he started classes. The brilliant William Billings organized a singing school in Boston when he was twenty-three; a year later, he published *The New England Psalm-Singer,* the first tune book produced by an American writer, featuring more than a hundred and twenty of his own compositions.

Puritan fears that music would distract from Holy Scripture were transcended by young composers who inspired the human heart and soul through the emotional power of melody as much as by the rubric of holy words. The story of the youthful choral music of New England in the eighteenth century is "the chronicle of a society which had to forge a musical life for itself out of the materials at hand and which would in due time build a musical culture that would be the equal of any in the Western world."[18] Due to the itinerant nature of the instructors, the young people who "graduated" from these schools in the mid-1700s came from villages all across the New England landscape. Rural communities saw the development of serious young composers whose inspirational work became popular throughout the region: singing masters such as Billings in Massachusetts, Supply Belcher in Maine, and Jeremiah Ingalls in Vermont published hundreds of a cappella fuguing tunes for groups of men and women to sing in harmony. These songs, often named after small towns such as "Northfield" and "Kittery," were taken up in church and tavern in the years before and after the Revolution and rank among the most beautiful compositions in American history.

Music bloomed throughout the New England landscape. Billings described the impact of the new melodies on the audiences of the day:

> While each part is thus mutually striving for mastery, and sweetly contending for victory, the audience are most luxuriously entertained, and exceedingly delighted; in the meantime, their minds are surprisingly agitated, and extremely fluctuated; sometimes declaring in favour of one part, and sometimes another.—Now the solemn bass demands their attention, now the manly tenor, now the lofty counter, now the volatile treble, now here, now there, now here again.—O inchanting! O ecstatic! Push on, push on ye sons of harmony.[19]

It was not unusual for a storekeeper or a boot maker to begin composing hymns and songs of the highest order and for rural men and women neighbors to express their deepest spiritual inspiration in choruses that echoed out from four-corners meetinghouses and brick-hearthed taverns. A unique culture flourished in New England villages and towns as inhibitions about the limits of America's rough-hewn culture began to be replaced by a growing national pride. At the same time, Boston grew to be the largest city in the region, its teeming, crooked, cobblestone streets weaving a maze among homes with diamond-paned windows, artisan's shops, warehouses, and markets.

By about 1690, there were two coffeehouses doing business in the town, the London Coffee House and Gutteridge's Coffee House, the latter across from where the Old State House stands today.[20] Perhaps the most dynamic of the old public houses was the Green Dragon on Union Street, where the patriots met to plan the Boston Tea Party in 1773. It was from its doors that a fortified Paul Revere departed toward Lexington on the fateful night of April 18, 1775.

A combined sense of self-reliance, devotion to principle, and love of liberty evolved in the eighteenth century and eventually took fateful form in the Revolution and in the founding documents of the Republic. The Scottish patriot Andrew Fletcher had once said that he would rather compose the songs of a nation than write its laws, and the fuguing tunes of New England remain evidence that music and nation building were both in full flower in America during the 1700s. William Billings wrote a hymn he titled "Chester" that became one of the foremost marching songs of the Revolution, establishing a tradition of New England topical ("protest") song composition that would continue over the ensuing centuries.

> Let tyrants shake their iron rod
> And slav'ry Clank her galling Chains;
> We fear them not; we trust in God—
> New-England's God forever reigns!
>
> Howe and Burgoyne and Clinton, too,
> With Prescot and Cornwalis join'd,
> Together plot our Overthrow,
> In one Infernal league combin'd.
>
> When God inspir'd us for the fight,
> Their ranks were broke, their lines were forc'd,
> Their ships were Shatter'd in our sight,
> Or swiftly driven from our Coast.

The Foe comes on with haughty Stride;`
Our troops advance with martial noise,
Their Vet'rans flee before our Youth,
And Gen'rals yield to beardless Boys.

What grateful Off'ring shall we bring?
What shall we render to the Lord?
Loud Halleluiahs let us Sing,
And praise his name on ev'ry Chord.[21]

Along with exalted verses like these, the salty and raucous traditions of seaport street singing and balladry flourished throughout the revolutionary period. Political songs from both patriots and loyalists were sung in the streets and bellowed out in the oaken barrooms of Boston. We are so accustomed to hearing a few fragments of "Yankee Doodle" that we overlook what a detailed picture the rest of the song presents of the homespun militia that flooded in from all over New England to Cambridge Common in the days after the battles at Lexington and Concord:

Father and I went down to camp
Along with Captain Gooding,
And there we saw a thousand men
As thick as hasty pudding.[22]

The Revolution stretched on for eight years, the longest war fought by Americans during the first two hundred and twenty-five years of our existence as a nation. A number of patriots enlisted in the army for lengthy terms, but most of the battles were fought by citizen-soldiers who left their homes and farms for a month or so, just long enough to walk to and from a battle that might have taken place a hundred miles or more from their homes. For example, once the summer's crops had been harvested, the Saratoga campaign saw the American army swell from a few thousand farmers in July 1777 to more than ten thousand at its climax that October. These men likely gathered around campfires to sing verses like the ones written to celebrate the victory at Bennington that August against the British regulars and Hessian mercenaries who had invaded their homeland:

Have ye no graves at home
Across the briny water,
That hither ye must come
Like bullocks to the slaughter?
If we the work must do,
Why the sooner 'tis begun,
If flint and trigger hold but true,
The quicker 'twill be done![23]

When the long war ended in an improbable victory, national unity became the watchword for all in the young country. Fourth of July celebrations were marked in songs and lengthy toasts. The "Yankee Doodle" tune was put to verses about the vigorous debate in Massachusetts regarding the ratification of the Constitution:

Now politicians of all kinds,
Who are not yet decided,
May see how Yankees speak their minds,
And yet are not divided.[24]

With freedom secured, the country embarked on the lively process of community building, and scores of composers across New England proceeded to create hundreds of songs and melodies. Folk dances of all sorts continued to be a major social force in the life of the young republic, and the fiddle, fife, and African banjo reigned supreme in dance halls for generations. A rich and broad collection of tunes had come over from England, Scotland, and Ireland, some of which were in print as early as the 1700s, while many originated centuries earlier.

In the euphoria that followed the Franco-American alliance during the Revolution, English traditional dances in "squares" were blended with French minuet styles to create a new form that became known as the "contra dance," which also combined jigs, reels, Scottish strathspeys, hornpipes, and French country dance steps. Old melodies such as "Childgrove" and "Sweet Richard" were joined by newer tunes including "Portland Fancy," "Hull's Victory," and the popular "Petronella." Immigrant Irish, French, and African American musicians became masters of the fiddle and bow. Even in the most remote districts, dances reigned supreme. A Yankee lighthouse keeper named Eliphalet Grover regularly rowed his way off Boon Island at sundown to play in dances near York, Maine. After leaving a rousing night of music, he would row himself, his little book of tunes, and his home-made spruce fiddle back home by the starlight reflected on the tides.[25]

Folk dancing was a major social function that spanned economic, political, and vocational distinctions throughout the founding years. The qualifications for a successful ministry, for example, might include competence on the dance floor, and a good clergyman often "found his place in the community via an Ordination Ball rather than by any such dour celebrations as are common today. As a minister, he was judged less by his pulpit pratings than by his ability to hold his Old Medford and handle a difficult figure. The officers in both the English troops and the Colonials were so crazy about dancing that some say, if you listen hard enough, the hills of New England will give forth a faint echo of Lord Howe's revels, or perhaps let go a few strains of Washington's favorite, 'Sir Roger de Coverly.'"[26]

An ardent love of community dances swept across countryside and city alike. The village year was marked by barn raisings, haying, husking bees, apple-paring parties, and other occasions when "many hands made light work," and hard labor went all the faster when it was enlivened by the notes of a soaring, keening fiddle. The construction of a number of taverns and community halls included a "springing dance floor" that "floated" on suspended stringers and even the crafting of a "fiddlers' throne," such as the elaborate platform that was constructed at the Mack Tavern in Deerfield, New Hampshire.

We get a sense of how devoted people were to folk dancing in a remarkable story of former days that Henry David Thoreau recounted in a letter to a friend in 1860: "An old Concord farmer tells me that he ascended [Mount] Monadnock once, & danced on the top. How did that happen? Why, he being up there, a party of young men & women came up bringing boards & a fiddler, and having laid down the boards they made a level floor, on which they danced to the music of the fiddle. I suppose the tune was 'Excelsior.'"[27] In the hills and backwaters where the rolling landscape tucked little towns snugly away from the influence of turnpike, factory, or railroad, tavern traditions of fiddle and folk dance lingered on for generations to come. Much later, these old tunes would be rediscovered and embraced by wealthy summer sojourners of the Victorian era in places such as New Hampshire's White Mountains and Monadnock Region and in the hill country of western Massachusetts and Vermont.

During the early 1700s, Massachusetts established itself as the headquarters of American international trade, securing its position on the strength and speed of vessels built in Yankee shipyards. Shipbuilders perfected their craft in maritime Massachusetts; for example, in Duxbury, in 1719, one Thomas Prince constructed a sloop made of wild black cherry timber, of the sort normally used for fine furniture. Big yards such as the ones in Portsmouth and Boston turned out thousands of vessels, their output added to by the Massachusetts ports of Newburyport, Essex, Salem, Medford, and the twenty-four shipyards that were hard at work in towns along the twelve-mile run made by the North River before it spread out into the Atlantic at Marshfield.[28]

> When the sun rose above the Marshfield hills, like a great red ball through the river mist, there began the cheery clatter of wooden shipbuilding—clean, musical sounds of steel on wood, iron on anvil, creak of tackle and rattle of sheave: with much geeing and hawing as ox-teams brought in loads of fragrant oak, pine, and hackmatack, and a snatch of chanty as a large timber is hoisted into place. At eleven o'clock, and again at four came the foreman's welcome shout of "Grog O!" For it took rum to build ships in those days; a quart to a ton, by rough allowance; and more to launch her properly.[29]

Yankee commerce stretched from Salem and East Boston to the mouth of the Columbia River, the docks of Canton, and the warehouses of Liverpool. Crews from dozens of nations singing shanties (or chanties[30]) scrambled aloft to tend thousands of yards of sails on graceful clipper ships that carried names such as *Red Jacket, Witch of the Waves,* and *Sovereign of the Seas.* Clinging with one hand to the heaving ship and working tarred ropes and flapping canvas with the other, the men perched on masts and spars that loomed a hundred feet or more above the wooden deck and the foaming waves below.

The work was done in time to the cadence of songs bawled out by the mate and answered by the crew:

> From Boston Harbor, we set sail;
> The wind was a-blowin' the devil of a gale
> With our ring-tail set all about the mizzen-peak
> And our dolphin striker a-plowin' up the deep
> With a big bow-wow,

Tow-wow-wow,
Fol-de-rol-de ride-all day![31]

State Street fortunes tacked their way into Boston in barrels full of silk fabric, crates of Canton china, and burlap bags of tobacco, coffee, and spices. Trade winds powered Yankee ships into many speed records that still have never been broken. The waterfront on Atlantic Avenue was a forest of masts and spars; on any given day, more than four hundred vessels might lay at anchor along its wharves, and the cobblestone streets of Boston rattled with cargo destined for all the bustling points on the broad New England compass.[32]

On the dozens of "spoke" roads that spread out from "the Hub," stagecoaches and cargo wagons brought passengers, newspapers, and a wealth of household items to destinations at general stores in all the four-corners and turnpikes from Boston to Stockbridge. During wintertime, the old thoroughfares teemed with horse-drawn sleighs and cutters jogging along in the icy air of night, their jangling bells alerting other travelers to their passage along the dark roads. Taverns and public houses thrived at busy intersections, places where a weary pilgrim could find a warm, dry stall for his horse, a hot noggin of "cherry bounce" for his spirit, a steaming bowl of stew or chowder, and the lively sound of music around the light of a sputtering fireplace: "There were popular ballads and folk songs . . . sailor's chanties along the coast, ballads of village murders, rockaby songs, sugar maker's songs, sung by weavers and carpenters, by farm wives and wandering fiddlers, by hunters, trappers, guides and lumbermen, snatches and refrains and longer pieces, brought from the Old World or natural outgrowths of the American soil."[33]

The Village era in New England was a time when people worked hard and played hard, singing at their toils in the days when "teamsters" were men who drove teams of horses, when "spinsters" were women who spun wool, and when "long shore men" were men who worked along the shore. Vibrant homespun speech was coupled with the cadence of stirring melody. In Yankee villages, the folk song culture of the new nation first began to hit its stride.

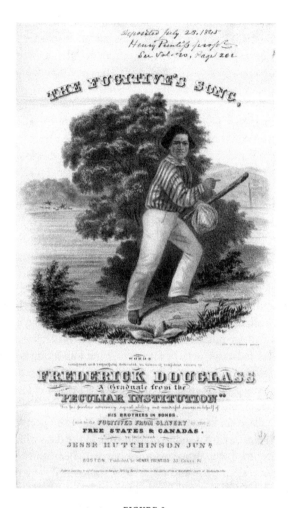

FIGURE 3.
Sheet music for "The Fugitive's Song" by Jesse Hutchinson, 1843.
Image of Frederick Douglass. Library of Congress,
Prints & Photographs Division, LC-DIG-ppmsca-07616.

CHAPTER THREE

THERE'S A GOOD TIME COMING

Reform in New England, 1810–1900

IN THE EARLY 1800S, by the fiftieth anniversary of Paul Revere's ride toward Lexington, new revolutions had begun to transform the old landscape of village and farm. Mills were set up wherever there was enough water flowage to turn a wheel and set gears to running. For all the bucolic charm and sturdy self-sufficiency of the Village era, a certain restlessness crept in and began to dominate New England life: "The air resounded with the saw and hammer, the blows of the forge, the bells in the factory towers. In all directions the people were building turnpikes, hundreds of miles of straight lines that cut athwart the old winding roads. The Green Mountain boys had erected their State House. Dwellings were going up in clearings and meadows, or, being up, were carted bodily off to better sites. Churches grew like snowdrops in early March. Villages, towns sprang from the fields. A current of ambition had galvanized New England."[1]

Along with industrializing activities, a goodly part of that galvanization also came in the form of religious revival. The iron hand of Puritan orthodoxy that had fallen by the wayside of American history had been joined by the discarded scepter of royal rule. Common people who had learned to invent their own way of government suddenly felt emboldened to find their own pathways to heaven. Particularly in the hinterlands, freedom of religion meant not only the ability to choose from one of the established churches but also to join or even invent a new one if the spirit moved in that direction. Being an American meant making decisions for yourself that had been left to the purview of one's "betters" for centuries.

While many men of property and education, like George Washington, Thomas Jefferson, and James Monroe, were deists who believed in a higher power while declining to choose a particular religious denomination, the majority of the solid villagers of New England stayed with the tried-and-true structures of an increasingly easygoing Congregationalism. The old skull-and-crossbones designs etched into Yankee gravestones were gradually replaced by stylized cherubs and weeping willows. A message of hope supplanted the fear of damnation in the neat, stone-walled village cemeteries where generations were gathered in the long reunion.

But out in the brushy hinterlands, at the new frontiers where wild things still howled in the night, the impulse to sanctification and salvation found earnest voice and novel direction. Baptists and Methodists gained in membership, and Shaker colonies sprang up in places such as Canterbury, Pittsfield, and Sabbathday Lake. New sects sprouted up like blackberry bushes in freshly cleared land, led by charismatic leaders preaching redemption, cleaving to an unshaken faith in the holy word, and expressing their spiritual rapture in tongues, in song, and in dance. Countless lone pilgrims made their way across the landscape, sowing salvation just as Jonathan Chapman of Littleton, Massachusetts, was strewing apple seeds. What these folks had in common was the conviction that a millennial reckoning was coming very soon, and that personal salvation was the only way to assure that you would have a place when the roll was called "up yonder."

Free of orthodoxy and unfettered by authorship rights, a traveling preacher would fill his saddlebags with hymnals printed on makeshift country presses and then head out for the remote farms of young believers, places where he was likely to be paid in pudding and corn-bread and given a bed in the loft. Within a day or two, once word was out, settlers would gather to hear spontaneous exhortations, to sing psalms set to old folk tunes, and to come to glory without inhibition, reservation, or judgment on the part of "superiors." On top of broad, cleared ridges, settlers gathered in northern New England and western Massachusetts to hold religious revival meetings that constituted a sort of spontaneous combustion of free-form religion. There were no walls but birch trees in such places, no rafters but clouds, and no expectations other than the sort of salvation that arrived in a direct line from the Divine. Nothing remains of these assemblies now but place names on modern maps: names such as "Zion Hill," "Camp Hill Road," and "The Mount."

Jeremiah Ingalls was a Massachusetts-born surveyor, cooper, and preacher who lived much of his life in Newbury, Vermont. He traveled extensively throughout northern New England in the years between the 1770s and the 1820s, teaching rural singing schools, marking town and settlement boundaries, and composing hymns that rivaled William Billings's work in their beauty and utility. In 1805, he published a hymnal that he called *The Christian Harmony* in Exeter, New Hampshire, which included his compositions "The Apple Tree," "Honor to the Hills," and "Northfield." The latter hymn eventually made its way, person to person, to the South, where it has been sung in Black churches and white shape-note congregations for more than two hundred years.[2] In this way, Ingalls served as the link between the New England revivals and the massive religious camp meetings that swept throughout the South, most notably in Kentucky, where twenty thousand gathered for a revival in 1801. As noted sacred music scholar William Pullen Jackson has said, "It was this remarkable Vermonter who, alone in his generation, borrowed the institutional singing-school song-book technic, harmonizings, book form, size and all, applied it to the country Baptist mass of folk song, published that mass of country song and thus lighted up for us the early, probably even the earliest times of religious folk singing in America."[3]

But by the 1820s, European music was becoming the order of a newer day in fashionable New England parlors, as the venerable fuguing tunes and old fife airs came to be considered out of date by young sophisticates of the Industrial Age. The old singing-school tradition was largely forgotten in the North by the time of the coming of the railroads, and churchwomen from New England congregations boxed up worn-out hymnals and sent them south as donations to poor African American slave churches. There, the old tunes would play a role in the development of Southern spiritual and gospel songs. In this way, Christian African American and Native American congregations joined their traditions with the singing and circulation of hymns that originated in New England.[4]

The first half of the nineteenth century also saw the rapid creation of the factory, the railroad, the telegraph wire, and the initial marketing of modern household comforts. The revolutionary period of enlighten-ment was supplanted by a dizzying period of industrial development. Thousands of inventions brought with them a host of unanticipated gains and losses. The degree to which the national expansion resulted in positive outcomes was happily accepted, even at the cost of ignoring collateral damage such as the spread of slavery, the continued sub-jugation of women, the plundering of the landscape, and territory-grabbing wars first with Native Americans and then with Mexico. On the balance sheet, to a nation that was on the make and in a hurry, it was considered "all good."

Not long after the factories of the Industrial Revolution began to displace most of the homespun ways of hearthside and farm, New England transcendentalists found themselves responding to the urge to "simplify" their lives. Many people in New England began to think that the great new industrial engine was actually on the wrong track and headed full-speed toward perdition. It was time, they thought, to revive the moral and creative principles that had been embraced in the Revolution. It was time, they said, to listen to the beating heart rather than the whirring machine. It was time to recognize the value in things that could not be locked in a vault, and it was time to reform, to sweep up the accumulated filth that several decades of greed and "progress" were heedlessly leaving in the wake of an unrighteous age.

Ardent bands of Yankee abolitionists, women's rights advocates, pacifists, and temperance workers chose the advancement of Amer-ican moral ideals as their life's work. For religious folks such as the Shakers and other millennial groups in rural Massachusetts and New Hampshire, this meant engaging in profound spiritual transformation. For the people who came to be known as transcendentalists, it meant embracing an emphatically secular set of reforms in academy towns and lyceum gatherings throughout the region, including, as in the case of the Thoreau sisters of Concord, acting as station keepers on the Underground Railroad that carried fugitive slaves from the South toward "the drinking gourd" of the North Star and freedom in Canada.[5]

There were antislavery activists all across small-town New England from the earliest years of the 1800s onward, hundreds of them offering their homes for use along the branch lines of the Underground Railroad. Abolition was not always a popular stance, but by the 1840s, it was the linchpin of a clear vision of a better day to come in America, based on the combined application of lofty ideals and practical gumption. The message of renewal was clear and consistent: we needed to get our national house in order. The means to do so lay in our spirits, in renewed commitment to the founding heritage, and, more often than not, in the revival of the traditional arts of music, dance, crafts, oratory, agriculture, and literature.

Hardly any statues were made of any of these reformers. They were almost all odd ducks of one sort or another, and whatever strange communities they retreated to were fraught with complications and contradictions that led them to be short-lived. But they were right. The ensuing chronic and tragic events of our national history—from the Civil War to modern institutional racism—have validated their fears and reinforced their aspirations.

It has been said that Americans never fail to "do the right thing" when it is the only option left to them, and so the issues of union and slavery festered for decades until they finally exploded in the Civil War, during which Americans killed about three-quarters of a million of each other. When patriots needed to brace themselves to make the sacrifices necessary to save the Union that Lincoln called "the last best hope of humanity," it was the music of the reformers that they marched to and the exhortations of abolitionists such as Harriet Beecher Stowe and Reverend Theodore Parker that they heeded.[6]

There is perhaps no better example of the fervor of this time and place than the career of the Hutchinson Family Singers of Milford, New Hampshire. The troupe, consisting of siblings Abby, John, Judson, and Asa, traveled the country in the 1840s as popular singing reformers. They exhorted their audiences to "get off the track" and join with them in espousing the causes of women's rights, abolition, temperance, and the Jeffersonian ideal of a peaceable, agrarian kingdom come. A full twenty years prior to the Emancipation Proclamation, the Hutchinsons were traveling the country and calling for an end to slavery in no uncertain terms:

We have come from the mountains, we have come from the mountains,
We have come from the mountains of the Old Granite State.
We're a band of brothers, we're a band of brothers
We're a band of brothers and we live among the hills.
With a band of music, with a band of music,
With a band of music we are passing round the world.

Liberty is our motto, Liberty is our motto
Equal liberty is our motto in the Old Granite State.
We despise oppression, we despise oppression
We despise oppression and we cannot be enslaved.
Yes we're friends of emancipation
And we'll sing the proclamation
Till it echoes through our nation from the Old Granite State![7]

Active at the midpoint between the publication of Thomas Paine's *Rights of Man* in 1791 and the release of Bob Dylan's "Blowin' in the Wind" in 1963, the Hutchinsons were one of the first popular singing groups in America. Of them, abolitionist William Lloyd Garrison said, "Never before has the singing of ballads been made directly and purposely subservient to the freedom, welfare, happiness, and moral elevation of the people."[8] Frederick Douglass, a former slave and the leading crusader for American freedom, wrote in appreciation of their work, "There was something almost miraculous in the singing of these three brothers and one sister. I have heard them, in a time of great excitement on the slavery question, calm to silence and order a turbulent and determined mob when it was in full blast and fiercely bent upon breaking up an anti-slavery meeting. . . . But the Hutchinsons were not merely a family of singers and sentimental reformers; they were actuated and guided by high moral principle."[9]

The persistence of New England abolitionists such as the Hutchinsons in raising the slavery question was one of the key precipitants of the Civil War. When Fort Sumter was fired upon on April 12, 1861, and Lincoln called for hundreds of thousands of volunteers to the Union Army, New England rapidly mustered regiment after regiment of young men in support of the effort. The song we now know as "The Battle Hymn of the Republic" began to take form in Boston that May at a

flag-raising ceremony at Fort Warren. There, enlistees started singing the abolitionist lyric "John Brown's body lies a-moulderin' in the
grave" to the tune of the old slave folk song "On Canaan's Happy Shore."
Immediately thereafter, troops throughout the Union began striding
toward the front lines in time to the new song, with its "Glory, glory,
hallelujah" refrain.

When she heard the sound of those Union troops singing in the
streets of Washington, DC, poet, author, and social reformer Julia Ward
Howe of Boston was inspired to compose "The Battle Hymn of the
Republic," new verses set to the stirring strains of the "On Canaan's
Happy Shore" / John Brown tune. Over the course of four long years
of war, Northern armies marched the long course from Bull Run to
Appomattox to Howe's composition and the cadence of songs such
as "Tenting Tonight on the Old Campground" (composed by New
Hampshire's Walter Kittredge) and "Tramp, Tramp, Tramp the Boys
Are Marching," and "The Battle Cry of Freedom" (both written by George
Root, a native of the hill town of Sheffield, Massachusetts).

ON APRIL 9, 1865, the American Civil War finally ended. A scant five
days later, Lincoln was assassinated by a die-hard racist who had made
a point of attending John Brown's hanging in 1859. A pall of moral
exhaustion fell over a bloodied and traumatized land. By the end of
the 1860s, the shadow empires of racism and elitism had struck back.
Reconstruction was castrated when it wasn't lynched, and the country
pretty much took up business where it had been left off before the
war. In a booming economy and in the sudden absence of national
purpose, a new Gilded Age began to fatten a limited number of very
deep pockets.

The federal government had borrowed from New York indus-
trialists much of the four million dollars a day that it required to
conduct the Civil War, and by the time of Lee's surrender, Wall Street
had overthrown State Street as the center of American power and, in
consequence, raw capitalism supplanted free enterprise as the economic coin of the American realm. In the aftermath of Appomattox,
many Americans were led to accept the Confederacy's mythology
of the "Lost Cause" of states' rights and decided that it was time
for a hearty handshake, a quick end to the Freedmen's Bureau and

Reconstruction, and a chummy resolution of what was suddenly convenient to see as having been nothing more, really, than a national family quarrel. If that seemed like a whole lot to sweep under the rug, well, the solution was clear enough: make a bigger rug. America proceeded to do just that for the next hundred years. There was a West to settle and to count profits from, and it was in that direction that the country proceeded.

Back in New England, forty-eight months of death and destruction in the Civil War had cut deeply into the virility and the spirit of the region. Boston was left in mourning, bereft of civic momentum. The region's little tidewater and hill country villages had seen hundreds of thousands of boys in blue volunteer and tramp away to the south; many never returned. Little towns of several thousand souls in the optimistic 1840s could count themselves only in the few hundreds by the Victorian era. Good, fertile farm land grew up into bushes and then trees; abandoned old houses rotted and collapsed into their cellar holes. In remote hill towns, tilting gravestones outnumbered the living. What remained of a once vigorous rural village culture endured only in the memories of elderly residents and in the stories of writers such as Sarah Orne Jewett.

After the war, the same New England composers who had penned songs to save the Union took it upon themselves to revive the poverty-stricken Northern countryside. Walter Kittredge's "Never Turn Back with Your Hand to the Plow" and George Root's "The Hand That Holds the Bread" were among hundreds of songs of rural revival sung fervently at local Grange meetings, along with sentimental pieces such as "My Old New Hampshire Home," which sold more than a million copies of sheet music nationally in 1898. In that same year, the governor of New Hampshire, Frank West Rollins, founded the Old Home Day movement, organizing festival observances in every town in the Granite State and reviving the folk customs of the Village era.

High on a hill in the Canadian border town of Pittsburg, New Hampshire, a bonfire was lit in the night that served as the signal to ignite a woodpile in the next town to the south, and in minutes torches flickered across hundreds of miles of hills and valleys all the way to the ocean and the Massachusetts border. The ensuing revival celebration, still observed annually every August throughout the region, featured sermons, songs, speeches on rural topics, displays of folk crafts and skills, and feasts of the old fashion, including clambakes tucked in seaweed, beans baked in the ground, and pies and puddings concocted from recipes written in butternut ink.[10]

Folk gatherings like these were the occasion for the singing of old songs such as "Cousin Jedidiah," "Old Pod Auger Times," and "Stay on the Farm."

> Come, boys, I have something to tell you,
> Come near, I would whisper it low.
> They say you are leaving the farm, boys,
> Don't be in a hurry to go.
> The city has many attractions,
> But think of its vices and sins.
> When once in the vortex of fashion,
> How soon our destruction begins!
> Stay on the farm, boys, stay on the farm,
> Though profits come in rather slow.
> Stay on the farm, boys, stay on the farm,
> Don't be in a hurry to go.[11]

Even as he preached his gospel of regional roots, Frank Rollins exhorted Yankee folk to embrace the presence of new immigrants in the country, calling for them to be welcomed with what he pointedly referred to as "a broad catholic spirit." "I think I see dangers to our beautiful country," Rollins wrote, "from the encroachment of materialism; and I believe everything which we can do to cultivate sentiment (and by sentiment I do not mean inane sentiment, but sentiment of the highest order, of the most advanced kind)—I say that everything which we can do to cultivate this, is to our advantage, and is an offset to the dangers of materialism."[12]

French Canadian, Irish, German, Jewish, Polish, Italian, Slavic, and Portuguese they came, not only filling factories with a new labor force but also, in many cases, taking up the core New England enterprises of fishery, lumber camp, and farm. In rich countrysides such as the Pioneer Valley of western Massachusetts and in city wards such as Boston's West End, Polish dances, Jewish klezmer tunes, and German polkas resonated across fields and tenements alike. New England folk culture took on broad new dimensions with the approach of the twentieth century.

Meanwhile, the moguls of the Gilded Age had little use for true free enterprise, replacing it with the management of corporate capital as the defining force in American life. A New England region that had long embraced both rural and urban traditions began to respond to new norms as suburban developments spread out along commuter railroad lines. The frontier had moved far to the West, with all of its energy and physicality, while new gentility and social strata came to the fore in the manicured neighborhoods of the Victorian Northeast. Neither the musty traditions of upcountry "hick" farmers nor the outlandish cultures of garlic-eating newcomers could pass muster in a social atmosphere that very quickly became indexed by breeding, connections, education, conformity, and financial capacity. All these factors combined to create an invisible yet unmistakable carriage of privilege. One either "had it," or, perhaps regrettably, one simply did not.

Instead of the hybrid vigor of old-timers and immigrants that Frank Rollins had envisioned, the Gilded Age began to play itself out along crabbed and spiteful parochial lines. Some Yankee nativists indulged in snobbish self-reference, backsliding into the sort of blooded entitlement that their grandsires had rejected in revolution only a few score years before. Irish and Italian immigrants were denigrated by the Brahmin elite for generations; these groups, in turn, nursed their grievances long after they had achieved majority status in the streets and at the polls. Fallen from its position as a visionary City upon a Hill, Boston became the home of the washed-up banker, the cop on the take, and the ward heeler on the make. The art of the shady deal was curated in the shadows of the Massachusetts State House and in the nooks and crannies of the barroom at the nearby Parker House. The common wealth was pillaged by charlatans who could smarm their way into tenured positions of high influence by simply "doing a few favors."

Yet at the same time that New England was losing her mantle of leadership in mercantile and political power, she maintained her patronage of the arts and learning. The region, and especially Boston, expanded its role as the home of symphony and symposium, art museum and athenaeum, antiquarian preserve and arboretum. Along the Charles, Harvard quietly and comfortably compounded the interest in the legacy left to it in the 1600s, joined in scholarly, elm-shaded incumbency by Radcliffe, Tufts, Boston College, Northeastern, Boston

University, and a host of other colleges, universities, and academies tucked snugly throughout the rolling New England countryside.

It was from this parentage of academia and the arts, energized by the contributions of scholars of both genders, that an appreciation of long-forgotten folkways began to emerge around the dawn of the twentieth century. Francis James Child was the son of a poor Boston sailmaker who began with an undergraduate scholarship and became a full professor of English literature at Harvard, where his passion and his enduring legacy was a five-volume compendium, *The English and Scottish Popular Ballads,* published in Cambridge between 1882 and 1898. Through exhaustive research, Child identified 305 distinct ballads from old British sources, dating from the thirteenth to the eighteenth century. Most were represented in multiple variations and fragments, resulting in the enormous size of the finished work. Inside the five volumes, the reader discovered tales of historic events, romance, chivalry, forbidden love, treachery, faithfulness, the supernatural, jealousy, nobility, and outlawry, drawn from written sources but assumed to be the products of oral tradition. Over the years, the "Child ballads" have been among the most enduring titles in the folk song canon.[13]

Child was succeeded in time and focus by a number of remarkable Yankee women scholars and collectors who ventured into the far corners of the region to identify, write down, and eventually record the folk songs of New England. Fannie Hardy Eckstorm was the daughter of a Maine fur trader who graduated from Smith College in 1888 and returned to Brewer, Maine, where she became the superintendent of public schools and founded that city's public library. She published a number of articles on birds and on Maine's fish and game laws, but her enduring interest was in the folklore and songs of the rural regions of her native state. Along with her friend, Mary Winslow Smyth, she traveled to remote fishing villages and logging camps, collecting sings and stories that she published in *The Minstrelsy of Maine* in 1927, and *British Ballads from Maine* in 1929. She documented rugged work shanties, French Canadian *chansons,* and newly discovered variations on the old Child ballads. Many of these tunes had made their way across the ocean hundreds of years before; like old seafaring ballast bricks, they had been pulled from the deep holds of sailing ships and mortared firmly into the warmth of Yankee hearths.[14]

Eloise Hubbard Linscott of Taunton, Massachusetts, graduated from Radcliffe in 1920. She pursued musical fieldwork throughout New England, collecting songs that she published in 1939 in her book *Folk Songs of Old New England*. Her first concentration was folk dance, and her collection of contra dance steps and tunes was gleaned from old callers and musicians from places such as Freedom, New Hampshire; Cumberland Mills, Maine; and Bernardston, Massachusetts. Linscott's collection of songs is remarkable for its diversity of sources, most of whose memories stretched back to the 1850s and some of whose family singing traditions went back to the 1600s. Like Fannie Hardy Eckstorm, Linscott had a warm place in her heart for the old North Country logging days, when, as she wrote, "five hundred loggers roared into town for a blow-in, their pockets full of pay, their calked boots scarring the tavern floors and plank sidewalks while they shouted and pounded at the bars." She described one of her many sea shanty tunes as "not those of the glee club nor of the barbershop quartet, but the heartbeat of a great ship as she rolls while the wind sighs in the rigging."[15] Eloise Linscott's collection of more than 2,500 recordings and manuscripts resides at the American Folklife Center at the Library of Congress.

Helen Hartness Flanders was a native of Springfield, Vermont, a 1909 graduate of Dana Hall School, and the daughter of a governor and wife of a U.S. senator from her state. In 1930, she was asked to join the Committee on Traditions and Ideals of the Vermont Commission on Country Life. In that role, she began collecting folk songs and recording wax discs in small hill town kitchens and farms in Vermont and New Hampshire, places where the ancient traditions lived on in parlors, on porches, and in the spirited dance get-togethers that were referred to as "kitchen junkets." Like many of her colleagues, she sought to collect the old songs before oral traditions were supplanted by the modern music that was beginning to beam across the countryside on the radio.

This remarkable woman collected and documented nearly 4,500 field recordings that are now housed at Middlebury College, at the American Center for Folklife at the Smithsonian, and at Harvard University. She wrote extensively on folk music, publishing a regular column on ballads in the Springfield, Massachusetts, *Republican* in the 1930s. During the following decade, Helen befriended singer Margaret MacArthur, who would go on to record regional songs well into the Boston-Cambridge Folk Revival.[16]

Given the huge amount of work that Eckstorm, Linscott, and Flanders did during the course of their dedicated and productive lives, it might seem puzzling that their names are not as celebrated as those of John and Alan Lomax and Cecil Sharp, who, after all, were collecting much the same material (particularly Child ballads) over the same period of time that these women were active in the North. It may be that the reason lies in the words "women active in the North." By the twentieth century, New England was already largely out of touch with its own roots, as, to a wide degree, it remains still. The great men folklorists seem to have been skilled self-promoters as well as adept field workers, active in the New York circles that supported their publicity and publishing. In any case, a study of American folk music would be incomplete without sufficient reference to the enduring work of these talented women.

In the realm of folk dance, New Hampshire's Ralph Page of Keene devoted his life to learning and then teaching the old contra dances that continued to thrive in isolated rural locations, preserved faithfully by aging fiddlers, seasoned callers, and generations of enthusiastic dancers. For Moses Asch's Disc Records and later for the Folk Dancer label, Page recorded a body of work that is now housed at the University of New Hampshire in his name, portions of which have also been included in the Folk New England collection at the University of Massachusetts Amherst. Page's career spanned most of the twentieth century and eventually took him around the world as an ambassador of American folk tradition for the U.S. State Department.

These and other dedicated Yankee folklorists ventured out on narrow dirt roads, seeking old-timers on isolated farms whose memories, if not their ankles or knees, were as limber as they had been fifty years earlier. There was a rich folk heritage and there were wonderful stories still alive in the New England countryside, not as celebrated but every bit as rich as the lore of the Old West:

> The old man was missin' a few teeth from the side of his mouth, and one of them old clay pipes fit just right into the space. It'd be snowin' to beat all, blowin' a gale outside, and he'd set there in the corner, pick up his fiddle, and motion to one of the older girls to go over to the old pump organ. Oh, they'd play away on those good old tunes over and over, father and daughter. Then the old man, he'd

look out the window at the snow blowin' around in the dooryard, and he'd puff on that old clay pipe and wink at me with a big grin on his face: "T'ain't snowin' in here, is it, Jimmy?"[17]

The first decades of the 1900s saw a vigorous expression of the roots and the folkways of New England emerge in a renaissance in many forms of the arts. Writers Robert Frost, Cornelius Weygandt, Ralph Nading Hill, Dorothy Canfield Fisher, Van Wyck Brooks, Archibald MacLeish, and Samuel Eliot Morison, among others, all drew inspiration from deep old New England cultural wells. Artists including Rockwell Kent, Maxfield Parrish, Daniel Chester French, and the members of the Wyeth clan distilled regional scenes and dynamics into dramatic statements in painting, woodcut, and sculpture. Composers such as Charles Ives and Aaron Copland combined polyglot musical influences into an almost mythical sense of the American land, expressing an inspired gratitude for the course of American history and the unique threads of American culture.

By midcentury, Historic Deerfield had been restored, Old Sturbridge Village established, and the New Bedford Whaling Museum founded. The cultural historian Edward Deming Andrews fostered a new appreciation of Shaker heritage and folk culture through his collections, lectures, and writings; in his work, Andrews did much to inspire the later establishment of museums in the former Shaker communities. By the 1940s, a sort of cultural Indian summer had settled over the northern countryside.

But, by and large, New England's traditional music did not share in this renewal. Conditioned by the modern standards of salon and concert hall, genteel New England declined to place much value on the cidery twang of old Yankee folk music. In conventional assumption, folk songs were likely to be thought of as the products of cowboy campfires, Negro juke joints, and Mississippi steamboats—all of them low in social status and far away from the places that "mattered." William Billings, the great folk hymn composer of the American Revolution, lay in his native Boston in an unmarked grave; his songs, unsung for generations, would largely go unrecorded until as late as 1964. Along with his spirit, the souls of thousands of Abenaki mothers, Yankee balladeers, French Canadian fiddlers, African American harpooners,

Finnish loggers, Boston schoolmarms, Portuguese fishermen, Irish stevedores, Vermont granny women, Jewish klezmorim, and singers from
all of New England's old cultures slept together in silent anonymity in
the region of their birth, their melodies forgotten along with the lives
that they had lived.

FIGURE 4.

Engraving of a nineteenth-century wood-fired railroad train,
from Clarence P. Hornung, *2,000 Early Advertising Cuts*
(New York: Dover Publications, 1995).

CHAPTER FOUR

THE SOUND OF YOUNG AMERICA

America Westward and Southward, 1800–1900

AT THE SAME TIME that the nineteenth century brought gentrifica-
tion to New England, the vast stretch of the American continent was
providing rough-and-ready room for the displaced world of homespun
and handmade culture. As if in answer to the rattle of cast-iron factory
gears in places like Lowell and Lawrence, wooden wagon wheels began
turning westward, carrying common folk toward a daylight shadowed
only by trees and mountains, out in "the territories." When the words
"frontier" or "pioneer" come into use, those of us who live in the modern
era may think reflexively of the American West, with all the iconography,
associations, and horse manure that come with it. Yet the real American
frontier of the nineteenth century unfolded serially across a westward
map that began in jumping-off points such as Deerfield, Massachusetts;
Albany, New York; Pittsburgh, Pennsylvania; and Nashville, Tennessee,
before reaching out to St. Louis, and then, much later on, to the streets
of Wichita, Dodge, Laredo, Fort Griffin, Tombstone, and San Francisco.

The movement westward expanded across territory that was being
taken over by force from its original inhabitants. As the West was settled,
the Native Peoples of the continent were swindled and displaced and
their ways of life eradicated in the name and under the benediction of
Progress. Fate cast an uneven hand as America was settled; events probably needn't have played out the way they did, but very few voices were
raised in opposition to revenge once the blood started flowing. Native
American tribes were systematically pushed aside by a civilization that

combined pious sentiment and insatiable yet respectable greed. Long before there was anything in America called an organized crime mob, the Native families were fingered, set up, and rubbed out by syndicates that moved in swiftly on their turf.

Fur and hide companies, lumber barons, cattle magnates, mining outfits, and railroad empires devoured the land, scattering behind them the bones of brave and buffalo. Reflections on "the Golden Rule" seem to have been restricted to a few hours on Sunday mornings, if that, in the context of creeds that were very rarely applied to "heathens." Above all else, ours was a culture on the make and in a hurry.

Into the newly opened country spilled thousands of immigrants heading toward stands of tall timber, expanses of fertile plains, and arteries of twisting rivers that stretched between the settled districts and the promise of California. Safety, freedom, and respect were as important as land and water for the travelers who struggled through what they sometimes saw as a blessed and sometimes experienced as a wearisome land. Broad stretches of prairie and plains were easy for people of modest means to come by beyond the settlements, where social constraints and stratification fell by the wayside. On the frontier, there were few limits placed on the deeply important American capacity to reinvent one's self, one's past, and one's future.

Wagon trains rolling westward served as portable villages for homeless immigrants. Pianos and organs would have been impractical on the trail, so the soundtrack to the western movement was scored by harmonica and fiddle, banjo and guitar. Each night, the new pilgrims circled around their firesides, deep in thoughts of the old homes that they had traded in for the hope of a new start out in the territories. The "rugged individual" may have come to be seen as an American archetype, yet, as a people, we have learned that we are at our best when we deliver ourselves from evil in the harmony of concord, creativity, and community. We have always had to dowse for our identities, quite often in the music of our restless and hopeful souls. Since we have been acculturated to take measure of our lives in wealth and status rather than in the reckoning of who we are and what we feel, music has served as a soul-saving guidepost in our tangled search for acquisition, validation, atonement, and peace on the American landscape.

Even in egalitarian New England, it was the oldest sons who inherited the farms, and generations of younger brothers and their wives were motivated to set out to "make a pitch" on their own. For those who had come to America as indentured servants, the frontier was a place where one could shake free of the stigma of what had amounted to contract slavery. A Northern "apprentice" could set out on the road with a set of skills that he had learned during his term as a "bound boy," perhaps as a leather worker, cooper, wheelwright, or carpenter. He might take on a new last name that advertised his status as a smith, a cook, or a joiner, particularly if at some point he had run afoul of the law.

Starting over was an easy thing to do, even for the poorest white people. When a Southern indenture ended either by term or by running away, paths led to the Appalachian uplands, where, on some hillside farm or in some lonesome valley, settlers could cultivate a garden of homestead kitchen staples while growing market crops of tobacco and corn. From the standpoint of transportability and profit, corn was best turned into cash in the efficient form of bourbon whiskey, the product of copper kettle and coil, for which there was always a steady demand, cash on the barrelhead.

By its nature, the frontier was to serve both as the perfect foster home for ancient tradition and as fertile ground for the hybridization of new folkways. Generations of local folk cultures that had been handed down through the years mixed together along the westward roads that stretched from central Pennsylvania across to Ohio, Indiana, and the Midwest, and from Baltimore and Virginia to frontiers in Tennessee, Kentucky, and Arkansas. In four-corner taverns, meetinghouses, ferries, and country stores, people gathered after work in woods and fields to get acquainted, tell tales, and sing their songs. A mix of ballads and dance tunes were the coin of the realm, with accompaniment by fiddle, gourd- (and later, skin-) bodied "banjars," and guitars. In time, songs and ballads that had been carried west from older homes were supplanted by a rich mixture of new reels, jigs, spirituals, love songs, shouts, and murder ballads that often ended with a powerful statement about the value of righteous living delivered from the gallows.

Down the Natchez Trace, out to Oregon, on to San Francisco, or down the Goodnight-Loving Trail, pioneers followed routes first set out by moccasins, stitched together by wagon tracks, and then spiked to rails and ties bedded on crushed rock. There were no newspapers or any other form of media out on the prairies. Few people had access to a mirror, let alone a photograph. Pioneers became adept at entertaining themselves with a combination of the oldest stories and songs that they could remember and the new ones they made up themselves.

In the 1840s, Stephen Foster single-handedly gave birth to American popular music. His songs swept swiftly across the continent, almost completely by word of mouth. Foster's "Oh! Susanna" was quickly amended from a Mississippi steamboat song to a celebration of the voyage of an East Boston–built clipper ship all the way around Cape Horn and up to San Francisco Bay:

> Oh, Susanna, darling, take your ease,
> For we have beat the clipper fleet—the *Sovereign of the Seas!* [1]

Other than the forty-niners who toiled in the goldfields outside Sacramento, the people heading west did not seek to become famous or rich but for the most part sought to create new lives for themselves on a new land, lightening the drudgery of hard physical work with the good times to be had singing and dancing. In 1849, a young man toiling in the gold fields of California wrote in his diary,

> I wonder if I am putting it too strongly to say that we American people never really got together until now? Surely there was never such a wide representation as is now seen on these California trails, for here are thousands from perhaps every state. You notice this, for instance, by the curiosity with which Yankees watch and listen to Southerners, or as both of these watch and listen to Missourians and the hill folks of Arkansas. Strange worlds—customs, dress, dialects and manners—here meet together. While travelers from both North and South have visited beyond the Mason Dixon line, and while minstrel troupes have carried darkey songs far and wide, I think negro melodies never acquired the popularity which is accorded to them here and now. [2]

Stephen Foster, who composed "My Old Kentucky Home," "Beautiful Dreamer," and "Old Black Joe," spent only a few weeks, late in life, in the Deep South. For the most part, he lived in Pennsylvania, Ohio, and New York City. When he was ten years old, his father suffered business failure and political reverse, and young Foster and his family had been exiled from their upper-middle-class mansion near Pittsburgh. As he wandered, depressed, rootless, and alcoholic, for the short term of his creative and tragic life, the composer shared with the Southern Black folk of his imagination a longing for lost hearth and home and the impulse to express his feelings in songs of sentiment and desire.

Foster's artistic world was largely his own inauthentic fantasy, but his wounded heart was real, as was his longing for surcease. His songs struck a chord that resonated across a transcontinental landscape of displaced and wayfaring pilgrims. The speed with which the new American music spread to the Pacific shore is all the more remarkable in light of the fact that there was no electricity, no radio, no recordings, no national entertainment industry, and no Internet pushing "hits" or "fashion" into the public consciousness.

Foster was not the first person, nor would he by a long shot be the last, to make musical hay by crossing the great national racial divide and infusing his music with the vigor of a hybrid American culture in the context of an imagined American past. Ragtime, show tunes, spirituals, swing, blues, jazz, and rock 'n' roll would all become vital expressions of blended cultural inheritance. Throughout our history, African Americans may have represented only somewhere between 10 and 20 percent of the population, but their cultural influence has always carried the electoral college of American music by a landslide.

The Industrial Revolution, the westward movement, and urbanization were all interpreted in their times as the avatars of unalloyed and unlimited progress. But the courses and character of these "advances" brought along with them collateral displacement and human trauma on a scale that hardly any people have ever attempted to culturally fathom in the short course of a few generations. We have often found ourselves too busy moving forward to really see where it was that we were going and whose buffalo we were goring in the process. Our "progress" has come at considerable deferred cost, and, at its heart, our nation has yet to really heal from or even truly understand the pain of our accumulated wounds, the costs of our short cuts, or the depth of our losses.

During the nineteenth century, Americans attempted to come to grips as best they could with the profound forces that were shaping a new fate for the nation. There was genuine excitement involved in developing a new national identity, and it found expression in a distinct American vernacular music. It did not take long for "syncopation to sweep the nation," as Bert Williams would later sing in his 1914 hit "You Can't Get Away from It," and for a racially hybrid American music to become both fashionable and profitable. But our history, particularly as regards race relations, seems to have always taken a half step or so backward after every step taken forward.

Beginning in the 1830s, the bizarre commercial concoction known as "the minstrel show" began to spread like wildfire across the land. In a society fractured along North/South and free/slave lines, the majority population's first impressions of people of color was largely through the thoughtless, unkind, and denigrated caricatures that were promoted in the popular minstrel show, and later in "moving pictures." Generations would struggle with the consequences of "darky" stereotypes that were dreamt up by some of the country's first ambitious popular entertainment figures (Thomas Rice, Dan Emmett, and Edwin Pearce Christy, among others) and that would echo on into the *Amos 'n' Andy* radio programs of the 1950s. An old saying had it that "a lie could run across town while the truth was still putting on its shoes," and such has been the long and unhappy course of imbedded cultural bigotry in America.[3]

On the positive side of the ledger, the magic of hybrid American music was out of the bottle, and, despite coming years of neglect and distortion, it was never going to be pushed back into the jug. In reference to the popular concert pianist Louis Moreau Gottschalk, a thirty-year-old Mark Twain had this to say in the *San Francisco Dramatic Chronicle* in 1865:

> I like Gottschalk well enough, he probably gets as much out of the piano as there is in it. But the frozen fact is, that all he *does* get out of it is "tum, tum." . . . The piano may do for love-sick girls who lace themselves to skeletons, and lunch on chalk, pickles, and slate pencils. But give me the banjo. . . . When you want *genuine* music—music that will come right home to you like a bad quarter, suffuse your system like strychnine whisky . . . ramify your whole constitution like the measles, and break out on your hide like the pin-feather pimples on a picked goose,—when you want all this, just smash your piano, and invoke the glory-beaming banjo![4]

When Mark Twain and his contemporaries thrilled to the notes of an opening banjo riff ringing out in a concert hall in the 1850s, they were experiencing the same sort of thing that Americans would feel a hundred years later when Chuck Berry's "Roll Over Beethoven" began to blast out of the speakers in a Chevrolet. But a whole lot of water would flow over the dam of industrialized culture in the intervening years before we, as a people, wholeheartedly began to throw ourselves into "digging these rhythm and blues."

During the very months and years in which the western movement played out, the matter of African slavery was being called into question by New England abolitionists. As the country grew in territory and influence, the conflict between bond and free, between North and South, and between the factory and the plantation began to tear the fabric of union to pieces. Dramatic struggles played themselves out in the halls of Congress, on far-flung roads where man catchers chased down fugitive slaves, and on the high seas, where the last active-duty assignment of the aging USS *Constitution* was to intercept a slave ship off the coast of Africa.

The issue of slavery had been kicked down the road by the founding fathers. Of our first twelve chief executives, only the two from New England (John and John Quincy Adams) had never owned slaves. Skilled and single-purposed Southern politicians dodged the question of human bondage and got the Constitutional Convention to agree to count every slave as three-fifths of a person in the reckoning of congressional representation, even though slaves were not allowed to vote. From the start, the slaveholding class maneuvered the South into overrepresentation in the American government, a hostage-holding position with a disproportionate influence in the affairs of state.

And so young America set forth on its course with a major portion of the power structure holding its first allegiance to slavery, while loyalty to the unified nation was a conditional second. Eighty years after the Constitution was ratified, when a majority of the country decided that slavery should gradually end, the leaders of the South chose to quit the Union and seize federal property, beginning with the pulverization of Fort Sumter in South Carolina by artillery fire on April 13, 1861. At that point, war became inevitable, both factions having convinced themselves that the other side would give up after a few picturesque battles. Forty-nine months of all-out destruction and over seven hundred thousand deaths ensued, exceeding the number killed in *all* other American wars combined, down to the present day. The combat ended in the spring of 1865 at Appomattox Court House, but the root causes of the conflict, its resentments, and its inclination toward easy mayhem were all left unresolved.[5]

The profound rupture of the Civil War brought with it a host of unintended consequences, many of which, ten generations later, remain the source points of our deepest divisions. Much of the Southern landscape lay devastated in the wake of more than four years of war and occupation. Fences had been pulled down and burned up for firewood, homes and barns plundered, plantations, factories, warehouses, and whole cities bombarded or put to the torch. Hundreds of miles of railroads, bridges, and roadways were destroyed, and the Southern economic system utterly dismantled. The South needed to be rebuilt as an entire region, but after the North extended reeducation and resettlement only to the freed slaves, die-hard elements of the displaced white population engaged in guerrilla terrorism and brutally derailed the entire enterprise of Reconstruction. The Northern impulse to reform and redeem lost its nerve, fell into moral exhaustion, and quit the field. Impoverished, defeated, and resentful, the white South resorted to the creation of the "Lost Cause" myth, and, in its political relations with the rest of the Union, perfected the arts of diversion, obfuscation, and veiled defiance.

The upshot of all this is still shaking out. Former slaves found themselves in a position of *partial* freedom. Because they were no longer property, they no longer had value, and in many instances were thus more vulnerable to acts of intimidation, assault, and murder. The slave who had once been a monetary asset in white society had now become a problem. Unschooled, mostly "illegitimate," and completely unfamiliar with accepted white middle-class social and intellectual structures, "the Negro" became an "issue" rather than an individual citizen.

Northern folks, many of whom felt that they had just bled white on the whole subject of race relations, could not, in most cases, be depended on to do much more than look the other way, sympathetic, of course, but in reality useless. The African American population was forced to depend on what few resources it could muster, acting on the evident fact that the only people they could trust, by and large, were themselves. In the fifty years following the Civil War, remaining in the impoverished South could seem worse than risky, while the idea of emigrating to the strange and complicated North was no more reasonable a prospect than would have been the thought of pulling up stakes in Alabama and moving to the shores of Labrador.

It would neither be the far North nor the Deep South that would be the next evolutionary move on the American racial checkerboard.

Redemption, if it could come at all, might be found in the border states of Missouri, Tennessee, Kentucky, and Maryland. With Abraham Lincoln long in his grave, the major force in nineteenth-century racial integration became the growing network of railroads that threaded their way across the landscape. Employment was readily available, all the livelong day, on the railroads that were being built, or rebuilt, between the recovering Southern cities and the thriving east-west lines that stretched out from Baltimore, Philadelphia, and Norfolk. The Illinois Central, the Louisville and Nashville ("the L and N"), and the Missouri, Kansas City, and Texas ("the Katy") became the deus ex machinae that took a growing number of freed slaves out of the bondage of the deltas and up north to a more promising land.

So it was that a Black laboring population made its way into the border states, "linin' track" into the steep and remote forested sections of the mid-South that the war had never scorched. There, huge stands of old-growth hardwoods still stood, ready to be chopped down by hand, hauled by horse power out to sawmills, and crafted into paneling, cabinetry, and furniture for the Northern gentry of the Victorian era. In the border cities of St. Louis, Memphis, Louisville, and Baltimore, African Americans took on menial jobs at lumberyards and on railroad crews or, through the application of long-mastered rural skills, as wagon teamsters, loggers, blacksmiths, butchers, and barbecue cooks. In short order, these professions became safe harbors for "the race," sources of steady income and social acceptance, providing footholds on the economic ladder of a fast-growing country.

Underlying all this, over the long centuries, the dominant Anglo-European culture had gone a long way toward eradicating the folkways of its own tribal Celts, Basques, Vikings, Picts, Saxons, and Scots. "Primitive" folk cultures had largely been replaced by highly organized, highly stratified, highly intellectualized, and conditioned social hierarchies. Sophistication, family "connections," politics, military power, and material wealth had long been the overwhelming cultural imperatives of Europe. In Anglo life, the personal ability to express emotion and to feel the "natural rhythms" of life in family and folkways had been relegated to a relative state of atrophy. A dominant white culture had developed that was, to a considerable degree, emotionally limited by its own subjugation to the constant and unrelenting imperatives of status and wealth.

The Age of Exploration had been, at the core, an age of exploitation. Native peoples from Africa and the Americas had been pirated away and enslaved, forced to mine the gold of the New World so it could be sent back in galleons to line the coffers of European royalty. Through the cruel agency of the slave trade, a nonindustrialized population of Africans had been imported to the Americas after being deprived of all their possessions except for the inherited, refined personal capacity to feel and express feelings. To an emotionally inhibited Anglo audience, the expressive power of African-influenced music was nothing short of magic. And so, in America, in their songs, their dances, and their jubilees, Black folk who were barely out of chains found themselves suddenly engaged in the long and unintended musical process of setting the white folk free.

As they headed up into the border states, former slaves in roustabout railroad crews brought along a heritage of work songs and spirituals, some of which had already been appropriated by white evangelical revivalists as "shout tunes." They carried with them, as well, old Yankee fugues that had been learned from brave New England schoolmarms during the brief years of Reconstruction. In addition to employment in transportation, cooking, and blacksmithing, opportunity beckoned for African Americans who could play the banjo or the guitar. A talented man could make good money by simply sitting in a press-back chair, plopping his hat on the ground in front of him, and playing hot music on street corners and in railroad stations for dimes adorned with the image of a woman in a flowing gown holding a shield labeled "Liberty." Steamboats on the Mississippi and Ohio Rivers employed musical groups of both races. "Sporting clubs" (the socially acceptable Victorian term for brothels) were places where a Black man could find steady employment as a ragtime parlor piano player, paid directly by the madam and tipped by lubricated white male patrons who found themselves to be in an expansive mood.[6]

It did not take long for ambitious and aware African American musicians to see the potential for greater status and greater income than would be available to them on street corners or in houses of ill repute. If you were inspired musically, if you believed that you had a gift in that regard, and if you perceived that it was only classical music that was really being taken seriously in gentrified American society, it would behoove you to enter into the realm of formal musical training. Thus, by 1871, the Fiske Jubilee Singers of Nashville began creating presentations of "Negro spirituals" in practiced nine-member harmony. Dressed formally in gowns and tuxedos, they played to packed concert halls throughout America and Europe.

Around 1879, Scott Joplin, the son of a railroad worker from Texas and a freed Black woman from Kentucky, sought out an immigrant German Jewish professor of music named Julius Weiss to teach him the basics of classical music theory. Joplin began writing his own piano compositions after a makeshift career around his native Texarkana, Texas, that included playing in red-light districts and, at one point, headlining a benefit concert put on to raise money for the construction of a statue of Jefferson Davis.[7] By 1893, Joplin was playing piano at the Chicago World's Fair, where a syncopated, hypnotic combination of interracial musical influences called "ragtime" was quickly becoming all the rage among the twenty-seven million Americans who attended the exhibits.

Already composing in the new idiom and fueled by the enthusiasm of the Chicago audience, the young pianist began performing around St. Louis, touring from there as far as Syracuse, New York. He entered into a publishing arrangement with John S. Stark of Sedalia, Missouri, a white Union veteran and native of Bean Blossom, Kentucky,[8] who extended a far more generous royalty arrangement to Joplin than was customary at that time. Over the course of nearly twenty years, Joplin wrote and published more than forty-five original pieces that would become the heart of the defining body of ragtime music, the first large-scale musical phenomenon of the twentieth century. The combination of African American syncopation, classical filigrees, polka-like bounce, and a delivery that combined elegance and high tempo was the perfect soundtrack for an age that defined itself in terms of progress and style. Ragtime reigned supreme from the 1890s up until the cusp of World War I, and before the fashion receded it had spread to every city, seaport, mining camp, boom town, and whistle-stop in America.[9]

None of this fuss was lost on the brother- and sisterhood of less-affluent musicians who worked the street corners of midcontinent, riverbank America. Pianos were expensive and cumbersome, but stringed instruments were available in every pawnshop, and washboards, jugs, and washtubs in every neighborhood and junkyard. Earl McDonald of Louisville, Kentucky, put a homemade orchestra together around 1902 that featured guitar, jug, fiddle, banjo, and mandolin. Around the same time, Memphis blacksmith Frank Stokes was inspired to strut out ragtime tunes on his guitar, and he began singing them with his partner, Dan Sane, out on Beale Street. There they were joined by local banjo player Gus Cannon, who put his own group together, calling them the Jug Stompers. A few years later, Will Shade, Minnie Douglas, and a host of other characters created the Memphis Jug Band, playing their own mix of ragtime blues and dance tunes. In short order, hundreds of other blues singers and bands developed in the same fertile territory between Memphis, Tennessee; West Helena, Arkansas; and the Yazoo Delta of western Mississippi.[10]

It would be hard to overstate the power, depth, and influence of the vernacular music that was invented and played in the Mississippi and Ohio valleys in the cusp decades of the nineteenth and twentieth centuries. In polyglot New Orleans, old masters Buddy Bolden and King Oliver were breaking in a young Louis Armstrong to the musical forms that later became the basis of jazz. As a young laborer, W. C. Handy had begun beating out rhythms with a shovel on a work crew; by 1893, he had put his first band together. It was around 1903, while waiting for a night train in Tutwiler, Mississippi, that Handy first heard the beguiling sounds of a slide guitarist playing the country blues at the railroad intersection "where the Southern crossed the Dog."[11]

The sound introduced Handy to a blues idiom that scores of Memphis musicians, including Frank Stokes, Pink Anderson, and Daddy Stovepipe, had created while playing in traveling patent medicine shows that were traversing in wagons down the long dirt pikes between dusty country towns throughout the South. Hundreds of these elixir-selling troupes crisscrossed the region in the Victorian era, employing blues and ragtime singers as well as dancers and comedians. Some performers were asked to act in all three capacities while selling homemade concoctions designed to remedy all sorts of human ailments, real or imagined. This sort of enterprise largely came to an end after the passage and the gradual enforcement of the Federal Food and Drug Act of 1906, but not before it had provided steady employment for scores of ragtime singers and served as a kind of traveling foster home for the young country blues.[12]

Riverboats plowed their way up and down the length of the old Mississippi, full of roustabouts, stevedores, travelers, waiters, cooks, and performers. As late as 1918, a fifteen-year-old Bix Beiderbecke is said to have encountered Louis Armstrong and drummer Baby Dodds playing on an excursion steamboat that was docked in his hometown of Davenport, Iowa. Long before the advent of modern media, hybrid musical partnerships were taking shape across the landscape that brought little notice at the time but would bear incredible fruit in later decades. Despite all the venal barriers that had been placed in its pathway, the old American truth was still marching on.

FIGURE 5.

Nineteenth-century engravings of a guitar, wax cylinder player, and banjo,
from Clarence P. Hornung, *2,000 Early Advertising Cuts*
(New York: Dover Publications, 1995).

CHAPTER FIVE

DOWN IN THE GROOVE

Recorded Music in America, 1890–1960

THE PROLIFERATION OF STREET singers, minstrel troupes, medicine shows, concerts, ragtime, and vaudeville established music as the most dynamic and defining popular force throughout American life in the nineteenth and early twentieth centuries. Musical performances all operated on an intimate level, since the audiences of that day were of necessity located in the same space as the performers. We will never know precisely what music sounded like during the first three American centuries for the simple reason that there was no popular access to sound recordings until about 1890. The creation of the "talking machine" changed all of that.

The earliest sound recordings available commercially were produced by the Edison Company on wax cylinders, the shape and roughly four times the size of a modern plastic prescription pill bottle. By the late 1890s, these were selling "like hotcakes," as they said in those days, primarily in the form of stirring recordings by popular marching bands such as John Philip Sousa's outfit, hits "waxed" by vaudevillians such as Bahamian star Bert Williams, popular parlor tunes, and "comedy" pieces. The latter were largely farces-in-dialect, spoken humor that mocked the stereotyped cultures of the Irish, Jews, and African Americans as drunks, swindlers, and lazy dimwits, respectively. If the cigar-smoking listener could imbibe a bit of racial superiority along with some knee-slapping humor, well, this was all in line with the social stratification that was chiseled into modern American culture in the disorienting wake of emancipation and immigration. There has always been good money to be made in the commercial transformation of the outrageous into the fashionable.[1]

Horizontal 78 rpm records soon superseded the fragile wax cylinders, much as MP3s would eventually replace the CDs that, in turn, had made long-playing records nearly obsolete. "Modern" people craved the spontaneity of music, and the parlor piano and its sheet music (played, perhaps, by the oldest girl in the family) quickly gave way to various species of talking machines that began to hit the markets prior to World War I. The early recording business was largely connected to the sale of cabinet record players, and so the consumer bought recorded music at furniture stores. At first, these discs were the equivalent of modern "loss leaders," so a customer might pay sixty dollars for an expensive oak phonograph console and "get five records free."

Libraries of recordings were accumulated by most middle-class families, largely continuing the market patterns that the cylinders had defined: marching bands, sentimental songs, vaudeville, and low-brow comedy. But at the same time, undercurrents in a society that was ambivalently in flux between down home and big city also began to gravitate toward regional "old-fashioned" music. Two very different records took the music market by storm in the early 1920s: "Crazy Blues" by the African American singer Mamie Smith and "The Wreck of the Old 97" by a white Texan who called himself Vernon Dalhart, combining the names of two Texas whistle stops and thus literally making a name for himself. It was clearly apparent through the success of these "hits" that poor folk of both major races were willing to spend a good deal of what little money they possessed on recorded music, and that together they constituted enormous purchasing power. To a few young enterprising record company executives, it also became obvious that handing a blues shouter or some hick fiddler a five-dollar bill and a half pint of whiskey as compensation for a performance would be a lot simpler than convening an orchestra of professional musicians in a New York studio, with its scheduling headaches, red tape, and financial overhead.[2]

Out of a sort of informed, ambitious sentimentality, academics and record companies began to scour rural districts at the turn of the twentieth century and to gather what remained of our indigenous national folk music while it lasted. Like the early ballad collections, the resulting trove of fieldwork provided the basis for the interpretation of American folk song tradition for decades to come. The most influential field recordings were made in isolated pockets of the South by Cecil Sharp, John and Alan Lomax, A. P. Carter, and Ralph Peer, leading to the modern assumption that the roots of American folk music originated in the Appalachian uplands and the Mississippi valley. These resulted in the first commercially recorded folk music, largely of tunes that had been performed in the 1800s in the hills and deltas of the South, but the "roots of the roots" had sprung from New England soil back in the 1600s, and surviving examples had been recorded by academic women beginning in the 1890s.

The great American migration of the Victorian era was from the South to the North. Poor whites and Blacks flocked to urban areas in the fevered generations that followed the Civil War, attracted by the facile promise of factory jobs and indoor plumbing in the crowded tenements of the industrialized centers above the Mason-Dixon line. For many of these homespun immigrants, displacement was followed by disappointment when it became clear that they would always be treated like outcasts in the cold heart of the privileged North. Race and class have long been among the tests of democracy that we are most likely to fail here in America; at times, the best that the middle class could manage to do was to extend "tolerance" to the poor folk that they encountered. Crucial status calculations began at the basics: Blacks were denigrated on sight, while a white hillbilly might not be socially disqualified until he opened his mouth and began to speak in a "cracker" drawl.

White society was conditioned to look down on poor Blacks not only for the color of their skin but for what were judged to be ignorant, promiscuous, and simpleton antics. In a bizarre and ironic form of "equality," the culture of the genteel mainstream also rejected poor rural whites for their unschooled speech and their ignorant, hillbilly ways. In consequence, humiliation, along with poverty and loss in love, became one of the basic reasons for impoverished Blacks and whites to sing the blues. At the dawn of the era of commercial music, record company scouts snatched up raw performances from the homelands of the Mississippi delta and the Appalachian highlands for sale to displaced urban poor folk who, like the prodigal son, only wanted to return to a place where they could feel that they belonged.

Headlong advances in wealth and industry may have led the charge of progress, but as far as the common people were concerned, they brought with them the sorts of perdition dolefully described in songs about ocean liners that hit icebergs, airships that blew up, and wrecks on the highway so horrendous that there was no room at the scene for the redemption of prayer. In blues bars, in hillbilly joints, and on the roadhouse dance floors of a thousand lost highways, American vernacular music helped folks come to terms with the contradictions and the heartbreaks of life in general and modern life in particular. Poor people tried to find some semblance of a satisfied mind in a troubled age that, for all its advances, seemed fit at times only to lurch from one high-anxiety crisis to the next.

The first record company talent scouts had no idea for certain what would sell to these common folk. All they knew was that there were hometown singers and vast markets somewhere "out there" in the vital expanses of America, huge paydays migrating across the uncharted cultural hinterland like uncounted millions of buffalo. Early artist-and-repertoire men such as Ralph Peer and Mayo Williams were modern businessmen, but they were also the grandchildren of settlers and hustlers who had plowed a lot of stony ground and dug a lot of dry wells before they ever got to cash in on pork bellies, hardware stores, or real estate.

Talent scouts from companies such as Okeh and RCA Records did not commission an opinion poll, since such things were unknown back in the 1920s. Instead, they followed the maxim they had likely heard from their fathers that success was the result of 90 percent perspiration and 10 percent inspiration. They bought tickets for good seats on the fastest trains they could find, took the wheel of the most rugged and comfortable roadsters they could rent, and drove off into the hinterlands to record almost everyone they could set a microphone in front of. With a prospector's confidence, they proceeded in the conviction that there were pure nuggets to be found out there somewhere among the gravel.

Indeed there were, all across rural America, since almost everyone in those days had learned to sing directly from people in their own family or their home town, and relatively few had yet heard a recording or learned to mimic the staged dialogue in moving pictures. For every successful Blind Lemon Jefferson there were a half a hundred Geeshie Wileys who, after the red light on a makeshift studio wall shut off, would pack up their notions and go back to living unheralded lives, selling only a few records or maybe none at all. But in those hopeful moments in front of primitive recording equipment, those singers left us with an account of what it sounded like, what it *felt* like, to live in the days before the fix was in, before machines had started calling out the tunes for people to dance to, and before Americans began to take the measure of themselves through the standardized cultural yardstick of popular mass media.

Between roughly 1920 and the mid-1930s, when the Depression took hold, American music companies such as Paramount, Okeh, and Gennett accumulated a vast trove of these traditional performances on disc. Some artists, such as Jimmie Rodgers ("the Singing Brakeman"), Bessie Smith ("the Empress of the Blues,"), and Bob Wills ("the King of Western Swing") became famous, while thousands of others (including the Dinwiddie Colored Quartet, Robert Johnson, and the Blue Sky Boys) made only a fleeting impression, if that. The market for rural music shrank after poor Black and white folk moved north to work in city factories; by 1940, the attention of both the record companies and the music-buying public was gravitating toward swing bands and crooners. Catalogs from the '20s labeled "Old Familiar Country Tunes" (marketed to poor whites) and "Race Records" (for the "colored" trade) went out of print, old 78 rpm records were set aside or destroyed, and popular culture moved far away from the backwater rural districts of the American South.[3]

Yet, even as commercial prospects waned for traditional musicians, interest in folk music began to quicken across America. Poets like Carl Sandburg, academics like John and Alan Lomax, and "true believers" like Pete Seeger brought field recordings and songs from the South and the West to the attention of big-city audiences. Educated, liberal New Yorkers, in particular, embraced this music in a logical expression of their New Deal convictions as interest in old-time tunes began to spread across political lines throughout the country. In 1933, Eleanor Roosevelt was among more than twelve thousand people who attended the White Top Folk Festival, held on a mountain meadow in Grayson County, Virginia. To her chagrin, the First Lady's servants were the only "colored folk" allowed to pass through the gates.

The economic disaster that followed the Roaring Twenties jolted America off the high wire of consumerism and modernity on which the country had teetered in the dizzy years following the Gilded Age. Millions of families fell a long, hard way down in a very short time during the Depression. The deep American faith in "better days to come" was suddenly compromised by the fear of humiliating economic ruin. Political ideologies lurched toward extreme positions that would exploit the insecurities of the twentieth century and rankle on beyond its end. The Far Right trucked in isolation and nativism, blaming the ills of the culture and the economy on people who were not "real Americans," whatever that was supposed to mean. The Far Left, in contrast, proposed a collectivist ideal on a scale ranging from a vague commitment to brotherhood to doctrinaire communism. In pursuit of an identification with "the common people," educated city liberals drew on the raw music of the heartland, calling as primary witnesses a few iconic rural troubadours.

Among these were such figures as Leadbelly, a Black ex-convict from Louisiana, and Woody Guthrie, a rambling white country singer from

Oklahoma. Both men were talented representatives of disparate American music cultures whose rise to folk music fame was made possible through the sponsorship of the Lomax family, combined with the friendship and support of Pete Seeger. More than any single person, Seeger was responsible for the safekeeping of folk tradition through the perilous course of twentieth-century civilization. After dropping out of Harvard, he had embarked on a lifetime of circuit-riding concerts that took him to nearly every campus in the land. Pete combined the attributes of the Yankee peddler and the Yankee reformer, making the sale and securing salvation in one fell swoop, through the sheer force of the amiable and indomitable character that he self-styled as "Johnny Appleseed, Jr."[4]

If the Depression had rekindled an activist strain in the American character, the events of World War II mobilized it out of a combination of idealism and self-defense. Emerging from the poverty, fear, and humiliation that followed World War I, Germany's Nazi Party combined ancient racial hatred with modern military technology, and brilliantly disguised its true nature with the invention of modern propaganda. Through the miracle speed and instant impact of radio and moving pictures, the German people became the first population, if not the last, to rapidly absorb inflammatory messages that in speech or in print might have been scrutinized and challenged, or at least discussed. Gathered in front of a silver screen or sitting by a radio speaker, reasonably educated human beings could be transformed into a population of slack-jawed sponges. If you told a lie often enough, and did so with purpose, style, and confidence, the alchemy of modern media could enable you to fool a lot more than half the people almost all of the time, even in the long decades before the invention of either television or the Internet.[5]

It wasn't until America was actually attacked at Pearl Harbor that the country awakened to the danger spreading from totalitarian dictatorships across both the Atlantic and the Pacific. Against all odds (and, literally, under the gun) Americans won World War II through the combined sacrifice of consumer rationing, the industry of farm and factory, and the rapid-fire development of technological advances of a people united in common cause both in combat and on the home front. It was not through superficial "support" but through personal sacrifice that the country came together in World War II, perhaps as it never had before. Americans forged a national unity that drew a straight line of descent from Washington to Lincoln and the Roosevelts; Americans of all nationalities and regions knew that they were in this fight together and without reservation. When our GIs moved into the hidden crevasses behind the Nazi lines, they unmasked the sickening reality of the concentration camps, and it became clear that Americans were fighting a war between ideals and evil, not just one of bombers and battleships.

When the treaty to the last declared war America would fight for generations was signed on the deck of the *Missouri,* Americans went back to work and, in greater numbers than ever before, to the business of raising families. Although the war had largely been fought against racism, it was easy for many Americans to avoid making personal changes in social behavior that reflected the postwar insight that bigotry was not only evil but also un-American. Change is hard, especially when status and fear are in play and are acting in competition with fairness, good will, and democracy. America was in need of an application of saving grace, a reason to venture, as Tracy Chapman would later sing, "under the bridge, over the tracks that separate whites from Blacks."[6] After the war, that intervention would begin to come, as it so often has in American life, through the magic that happened when people "faced the music and danced."

Crooners and swing bands may have gotten the nation through the war, but with the coming of peace, Americans were beginning to change their tunes. The biggest hit musical of the 1940s was not about a tail gunner or a physicist but about a sodbuster singing about how tall his corn was gettin' to be. The irrepressible vitality of country and western music (with its mix of fiddles and amplified steel guitars) and bebop (an African American mix of jazz, swing, and rhythm and blues) came to the fore. Postwar jukeboxes filled up with records by Hank Williams and Louis Jordan, both men up-to-date musicians rooted in deep regional musical traditions. Now secure in their modern homes, many Americans sought connection to the simple verities of the past. The generation that was born into that sort of optimism had reason to believe that, as a country and as a culture, all of us were bound for glory. Any time and place that produced both the Mills Brothers and the Sons of the Pioneers had a whole lot going for it.

The power of music accelerated in the recordings of the early twentieth century and came to the fore in modern jazz and swing music. The war had been fought to a soundtrack produced by inspired and, at times, integrated swing bands. "Swing" itself, like ragtime and jazz before it, had largely been the product of African American roots, and white bandleaders as disparate as Benny Goodman and Bob Wills were forthright in expressing the debt they owed to Black musicians.[7] Nat "King" Cole, Ella Fitzgerald, and Sister Rosetta Tharpe began to be heard openly by a white audience that came to the realization that, in American culture as in American music, "it don't mean a thing if it ain't got that swing."

About the same time that America was beginning to acknowledge its debt to African American music, the country started to develop a peacetime taste for "Americana," a connection to roots and traditions through what were often somewhat sanitized versions of old folk songs. Western movie jamborees, summer camp choruses, and "fireside" sing-alongs in centrally-heated living rooms all combined to create the climate for an American folk song revival after the war. Some of this impulse was expressed by traditional, conservative artists such as Fred Waring and the composer Roy Ringwald (who together produced the patriotic *Song of America* album in the early 1950s), singers such as Kate Smith, and, in the country music field, Roy Acuff and Tennessee Ernie Ford. Further to the left on the cultural spectrum were the Weavers, a group of New York musicians and activists (Pete Seeger and Ronnie Gilbert being the best known) who sang traditional songs including "Follow the Drinking Gourd," "The Sloop John B," and "Kisses Sweeter Than Wine." In 1950, their recording of Leadbelly's "Goodnight, Irene" reached the top of the pop music charts and remained there for an unprecedented thirteen weeks. The success of the Weavers inspired dozens of other city singers to look to traditional folk sources for material that could be arranged and presented to meet the tastes of the modern audience.[8]

Of all the "established" folk musicians of the early 1950s, few would prove to be more influential than a Harlem-born man of mixed racial heritage named Harry Belafonte. At about the age of five, he went to live with his grandmother in Jamaica, returning to graduate from high school in New York City before enlisting in the U.S. Navy. After the war, he resolved to pursue an acting career with his friend Sidney Poitier. Belafonte began singing in supper clubs to earn funds to pay for acting classes, at one point fronting a combo that included Charlie Parker and Miles Davis. He developed an interest in folk music and delved into the trove of traditional songs collected in the Library of Congress. By 1952, he was performing at the Village Vanguard in New York and then signed a contract with RCA Victor Records.

Belafonte's first single was "Matilda," which introduced African-influenced "island" music to a mainstream audience that suddenly could not get enough of it. In 1956, his record album titled *Calypso* became the first million-selling LP, spending nearly eight months in the number-one position and a total of ninety-nine weeks on the U.S. album charts. Songs including "Day-Oh," "Jamaica Farewell" ("I had to leave a little girl in

Kingston town . . ."), and "Jump in the Line" seized the imagination of a youthful audience. Belafonte's captivating personality seemed to strike as strong a chord as his music did. Sixty years later, the Boston folk singer Dayle Stanley would cite him as a major influence in her decision to begin singing in 1961: "He aroused tremendous passions in me towards folk music," she recalled.[9] She was decidedly not alone in that response.

By the mid-1950s, a host of young folk singers were plying their trade on both coasts. Following in the steps of Harry Belafonte, a West Coast group calling themselves the Kingston Trio presented an upbeat, "clean-cut," and energetic image to good effect on the campuses and in the record stores of America. They availed themselves of a combination of traditional material and new folkish songs. With the release of their first album in 1958, featuring the old Appalachian tune "Tom Dooley," they became instantly successful on a scale that would not be replicated until the days of the Beatles and then Michael Jackson. Because of their mainstream success and polished arrangements, older urban folk song enthusiasts judged them to be "too commercial," but for many a young folkie, a Kingston Trio album was the beginning of a lifelong interest in traditional music. The group's prominence grew to the point where they released a hit song, "The New Frontier," based on the spirit and the text of John F. Kennedy's 1960 inaugural address.[10]

A musical appeal to national ideals and roots struck a perfect chord in postwar America. For the bravest and the most committed, enlistment in the Peace Corps or in the peacetime military might be the perfect expression of national hopes and dreams. For most, however, the new frontier was symbolized by the high technology of "the space race," which was promoted on television as the ultimate expression of Manifest Destiny. Despite the hype and excitement, sending a handful of brave astronauts up above the troposphere was not really the equivalent of the landing at Plymouth Rock, the emancipation of the slaves, or the wagon trains rolling westward. The space race was a televised spectator sport for most Americans; in reality, there was not much potential for a frontier experience to be found in an easy chair. There had been no potato chips at the Alamo. There were no on-the-scene announcers around to cover the progress of Lewis and Clark. Sojourner Truth's message of freedom had not been interrupted at halftime by a helpful word from her sponsors.

Despite all the advances being made in postwar America, something vital was missing. Something real and courageous and beautiful had been drained away from the modern American character. It was time to find out where it had gone.

FIGURE 6.
Contra dancers at the Tunbridge (VT) World's Fair, 1941.
Photo by Jack Delano, Library of Congress, Prints & Photographs Division,
FSA/OWI Collection, LC-USF34–045838-D.

CHAPTER SIX

ROLLING HOME TO OLD NEW ENGLAND

The Beginnings of the New England Folk Revival, 1940–1962

OVER THE COURSE OF a few generations in the 1800s, the advance of the Machine Age had displaced almost two hundred years of American folkways in settled New England. The oldest part of the country had the deepest heritage to lose in the modern era, and the combination of industrialization and middle-class convention created an entirely new normal in Yankee society, particularly in genteel suburban sections. Massachusetts men whose great-grandfathers had been ship captains were taking daily commuter trains to and from jobs in office cubicles. Not only had the old farm songs and sea stories disappeared but in addition whole landscapes and entire skill sets and livelihoods had been eradicated. The hand-hewn timbers of tradition were replaced by the particleboard of popular culture, and the birthright of regional memory retreated into the shadows.

Progress had come with a whole lot of traumatic baggage, in the forms of World War I, the Depression, and then World War II. For thoughtful people, the sickening realities of the Holocaust and the disturbing invention and deployment of the atomic bomb called the very fate of the human race into question. Popular culture, a burgeoning celebrity-based entertainment industry, and a booming economy all kept people busy. But along with new concepts such as "washing machines," "convertibles," and "game shows," terms like "stress," "rat race," and "nervous breakdown" also began to appear in the lexicon of modern times.

And so, after the Machine Age had obliterated the world of hearth and homespun, people began to entertain the romantic notion that, somehow, "things were better in the good old days." The morning sun seemed to beam all the brighter on an imagined pastoral landscape even as it dimmed in the haze of urban smokestacks, a welter of interstate highways, and a pall of diesel fumes. A rekindling of regional New England culture began to take place over the course of the twentieth century, even if it was sentimentality rather than vitality that fueled renewed interest in the surviving rural ways. People began to collect antiques, to rusticate in rural summer homes, and to develop a taste for singing along with old-time tunes. Of all the musical connections that kept the faith with the rural past, one of the most long-lived and vibrant was the field of traditional folk dance.

Before karaoke and singles bars, before chat groups and lonely hearts clubs, New Englanders were accustomed to take to the dance floor to mingle with other people. Over time, contra dance tunes and heirloom dance steps became artifacts that accumulated like mismatched furniture in a rambling old house, with a few English morrises in the hall, a fancy French piece tucked under the stairs, a sturdy Scottish strathspey in the parlor, and an Irish jig perched near the stove. The instruments were a mix of cultural influences straight off the decks of Yankee immigration: fiddle, guitar, flute, piano, and, here and there, an accordion. The caller lined out his dance steps, almost acting in the style of an auctioneer, as if to say, "Now, folks, what'll ya give me here tonight for the old Portland Fancy?" The dancers were often well-traveled: Monday nights they were at the Scottish dance at the Sargent Gym at Boston University; Tuesday was the Ralph Page dance at the Boston YWCA; Wednesday nights an English dance convened at the Cambridge YWCA, where the Taylors held folk dances on Thursday; and on Friday, Ted Sannella called a dance in Porter Square. Whether your family members voted for Daniel Webster or Al Smith, the dances pretty much remained the same. At least, they were recognizable.[1]

Back in the 1850s, there had been many noteworthy dance outfits, including Goddard and Twitchell's Quadrille Band and stalwarts such as the fiddling snowshoe maker Mellie Dunham, who lived long enough to make several hit 78 rpm records on RCA Victor. Then along came people such as Ed Cole of Freedom, New Hampshire, who was remembered as a good man who liked his pint, and an elderly Monadnock-area summer resident by the name of Mr. Hazard, who wielded a Stradivarius and had played in William Tecumseh Sherman's military band on his march through Georgia. Happy Hale, an African American from Bernardston, Massachusetts, smoked a big cigar while he was calling, and old Ed Larkin played at the Tunbridge World's Fair up in Vermont, where they used to say that the drunks were packed in so thick, there was no room for them to stagger.

Ralph Page of Keene carried the old traditions forward into the 1940s and '50s, with an orchestra that included the affable Bob McQuillen on accordion and the incomparable coupling of Johnny Tremblay on piano and Dick Richardson on fiddle. Ted Sannella was a Revere native and Tufts graduate who operated out of a home base in Concord, Massachusetts, and he called dances in Cambridge and down on Westport Point. Up in the hills of Nelson, New Hampshire, the Tolman clan presided in the town hall for generations, with Francis on piano, Renn and Newt on flutes, and Albert Quigley playing away on the fiddle. As a boy, Newt had played the flute at a recital for John Philip Sousa. He was quite a character; he drove an old Rolls Royce over all the local dirt roads and eventually played with Dudley Laufman at Club 47 and on the stage at the Newport Folk Festival.

Among the many things that set contra dancers apart from the general population was that they were all active performers, each in his or her own right. The era of Victorian gentility and the rise of recordings left most of the population in a passive relationship with music, but if you were a contra dancer, you were all in, body and soul. Ralph Page drew enthusiastic crowds to his rural "kitchen junkets" and to the dances at the Boston and Cambridge YMCAs throughout the 1940s. Page joined forces with Mary Gillette and Grace Palmer of Boston to form the New England Folk Festival in October 1944, which has convened annually ever since at various locations in Massachusetts, New Hampshire, Connecticut, and Rhode Island. The Boston folk dance scene was supported by people such as Louise Todd of Lexington, who taught folk dancing and collected hundreds of records from Europe and the British Isles, as well as those featuring American square dances. Throughout New England, energetic young couples flocked to old town halls where they fell in line to the exhortations of callers including Page, Sannella, and Laufman to "Awnah ya pahtnah, bow to ya cawnah, and praw-ma-nade!"

Decidedly liberal and socially conventional, most of the early folk music enthusiasts came primarily from the educated class, solidly patriotic professional people who mixed progressive political convictions with an interest in both national and international folk traditions. Their devotion to brotherhood bucked the national bout of hysteria that occurred during the McCarthy Era of the early 1950s. Lefty folk singers were easy targets in those times; the Weavers, for example, who for a while led the pop musical charts, were effectively put out of business because of their political convictions, and hundreds of liberal artists and writers were blackballed. Pete Seeger, who may well have been a member of the Communist Party for a time, was hauled before the House Un-American Activities Committee and cited for contempt of a Congress that, under any reading of the Constitution, richly deserved that response.[2]

If the country as a whole had become repressive and grim, the city of Boston presented a particularly instructive case study in reactionary culture and politics. Any sort of artistic renaissance was going to have to overcome serious headwinds in the grimy streets of the postwar Hub. Power was wielded in the iron hands of an unholy alliance of bureaucrats, clerics, and small-time hoods, united in distrust of change and sharing the tired turf and the stale spoils of incumbency. The former "Athens of America" was not an easy place to be a Jew, it was not an easy place to be a person of color, and it was not an easy place to be an independent-minded woman. The courts, the licensing boards, the press, and the neighborhood police precincts were eager not only to enforce the laws but also to make life difficult for nonconformist types, lumping "eggheads," "musicians," "beatniks," "fags," and "pinkos" together with "the Negroes" as "troublemakers." All were easy targets for official harassment. There was a mean streak abroad on the streets of midcentury Boston; the beans were undercooked, and the codfish had gone a bit rank. You kind of had to watch your step.

Bucking this trend, a young, liberal World War II veteran named Manny Greenhill took it upon himself to make Boston a safe place for traditional music once again. Greenhill had grown up in a musical family (his father had been a *capellmeister* in Russia), and, as a young man in Brooklyn, he had been mesmerized by a Libby Holman and Josh White performance at New York's Cafe Society. He packed an audio disc of White's "House of the Rising Sun" and "John Henry" with him when he enlisted in the U.S. Army. Then, after three years of service in World War II, he decided to move to Boston, where he opened a business called the Foreign Language Press.

On his own inspired initiative, he began to organize "Midnight Owl" folk music concerts, first in March 1958 at the old Hotel Ambassador off Cambridge Common and soon thereafter at Bates Hall in the YMCA on Huntington Avenue in Boston. Greenhill created a management company called Folklore Productions and expanded his schedule to bring a rich variety of artists to his Folklore Concerts Series held at Boston's Jordan and Symphony Halls. Performers included ethnic singers the Clancy Brothers, Theodore Bikel, Martha Schlamme, Geula Gill, and others, as well as Black artists Odetta, Mahalia Jackson, and Josh White at a time when "Negro" performers were generally not included in mainstream events. Manny Greenhill was a Bostonian equivalent of Pete Seeger, and the Folk Revival in Boston and Cambridge was very much the result of his convictions, his talent, and his personality. Among Greenhill's most influential bookings, the New Lost City Ramblers displayed both scholarship and virtuosity as they crisscrossed the country, creating enthusiasm for traditional string band music wherever they played.[3]

The popularity of commercial folk tunes and the availability of field recordings made by the Library of Congress was resulting in a growing interest in traditional music in the Greater Boston area. New Englanders began to share records and to attend folk concerts as well as contra dances. The Folk Song Society of Greater Boston was formed in 1959 and attracted progressive-minded audiences to its membership. Many people sought to bear witness to brotherhood, and a distinct new strain of the old Yankee reform spirit was awakened and extended, however tardily and however episodically, to the cultures of a broad swath of ethnicities and races. The new folk music movement would eventually become known for its secular nature, but at the roots, it owed a good deal to the Jewish, Quaker, and Unitarian congregations of Greater Boston.

In growing numbers, these began to be joined by college students. By the mid-1950s, the precursors of the baby boom generation were flocking to the universities of Boston in unprecedented numbers. Born just before the war, many of them had spent childhood summers at progressive summer camps where folk song and folk dance were both featured parts of the core curriculum. As an example, in 1954, Harvard student Tony Saletan was hired to be a summer camp counselor at the

Shaker Village Work Camp in New Lebanon, New York. In preparation for a job as camp song leader, he delved into the stacks at Widener Library, where he discovered and adapted the song "Michael Row the Boat Ashore" from an 1860s volume of slave tunes before passing it along to Pete Seeger. Tony also popularized the African song "Kumbaya" while singing it with his campers. These songs and others, such as the old English ballad "The Golden Vanity" and the Jewish folk tune "Dona Dona," became summer-camp favorites in places such as Pine Woods Camps in Plymouth, Massachusetts, where Saletan also taught, and at the Farm and Wilderness Camps in Plymouth, Vermont, where Dudley Laufman called contra dances in the summertime for young Quakers and others.

John Cohen was one of the young musicians whose parents had predisposed him to a love of traditional music through their record collection and their enthusiasm for folk dance. His experience at summer camp in the Hudson River valley directed him toward a lifetime devoted to traditional music. Late in life, he recalled that one of his camp counselors, who had met an old mountain man in Kentucky who made five-string banjos out of primitive components, taught young John how to make a fretless banjo out of local wood, tacks, and a possum hide. That experience, along with exposure to Woody Guthrie's *Dust Bowl Ballads* and a reissue album of hillbilly songs, sent Cohen back from summer camp a changed man at the tender age of sixteen.[4]

When it came time to attend high school, teenagers of comfortable circumstance, liberal persuasion, and artistic temperament gravitated toward private prep schools such as the Cambridge School of Weston and the Putney School in Vermont. Within such creative enclaves, a generation of young people found themselves drawn into deep fascination with the old tunes and folk dances. Adolescence and folk music were twin doors into a world that suddenly felt like a hybrid mixture of Memphis and the Middle Ages. Not only was it a time of wonder, it was a time when young people felt called on to explore new frontiers and to enlist themselves in new crusades.

Idealistic young folks were in for a rude awakening when they eventually went on to college. The buttoned-down campus of the 1950s was no place for dreamers. "Progress" was America's most important product, after all, and four years as a university man were constructed to function as the down payment on a forty-year career as an engineer, a corporate functionary, or a Madison Avenue executive. If you were a woman, your role would be to construct a physical and social persona that could provide an attractive and effective complement to "the career man."

The assumption that technology would provide all the solutions to America's problems was being confidently promoted as an accepted fact. In the '50s, the "Navajo" missile, the race to the moon, and thousands of technological advances were supposed to save the country. Yet they clearly were not doing so, since the chronic national challenges of race, gender, and class fell into realms of history and human relations that could not be addressed by throwing a switch, pushing a button, or solving an equation. That was the point that many young people were feeling: a whole lot of the most important things in life were *not* rocket science.

Orthodox thinking and conformity began to fracture and fail in the minds of some young college students. For many, freshman orientation felt like a brisk group exercise in right-brain lobotomy. As a result, some creative young people made quick work of their college careers in Boston, entering on one side of the academic omnibus on cue and then exiting out the far door before it left the stop, much in the manner of Buster Keaton in a silent film. Although the people involved might not have perceived it at the time, folk music became a sort of foster home for a whole generation suddenly exiled from the structures of family and social conformity.[5]

In the late 1940s, a few youthful freethinkers had established a beachhead not far off Harvard Square in a communal house known as Old Joe Clark's, named after the old folk song. Loosely associated with the Outing Clubs of MIT and Harvard, this somewhat informal group-living arrangement began decades before the publication of the first *Whole Earth Catalog* or the beginnings of the 1960s counterculture. Neither beatnik nor hippie, the inhabitants were peacetime soldiers of fortune, among the first of what would eventually come to be called "folkies." Old Joe Clark's was a kind of Lhasa-on-the-Charles, a place where young expeditionaries could drop in and out from hiking the Appalachian Mountain Club huts of the White Mountains, skiing in Vermont, or hitchhiking to places such as Amherst, New York, Madison, or across the continent to Berkeley.

Sylvia Miskoe was a young folk dancer and accordionist who came from her native New Hampshire to the Boston area in 1957 to work for the Harvard Public Health agency. She remembers Old Joe Clark's as a bit of a moveable feast of communal living: "The first house they lived in was on Arrow Street, then that got sold, so they hustled around and got a great big house on Thomas Park, which was above Harvard Square, and then that got sold. So they decided they would buy a house, and they incorporated Old Joe Clark's. They sold shares—$10 a share—and that was part of paying for the mortgage. . . . We did dancing in the living room or some jamming . . . you had the singing people and the dancing people."[6]

On any given Friday night, the house steamed and whistled like a coal-fired locomotive, and in every room, a different kind of live music boomed on into the early morning. Low-down blues, cowboy songs, Irish come-all-ye's, bluegrass breakdowns, Scottish balladry, and old-timey fiddle tunes were punctuated by the sound of enthusiastic contra dancers clomping around in circles on the living room floor. The common denominators were folk music, beer, and nonconformity. The women who ventured into this Cambridge logging camp were of necessity a hardy lot, as male privilege was not among the conventions that were discarded in postwar bohemia. The easy benefits of premarital sex tended to accrue to only half of the participants; birth control in any form was illegal at best and fatal at worst. Impulses toward progressivism and equality that drew young people of the day to folk music were rarely extended to women or women's issues, realms in which the folk scene remained more rooted in the Middle Ages than the Progressive Era.

Sprinkled among the youthful college dropouts of New England were a few veteran musicians and artists who had been marching along to the beat of their own drummers for quite some time. Among these were Paul Clayton, Rolf Cahn, and Eric von Schmidt. Clayton was born in 1931 and grew up in New Bedford, Massachusetts, one of the oldest and most racially diverse cities in New England. He had been drawn into the magic of old whaling songs and sea shanties while still in high school. After discovering a trove of old tunes at the New Bedford Whaling Museum, he had begun collecting and performing folk songs on the local radio station, WFMR. Paul went on to the University of Virginia, studying under folklorist Arthur Kyle Davis and collecting songs from the traditional Southern musicians Etta Baker and Hobart Smith. He also came to the attention of the ballad scholar Helen Hartness Flanders, who taped about a dozen of his songs.

After college, Clayton gravitated to New York, where he began performing in Greenwich Village and recording albums of seafaring and logging ballads. Paul became something of a lone pilgrim of Northern folk song, one of the earliest and best-trained of the new interpreters of traditional music in New York and Boston. He was an important teacher and role model for younger musicians (most notably Bob Dylan) through his personal performances and the more than twenty record albums he recorded and released between 1954 and his early death in 1967.

Rolf Cahn was born in 1924 in Germany to a Jewish family who fled Hitler's regime in 1937. During the war, he chose a dangerous and unconventional role for himself in the struggle against fascism: barely twenty years old, Cahn enlisted and was trained in the Office of Strategic Services (precursor to the CIA) and then parachuted behind Nazi lines in Europe, where he blew up bridges and acted as a commando for the duration of the war. On returning to America, he devoted himself to radical politics and to folk music, first in California and later in Massachusetts. Rolf was an eclectic and a disciplined musician, mastering the flamenco guitar and developing a deep connection to African American blues songs.

A committed and confident artist, Cahn helped to define the scenes in both Berkeley and Boston, combining the roles of teacher and performer for the young acolytes of folk music. In their definitive account of the folk revival, *Baby, Let Me Follow You Down,* Jim Rooney and Eric von Schmidt recalled that Cahn was the first folk and blues guitar teacher to come to Cambridge. "Eminence, rabbi, guru, whatever, Rolf could be intense and volatile or tender and charming. Like most good teachers, he was always searching and learning himself."[7]

Eric von Schmidt was born in Bridgeport, Connecticut, in 1931, the son of illustrator Harold von Schmidt. By his teen years, Eric was already an accomplished graphic artist in his own right. Following a stint in the U.S. Army and a Fulbright scholarship that supported art study in Florence, von Schmidt moved to Cambridge in 1957. There he developed an uncanny ability to interpret African American blues in a manner that was authentic, heartfelt, and, above all, magnetic. The strength of Eric von Schmidt's personality became a defining force in what would soon become the Boston-Cambridge scene.

Bob Dylan would later write of him, "Here is a man who can sing the bird off the wire and the rubber off the tire. He can separate the men from the boys and the note from the noise."[8] Wherever he appeared, pulses quickened, and improbable things began to happen.

Eric von Schmidt also became the player-coach of a whole roster of promising rookie folk singers in Cambridge. A bit later on, David Wilson would say of him, "He is as close to being the font, the musical inspiration, for this most fertile of folk music communities as any one person can be."[9]

The street-level tone being set by these artists was decidedly bohemian, but prior to about 1960, the prevailing style of folk musicians remained as conventional in appearance as it had been in the previous decade. The mainstream folk music audience that had bought Weavers records in huge quantities in the early 1950s, still very active, was also basically conventional in style and taste. Oscar Brand, Jean Ritchie, Josh White, and Theodore Bikel were mainstream singers of traditional folk material who all met with success in performance and in sales of the recordings they put out on Elektra Records, a small New York label.

Folk music was regaining its long-dormant place in New England life at about the same time that a powerful new musical expression ventured up from the rural South to the youthful, middle-class North in the dynamic form known as rock 'n' roll. Starting in the late 1940s, African American "jump" bands and vocal groups had begun popularizing a hipster musical form known as bebop, and a number of poor white Southern boys (several of whom had grown up on public welfare) began mixing Black rhythm and blues with hillbilly music, much as had been done for decades in the levee camps, railroad yards, and juke joints of the mid-South. Elvis Presley, Carl Perkins, and Johnny Cash were only a few of the impoverished kids drawn to express the limitless exuberance of youth through the magic of racially hybrid music. They all made their first records in Memphis (not far from where bluesmen Frank Stokes and Gus Cannon were still living) at Sun Records Studio, which was owned by Sam Phillips (who, along with composer W. C. Handy, was a native of Florence, Alabama).[10]

"Country bop," "rockabilly," and even a "folk music fireball" was what they called rock 'n' roll when it was first recorded at Sun Records in the early 1950s, and it took the country's teenagers by storm. In its wake, the music opened the door to the emancipating possibilities of racial integration, since the powers that be could not prevent white kids from flocking to Black dances. It was not by accident that the Ku Klux Klan began taking out advertisements in newspapers warning parents to steer their children clear of "Negro jungle music." On the winds of AM radio, incendiary musical sparks from the mid-South blew up and into the tinder-dry suburbs of Cleveland, Philly, New York, and Boston. Hillbilly and bebop culture were suddenly free to come out onto the pop charts, and when erstwhile collegiate bluegrass players attempted to launch their voices into high and lonesome harmony, it might be the Everly Brothers that they would be using as role models as much as it was traditionalists like the Monroes and the Stanleys.

THERE WAS SOMETHING IN the nature of folk music as it was understood in the late 1950s that gave young people the notion that, like making scrambled eggs or playing baseball, traditional singing was something anyone could set out to do themselves, right at home or in their dorm room. Learning to play a musical instrument became a reasonable prospect, not in the expectation of fame and fortune but because it seemed as though it would be a lot of fun. Mastering guitar chords, banjo licks, or contra dance steps was a lot like learning to walk, coaxing clumsy limbs and digits into new steps and patterns that produced primitive but encouraging results and gradually became second nature for those who stuck with it.

A young folkie could be transformed from a shy introvert into a party-hogging ham faster than you could say "Careless Love." In the perilous and uncharted territory that had to be traversed in early encounters with the opposite sex, proficiency on the guitar became a potent and magical attractant for both young women and men. The motivation for embracing folk performance often became a combination of a commitment to "help make a better world" and the desire to "get girls" or to "attract boys."

Boston and Cambridge became a tale of two squares, Harvard and Kenmore, as a smattering of small coffeehouses ran the gauntlet of the licensing boards and became off-campus hangouts where young people of an artistic bent could congregate. In 1955, Tulla's Coffee Grinder was up and percolating on 30 Dunster Street, just off Harvard Square. The coffee-drinking clientele there played chess and listened to classical music, with an occasional flamenco guitar performance thrown into the mix by Harvard student Dick Zaffron. In July 1957, the Turk's Head Coffee House opened at 71½ Charles Street in Boston, at the foot of Beacon Hill. Proprietors Bill Baldwin and David Welsh set about to do business after securing a galvanized sink and an ancient stand-up espresso machine.

On a street full of antique stores and real estate agencies, the Turk's Head was tucked below a granite portal, and, several stone steps down from the sidewalk, a narrow, brick-arched passageway opened toward a green-walled garden. A left turn and a downward step led into a brick-lined room about two-thirds the size of a subway car, with just enough space for a small stage, a tiny kitchen, and a few tables. A pair of tiny horizontal windows below the ceiling revealed a curtained, shoe-level view of Charles Street. It was to become the perfect setting for strong coffee, earnest conversation, and songs from other centuries.

By 1958, a scene was brewing just off Kenmore Square at the Cafe Yana, which developed a specialty in the mixture of caffeine and folk music. Early on, it was located near the railroad tracks on Beacon Street; it would later move to Brookline Avenue, closer to Fenway Park. Situated as it was near the Boston University campus, the Yana became a handy port of call for the youthful round pegs who found themselves chafing at the square holes of BU. In one small step for womankind, college dropouts Betsy Minot (later Siggins) and Debbie Green waitressed at the Yana for a few weeks before bringing banjoes and guitars to work. On stage, Green mustered the courage to play a repertoire of songs she had learned at the Putney School, including old Child ballads and Appalachian love songs that she had set like old gemstones into memorable new arrangements.

Jim Kweskin soon arrived from Stamford, Connecticut, where he had honed a deep interest in ragtime music and the old blues. Kweskin had already delved deeply into traditional music, collecting songs and styles from a variety of sources and performing in the coffeehouses of Greenwich Village. From nearby Acton, Massachusetts, Peter Childs had gone on to Oberlin College, where he was inspired by a Pete Seeger concert to pick up the guitar. Childs soon constructed an eclectic repertoire of traditional blues, ballads, and songs that he brought back with him to Boston and the Yana.

Public performance was the product of weeks of practice in dorm rooms and at parties. College students and dropouts alike gravitated toward cheap apartments in various locations between Kenmore Square and Charles Street, and, on Friday and Saturday nights, those places became the crossroads of camaraderie, flirtation, wine, and music for a host of erstwhile minstrel girls and roving gamblers. Elsewhere in America at the time, you might have had to be a football player or a cheerleader to become a social force on campus, but in the valley of the Charles, there was a very different sort of deal going down. The universal plots of youthful drama were played out every weekend in performances that were scored by traditional music. Some nights, a hopeful rendition of "Freight Train" might fail to gain any traction at all over the buzz of ambient party conversation and would be abandoned before it could chug its way into a third verse.

Other times, every voice in the room joined in as the singer sang about hoping to "be your salty dog," and all that could be heard, otherwise, was the clink of discarded empties. Every once in a while, the room would fall silent as the alchemy of music and emotion pulled everybody into the same quiet place of wonder, the same sense of freedom, and the same belief in the magic of song. Something was happening here.

In February 1958, southwest of Harvard Square, two young entrepreneurs, Joyce Kalina and Paula Kelley, opened the doors of an establishment that they named Club 47 Mount Auburn. There, out beyond the Lampoon building, they filled a spacious room with tables where students could play chess, engage in conversation, and listen to a modest program of jazz music that eventually expanded into other realms. Within a matter of a few months, the room at Club 47 was being commandeered by a growing list of student-age folk performers who followed in the footsteps of veterans such as Rolf Cahn and Eric von Schmidt. Those were heady times; it took real courage to buck the prevailing winds of middle-class conformity when there was precious little in the way of role modeling or encouragement. It was, as singer-songwriter David Mallett later described it, an "innocent time."[11]

Joan Baez, another Boston University dropout, was a friend of Betsy Minot and Debbie Green who overcame stage fright just enough to sing at Tulla's and then joined a dozen or so friends who began to "come for to sing" on the stage of Club 47. These included the Charles River Valley Boys, Eric von Schmidt, and African American singer Sylvia Mars, who as a child had sung and danced for textile mill workers coming off their shifts in her hometown of Abbeville, South Carolina. Sylvia became a regular at the club, singing spirituals and Bessie Smith blues songs to an appreciative young audience. About the same time, Tom Rush, a Harvard student from New Hampshire, took on the announcer's role in Pennypacker Hall on WHRB's *Balladeers* program, where he started playing a repertoire of blues tunes he had picked up on old 78 rpm records from the 1920s and '30s.

In 1959, a number of the young people who were hanging out at the Cafe Yana heard that there was a property available across the railroad tracks, a bit closer to the Boston University campus. In short order, singers Fred Basler and Peter Lanz decided to take the plunge and secured the place for a coffeehouse, festooning the walls with fishnets, throwing together a makeshift kitchen, and christening the room The Golden Vanity. The opening act was an impromptu duo of the veteran blues harmonica player Sonny Terry and the local singer Eric von Schmidt. Fortified with much gin and supported at least part of the night by a kitchen crew consisting of folk singer Robert L. Jones and artist Bob Neuwirth, the two played three sets to a packed house, thus launching the Golden Vanity into the lowland sea of the Back Bay.

Before long, the Vanity became established as a major component in the budding folk music scene, and performers of all abilities, characters, and tastes began to take the stage. Other than on a very few muddied reel-to-reel tape relics, there is little record of these times apart from the memory of the participants whose lives were transformed by the music being played. The newly minted Charles River Valley Boys came over from Harvard, Eric von Schmidt was a "regular," and others came and went from the stages of the Salamander on Huntington Avenue, the Turk's Head on Charles Street, the Yana, and the Ballad Room in Copley Square. One night, someone thought to bring a tape recorder to the Vanity and caught a snippet of Joan Baez singing "Pastures of Plenty," "The Nightingale's Song," "Enchantment," and "Girl of Constant Sorrow." At one point, Joan asked Betsy Minot to come up and sing harmony on "Long Lonesome Road" and "Jackaroe" before the two were joined by a male singer, possibly David Gude, on "All My Trials." The feeling was far more that of a living room than a stage.[12]

In the fall of 1957, Bob Siggins, from Nebraska, and Texan Clay Jackson met on the cross-country railroad train that was taking them both eastward to the green expanses of Harvard University. Once there, they encountered old-timey music enthusiast Eric Sackheim and mandolin player Ethan Signer, and soon they were all learning to sing and play a mixture of old string-band numbers and hard-driving bluegrass songs. In 1959, as the Charles River Valley Boys, they began to appear regularly at Tulla's Coffee Grinder and on the airwaves of WHRB, where they met emcee Tom Rush and his assistant, Betsy Minot. The CRVB may have been undergraduates at Harvard, but they soon developed a masters-level grasp of about a hundred and fifty years' worth of old-time American music. Early in 1960, the group encamped at the Harvard radio station and set on tape a seventy-six-song collection of early string-band tunes, a one-of-a-kind Cambridge anthology of rural American folk tradition.[13]

Betsy Minot and Bob Siggins became an "item" and were married in a ceremony that included Joan Baez as a bridesmaid. In 1961, the young couple and some of Bob's fellow musicians took time off from their studies to jaunt across the water to Europe, and, in the course of the journey, cut a record called *Bringin' in the Georgia Mail* at Dobell's Record Shop in London. Soon after their return, the CRVB began working on the album that would become *Bluegrass and Old-Timey Music* and launched into a performance schedule that made them one of the best known of the Boston-Cambridge folk groups. They became mainstays at Club 47, where Betsy (now Siggins) began to take on a wider role, partnering with entrepreneur Byron Lord Linardos in the management of the club as it reorganized into a "membership" nonprofit organization in order to anticipate and, if possible, avoid the hurdles that were regularly put into its path by the Cambridge Licensing Authority.

Jim Rooney happened to show up at Club 47 for the first time on a day when the house was surrounded by Cambridge police squad cars, and officers were in the process of padlocking the doors for some trumped-up reason. With the help of other Boston and Cambridge coffeehouses, the hassles were cleared up, and Jim continued on the course of his lifelong musical journey on Mount Auburn Street. Sometime around his freshman year at Boston's Roxbury Latin School, Rooney had fallen hard for country music through exposure to *The Hayloft Jamboree* radio show on Boston's WCOP. By 1953, he owned a guitar and was following in the footsteps of Hank Williams, singing on the radio and appearing on the *Jamboree* in "powder blue pants and a fancy shirt."[14]

Eventually, he made his way to Amherst College, where he met Brockton boy Bill Keith, who, as luck would have it, had just learned the banjo parts to all the Flatt & Scruggs songs that Jim had recently learned to sing. A fateful partnership in music ensued. When the two friends decided that they wanted to organize an Odetta concert in Amherst in 1960, they got in touch with Manny Greenhill in Boston, who suggested that they needed to have a local organization designated as the concert sponsor. So, together with University of Massachusetts students Buffy Sainte-Marie and Taj Mahal, Keith and Rooney incorporated the Pioneer Valley Folklore Society, and, in due course, these two opened for Odetta. A fuse had been lit on the banks of the Connecticut River.[15]

Unlike others on the scene whose academic careers became collateral damage of the Folk Revival, both Rooney and Keith planned on continuing their educations, and for them the move over the Mass Pike to Cambridge was tailor-made. The duo played the Ballad Room in Copley Square, the Boston YMCA for Manny Greenhill, and the Agassiz Theatre for the Harvard-Radcliffe Liberal Union. They opened for Joan Baez at the 1960 Dartmouth Winter Carnival, played at Cafe Lena's in Saratoga, New York, at a place called the Red Onion in Toronto, and eventually at the Philadelphia Folk Festival, where they stunned the crowd with Bill's banjo picking on an old fiddle tune, "The Devil's Dream." But their shoes kept walkin' back to Cambridge, where Keith & Rooney settled into a life of fame, if not fortune, as regulars at Club 47 Mount Auburn, singing songs such as "Pretty Polly," "Salty Dog Blues," and "The Willow Garden."[16]

They became among the first beneficiaries of Paul Rothchild's eventual success at getting a Charles River Valley Boys record out on his fledging Prestige/Folklore Record company. The second title on the new green label was Keith & Rooney's *Livin' on the Mountain* album, fourteen fine bluegrass and old-timey songs featuring Bill and Jim's favorite material backed up by Fritz Richmond on washtub bass, Herb Applin on guitar, North Carolinian Herb Hoovin on fiddle, and, on mandolin and singing tenor, a guy from Watertown named Joe Val. "I love to watch peoples' faces when Joe hits the high notes and their glasses begin to break!" wrote Rooney in the album's liner notes. "Certainly one important reason for whatever success we had was we really liked the songs we recorded. . . . We caught the bird on the wing once and with a little luck maybe we'll catch it again someday." That wonderful record is little noted today, but it initiated a regional recorded bluegrass history that still resonates, going on sixty years later.[17]

The Boston singer who became known to thousands of folk enthusiasts as Jackie Washington had been born Juan Cándido Washington y Landrón. Jack was a Roxbury native who, as a child, had been directed by a white school teacher to change his name to something that sounded more "Anglo." He began performing for family and friends in his youth, and it was on the regional version of a "chitlin' circuit" in "the "Negro sections" of places such as Lowell and Brockton that he crafted his considerable musicianship and stage presence. He remembers hoofing the boards alongside preachers, comics, gauzily clad showgirls, and a singer with a Caribbean island persona calling himself "Calypso Gene," who would later be known as Louis Farrakhan. Long before he "came for to sing" folk songs, young Jack was the master of the Black culture that had flourished in the era of Louis Jordan, Cab Calloway, and all the architects and practitioners of jump band music during and after World War II.

While a student at Emerson College, Jack encountered the largely white world of folk music through friendship with musicians Tony Saletan and Irene Kossoy. He joined the couple in forming the Boston Folk Trio and, in the process, absorbed the conventions of the budding Folk Revival. He was a very early presence in the new folk scene, and, as an already-seasoned performer, he became a regular at Club 47 Mount Auburn. At heart, Jack was and always will be an actor, yet his voice was a perfect instrument for the repertoire of folk material that he carefully curated in both performance and on records. He signed early with Vanguard Records and was booked by Manny Greenhill's Folklore Productions into an ambitious performance schedule that eventually brought him to scores of venues around Boston and, later on, into a friendship with Pete Seeger.

By virtue of his personality and his talent, Jack Landrón could grab hold of an audience like no other performer of that time. His playlist ranged from "Sweet Mama" and "Tell Old Bill" to defining versions of "Oh, Babe It Ain't No Lie," "One Man's Hands," and, later, Malvina Reynolds's "It Isn't Nice." In 1963, when he was roughed up by the Boston police, the folk community rallied around him; the incident was an early indication for any white folks who were paying attention that things were not hunky dory for people of color in the old City upon a Hill.[18]

After an impromptu 1961 set at the Golden Vanity, Tom Rush went from being a play-by-play man on the radio to batting cleanup on the stage of Club 47 Mount Auburn. The transformation could not have been more impressive if it had occurred at midnight on a Mississippi crossroads, although it probably happened in some combination of Rush's native New Hampshire and his dorm room at Harvard. Tom has always had an uncannily good eye for material, and he chose traditional songs with an irresistible combination of novelty and integrity; nobody else combined the works of Carl Perkins and those of Pink Anderson in a playlist.

In short order, he became a defining presence on the scene, not just in Cambridge and Boston but throughout all of New England. On any given evening, Tom could usher an audience of callow college students and moon-faced suburban kids onto a musical tour bus that took them over the Mass Pike, down into the steamy juke joints of Mississippi, along the grimy streets of Memphis, through the bullet-pocked cow towns of the old West, and then get them all back to the Unicorn safe and sound, and, somehow, a little more American than they had been when they had come in and hung up their pea coats. Like Geoff Muldaur and Jack Landrón, Tom could take instant title to a room, wielding his big old Epiphone Texan like a magic wand and holding an audience spellbound for the duration of a set.[19]

Geoff Muldaur was a young musical soldier of fortune from Pelham, New York, who had been steeped in African American music through the magic he discovered in his older brother's collection of jazz 78s. He jettisoned his college career and ran off with the circus of an American traditional music that he very quickly mastered at the high-wire level. Geoff's connection to the old songs was deep and instinctive, and he combined taste, virtuosity, and commitment with a wry but boyish hipster's stage presence. At Club 47, he sang in a unique voice inspired by the living traditions he had absorbed from scratchy old records and by an impulsive pilgrimage that he had taken from New Orleans to East Texas to visit the grave of blues singer Blind Lemon Jefferson.

On such songs as "Trouble Soon Be Over," Frank Stokes's "Downtown Blues," and the Kweskin's band's "Wild about My Loving," Geoff set riveting vocals into brilliant and inspired arrangements that he presented with the conjoined force of a magnetic voice and an engaging personality. Geoff Muldaur sings right into your soul, and when you are listening to him, you don't have to imagine what it was like to be in a room with a craftsman like Gus Cannon or a wizard like Hoagy Carmichael. With his friends Eric von Schmidt and Jim Kweskin, Geoff became a consulting architect of the Cambridge scene.[20]

Alvin Hankerson was a Florida-born bluesman who had come to Boston in 1945, working as a barber in Roxbury and singing with a band part-time under the name Guitar Nubbit. At some point, while buying 45s at Skippy White's Mass Records, Nubbit told White that he played the blues, and the music dealer asked him to bring in some tapes. One thing led to another and, in 1962, White's Bluestown Records began recording him and released his "Evil Woman Blues."[21] About this time, Nubbit attended a Lightnin' Hopkins concert and afterward talked with the Texas bluesman as well as Boston promoter Manny Greenhill.

Greenhill encouraged him to go over to Cambridge and play at a Club 47 hootenanny, where Nubbit was given a regular Tuesday night slot and was featured on a poster (see page 92) listing sixteen regular performers. In addition, he played at the Silver Vanity in Worcester and may have appeared at the King's Rook in Ipswich. There is more than a little irony in the realization that, even as academics from Cambridge were setting out to rediscover African American blues artists in Mississippi, Guitar Nubbit was hiding in plain sight in Roxbury. (Skippy White and David Wilson were among the few white Bostonians who seem to have been familiar with his music.) Between 1962 and 1965, Nubbit recorded a few dozen songs on White's Bluestown label before apparently giving up on his folk blues career. His recorded output eventually was "discovered" in England in the 1980s, but he remains a largely unappreciated figure from the early Boston-Cambridge scene.[22]

Dayle Stanley began singing at Club 47 early in 1962, at first sharing evening billings with singers Tom Rush, Mitch Greenhill, or Geoff Muldaur, and then later appearing on her own more than three dozen times in 1962 and 1963. Her repertoire included ballads such as "Fennario" and "The Cruel Mother," work songs like "Look Over Yonder" and "Swing That Hammer," and the well-known folk songs "Shenandoah" and "Pretty Saro," as well as the rural New England hymn "Come, Shaker Life." She was one of the first singer-songwriters in Cambridge and Boston, composing such pieces as "The Years" and "Nobody Knows That I Have a Name." In addition to Club 47, she played at the Unicorn, the King's Rook, and the Orleans. On tour, she performed at Gerde's Folk City in New York, the Flambeau in Baltimore, and the Main Point in Bryn Mawr, Pennsylvania. Dayle appeared at a number of civil rights benefit concerts, most notably at the Sanders Theatre in August 1963, where funds were raised to enable young activists from Boston to travel to the March on Washington. Her rich voice held audiences spellbound, and she became one of the most popular singers in the Revival.[23]

About the same time, a young Canadian, Bonnie Dobson, brought a repertoire of international songs to the club that included the work of traditional singers from the Maritimes, many collected by the folklorist, academic, and record producer Kenneth Goldstein. Bonnie left Canada in 1960 while still in her teens, playing the Folklore Center in Denver, the Ash Grove in LA, and Gerde's Folk City in New York before coming up to Boston. She performed moving versions of traditional songs such as "Schule Aroon" and "Peter Amberley" and Ewan MacColl's "The

First Time Ever I Saw Your Face." She wrote some of her own material as well, most notably "Walk Me Out in the Morning Dew," which was printed on the cover of the New York *Broadside* even before songs by Bob Dylan and Phil Ochs began to appear there. Bonnie's recordings, like Dayle Stanley's, were featured on the WBZ *Hootenanny* radio program, which was broadcast on Sunday evening from 6 to 8 p.m. over a fifty-thousand-watt signal that blanketed much of the Northeast.[24]

For all these convinced bohemians and freshly minted college dropouts, there were no correspondence courses or handy websites available to act as portals into the uncharted frontiers of traditional music. The ballad collection of Francis James Child was readily available in print, if lacking in tunes, and the chief source of recorded folk material was Folkways Records in New York City. Folkways, the work of Moses Asch and Marian Distler, specialized in producing "long playing, low selling records" of everything from reissues of 1920s blues men to the tunes and shanties of whaling crews. In the early 1950s, an odd soul by the name of Harry Smith came to Moe Asch's office and proposed the production of a long-playing sample of his enormous collection of 78 rpm records from the 1920s and '30s. Blissfully free of reference to copyrights or permissions, Asch put out this *Anthology of American Folk Music* in a six-record box set that became the primary entry point into traditional song for a host of young musical explorers as they attempted to invent a post-postwar American landscape and then to navigate through it.

Harry Smith's *Anthology* looked, at first glance, like a quirky menagerie of musical oddities, but on examination, it actually proved to be an uncannily powerful cross-section of American traditional culture. Its eighty-four American folk, blues, and country tunes inspired young musicians to transcribe the lyrics and "figure out the chords" on all the old songs, and, soon thereafter, hopeful new arrangements from the collection were being played in dorms and in coffeehouses. Even though there was enough material on those six records to keep most young singers busy, the *Anthology* served to whet the curiosity of a few true believers who began to comb secondhand stores in search of older and even more obscure recordings. Sixty years later, John Cohen remembered how rich the material had seemed to him, and how he suddenly felt called to proselytize and make people aware of the world of these wonderful old songs.[25]

For young enthusiasts like these, the weight of modern assumptions about time and space lost credence as soon as a record needle hit the grooves of an old 78 and ancient sounds began to issue forth from modern hi-fi speakers. There was a hypnotic power in the voices of antique rural America, singing songs that went back to origins in Ghana, Nova Scotia, New Mexico, or Scotland, and, in time, anywhere from the 1920s back to the 1400s. After the magic lamp of the record player had been rubbed, the voices of resurrected souls could be heard not just speaking but singing and feeling, picking up the game where one day, long before, they had left it off. Death may have had its sting, but it did not have the last word.

A kind of alchemy operated at the heart of the matter. Many young listeners, accustomed to the polish and production of modern music, were taken aback at first by the starkness and atonality of some traditional singers, not to mention the accumulated decades of nicks and scratches on the recordings themselves. A voice like Almeda Riddle's or Blind Willie Johnson's carried the banner not of celebrity or fashion but of mystery and magic. This was very powerful stuff, and to simply call it "a hootenanny" or "the folk music boom" was to miss the caliber of emotional intensity expressed by the artists and the depth of the impact they were having on young listeners. Coffeehouse candles in empty Beaujolais bottles began to take on a votive quality, and young devotees started to imagine that they could actually learn, first to feel and then to play and sing these kinds of songs themselves.

When a beautiful young woman sang that she would "never prove false to the boy I love, till the rocks melt with the sun," her youthful listeners fervently wished that someone would feel that way about them. When an elderly blues player declared, "Death don't have no mercy in this land," no one had to ask for whom the bell tolled from the depths of his big Gibson guitar. When bluegrass brothers sang in high and lonesome harmony about a tearful old farm couple kissing their city-bound boy goodbye, it wasn't the kind of thing anybody could treat like background music. When a single voice called out, "Come gather 'round people, wherever you roam," it was a direct take-it-or-leave it proposition that stood out in bold contrast to the never-ending modern Muzak of celebrity, entertainment, and advertising. If you really listened, you heard, and if you really heard, you would never be the same.

CLUB 47

COFFEE HOUSE AND ART GALLERY
UN 4-3266 - CAMBRIDGE, MASS.

FOLK SINGING with
Jackie Washington   Dale Stanley
Guitar Nubbit   Rolf Cahn
Keith & Rooney   Tom Rush
Eric von Schmidt   Sylvia Mars
Bonnie Dobson   Greenbriar Boys
Charles River Valley Boys
Bob Jones   Paul Arnoldi   Pete Stanley
Mitch Greenhill   Jess Muldor

FIGURE 7.
Club 47 Mount Auburn poster, c. 1962.
Department of Special Collections, W. E. B. Du Bois Library,
University of Massachusetts Amherst.

CHAPTER SEVEN

TENTING TONIGHT ON THE BANKS OF THE CHARLES

Boston and Cambridge, 1960–1963

WHAT BEGAN IN THE Charles River valley as a diversion turned into a fascination, then a credo, and then a movement. The ardor and growing musical ability of the young New England folkies was personified in the talent and the burgeoning career of Joan Baez. On the nights that she performed at Club 47 and the Golden Vanity, word of mouth alone filled the house as nothing had ever done before. Her material was authentic, her arrangements were impeccable, and she sang in a voice so powerful it seemed as though it could move mountains and sweep back the running tide. It was unprecedented for a woman performer to assume such a position of moral leadership. Seeing Joan Baez appear ten feet away from you at a coffeehouse in Harvard or Kenmore Square was a little like sipping a cup of espresso while watching Marion Anderson sing at the Lincoln Memorial.

Joan's trajectory from college dropout to best-selling recording artist took a little less than two years to play out in the months between the autumn of 1958 and the summer of 1960, in a dynamic that combined artistic inspiration, ambition, and stage fright. Her initial appearance at Club 47 was witnessed primarily by her parents and her sisters, but word of her talent spread rapidly. Joan's weekly gigs were soon jammed with students who, at that time, were likely to be dressed in tweed jackets and ties or blouses and skirts, with penny loafers or flats. Her material at first included tunes likely learned from Harry Belafonte and Burl Ives records, but through friends including Debbie Green, Rolf Cahn, and Betsy Minot, she rapidly developed a wide repertoire of traditional ballads and songs. At times, she joined in with singers Bill Wood or Ted Alevizos, at other times she sang solo, her audience alternating between sitting in stunned silence and singing along with her on songs such as "Passing Through" and "Don't You Weep after Me."

Joan's parents were convinced Quakers, and her political and moral convictions were of a piece with her music. She was deeply intelligent, she was strikingly beautiful, and, despite her humorous asides on stage, she was deadly serious about her sense of mission. Her voice and her presence shattered all conventions in a time and a place where conventions ruled the day. No one could ignore Joan Baez.[1]

Like many of the other participants in what was becoming the Boston-Cambridge Folk Revival, Joan entered the world of traditional music through a process of artistic maturation that took the course of only a few months. Tapes of her performances at the Golden Vanity and Club 47 include "Dink's Song," "Delia's Gone," and "La Bamba," as well as titles she would later put on record, such as "All My Trials," "Dona, Dona," and the Child ballad "Henry Martin." Within the year, Joan went from singing among the squeaking chairs and espresso machines of Cambridge and Boston coffeehouses to an invitation to join well-known folk singer Bob Gibson on center stage at the first Newport Folk Festival in 1959. Her two-song performance there stunned the audience and brought Joan to the attention of the New York folk crowd.

Columbia Records beckoned, but she signed with Odetta's label, the little-known Vanguard Recording Society. Albert Grossman, the walking definition of "big time folk music," offered his services as her manager, but instead she joined in with Manny Greenhill's stable of Boston artists at Folklore Productions. In July 1960, she found herself in the ballroom of the Manhattan Towers hotel, which had been converted into a makeshift recording studio that sported two microphones and a tape machine. She later remembered, "I just did my set; it was probably all I knew. Just put 'em down. I did 'Mary Hamilton' once, that was it. That's the way we made 'em in the old days. As long as a dog didn't run through the room or something, you had it."[2]

Indeed, she did. Her first album was released to widespread acclaim, and soon it conquered college campuses across the nation. The embers that had long been burning in the work of Odetta and Pete Seeger and the kindling that had been stacked up by the Weavers and the

Kingston Trio exploded into what would soon take on the form of a musical conflagration.

Bill Keith remembered opening for Joan at Dartmouth Winter Carnival with his bluegrass sidekick Jim Rooney in 1961. Both Amherst men had been up late the night before, sampling the fabled ales of Dartmouth. They had figured that the 10:30 a.m. Saturday concert time and a sudden snowstorm would combine to dampen the turnout, but they were wrong. "You couldn't have put another person in there sideways," Bill recalled in *Baby, Let Me Follow You Down*. "We went out there and did our set and couldn't believe the response, but that was nothing compared to what they did for Joan. After every song, they'd stamp and whistle and applaud like it was the end of the world. I guess that's when we realized how big a star she was going to be. It was phenomenal."[3] Shortly thereafter, she claimed the mantle of best-selling female recording artist in America, a distinction that she took over from pop singer Brenda Lee.

The Harvard Square scene was continuing to percolate, both musically and culturally. In February 1963, David Wilson was asked to put a roster together for a benefit for the Community Church Art Center in Copley Square, and he remembers suggesting that Jim Kweskin join forces with Geoff Muldaur for the concert. Soon thereafter, the two came together to form the nucleus of the group that became known as Jim Kweskin and the Jug Band. While other artists sang material from the rural hinterlands, the Jug Band sang the downtown blues of the Ragtime era, channeling the sweet street-soul of the nineteenth-century border towns of St. Louis, Louisville, and Memphis. In short order, they began synthesizing this complex musical ancestry into an aesthetic of retro-hipness that was something of a stroke of genius. Kweskin's ragtime guitar and good-time delivery on such songs as "Boodle Am Boom" and "Somebody Stole My Gal" made an irresistible combination, and Muldaur's voice, bluesy phrasing, and blow-you-away timing were every bit as distinctive and riveting as Bob Dylan's or Dave Van Ronk's. Anchored by Fritz Richmond's virtuoso washtub bass and filigreed by Bill Keith's banjo, the Jug Band became all-stars in their rookie year.

The Tiffany glass ceiling of the Kweskin fraternity was blown away by the addition of Maria D'Amato, the first of the red-hot folky mamas. She was a native of Greenwich Village who loved music as a child, became part of a doo-wop group in high school, and was then drawn to the folk music being played around Washington Square. Maria was enthralled by the blues singing of Bessie Smith and, later, became a student of the Appalachian fiddling of Gaither Carlton, Doc Watson's father-in-law. She was steeped in some of the richest musical strains in American culture.

Looking for all the world like the sort of young gal who would turn heads at the health food store ("I'll have what she's having . . ."), Maria rocked out in the traditions of Smith, Sippie Wallace, Minnie Douglas, and the other classic women blues singers of the 1920s and '30s. Boston, Cambridge, and, in particular, Geoff Muldaur were smitten. He and Maria became a couple, and she jumped ship from the Even Dozen Jug Band in New York to join the carnival in Massachusetts. The Kweskin Band's droll and deadpan delivery, coupled with their infectious material, impeccable musicianship, and funky threads, made its performances unforgettable. Its first record was devoured by isolated young folkies like Janis Joplin of Port Arthur, Texas; Dan Hicks from Little Rock, Arkansas; and Jerry Garcia out in Menlo Park, California. Something, indeed, was happening, and it kind of didn't matter what it was, as long as, hey, everybody was having a good time.

Up from New York, folk musician Tim Hardin, old-timey fiddler Peter Stampfel of the Holy Modal Rounders, and twelve-string guitar player Mark Spoelstra all took up residence for a time in Cambridge. Bob Dylan and Dave Van Ronk became regular visitors, sleeping on couches following after-hours parties near Club 47 and the Unicorn Coffee House, which opened on Boston's Boylston Street around 1961. Musical cross-pollinations became coin of the realm. Dylan would make prominent mention of Eric von Schmidt on his first album in 1961; in 1963, *Mark Spoelstra Recorded at Club 47 Inc* featured cover artwork by von Schmidt and Byron Linardos. For the Holy Modal Rounder's first album in 1964, Stampfel borrowed the old folk song "Bound to Lose" that he'd learned from Bob Dylan, who, himself, had picked up more than a few songs from the Boston-Cambridge community.

It was one thing for a young folkie to learn the chords and words to a song such as "Salty Dog Rag" or "The Trees They Do Grow High," but performing in public, under a spotlight, in front of an audience of strangers, was another kettle of fish. What might have been imagined as a moment of glory in front of the microphone could come to feel more like standing blindfolded a dozen feet away from a firing squad. Nervousness often led to interminable spoken introductions that hauled the audience through a sea of verbal footnotes or tangential anecdotes before a song actually started. One night at the Turk's Head, guitarist John Fahey became so engrossed in his own banter that he forgot to play any music at all. Perhaps the best role model for young performers was Mississippi John Hurt, who just walked to the stage, thumbed his big Guild guitar, smiled, and said, simply, "Good evenin', people. Glad to be with y'all!"

Some folks specialized in storytelling: Jack Elliott had a few numbers that consisted mostly of poetry set to guitar picking. Others, like Tom Rush, developed the ability to engage an audience in laconic monologues that connected songs and provided vamping space during tunings. Jack Landrón, a master showman among the local folk musicians, recited stories, did impressions, and told jokes between songs to audiences that hung on his every word. When Peter Stampfel and Steve Weber (the Holy Modal Rounders) appeared on stage, Stampfel gave the impression that he was the strangest old codger north of the Carolinas, a geezer who was managing to perform for an audience and somehow get the last laugh on them at the same time. How the duo managed their deadpan delivery of outrageous material such as "Euphoria" and "Mister Spaceman" is still a mystery. When Jim Kweskin and Geoff Muldaur appeared together, audiences were treated to vaudeville-hipster schtick of the highest order.

Fritz Richmond, a Newton native, was one of the most dynamic figures in the Boston-Cambridge Folk Revival. His musical skills were unparalleled, and his range of activity on the washtub bass appeared limitless. Embracing what seemed superficially like a "gimmick" instrument, he achieved virtuosity in partnership with nearly every major folk performer on the scene. Fritz, like a number of other folkies (Robert L. Jones, as well as Mitch Greenhill, Hardin, Keith, von Schmidt, and Wilson), had served a stint in the military before returning to the Boston area, just as the Folk Revival was picking up speed. Tom Rush tells a tall tale of GI Fritz attempting to hook up a telephone pole to a Quonset hut with a huge piece of cable to see what kind of sound he could come up with.

The mechanics of the instrument are basic enough. Setting one edge of an upside-down galvanized washtub on a two-by-four so the sound can resonate, the player hooks one end of a steel cable to the tub and the other to the top of a stout five-foot-tall stick, which leans on the other edge of the tub to create a triangle. With one foot up on the tub, he "twangs" the cable with a dominant hand, while, with his other hand in a leather glove studded with nickels, he grasps and tilts the stick backward and forward to tighten or loosen the wire, thus modulating the tone that booms out into the room. But, as anyone can demonstrate, the ability to actually hit *notes* on the thing, and then to be able to improvise and syncopate with it, was a whole lot harder than it looked. In fact, it was something almost nobody else knew how to do.

No one recalls in what coffeehouse or at whose apartment Fritz Richmond first set up his cable-and-tub contraption, but whomever he backed up (and we can imagine that it was the Charles River Valley Boys) probably swung along in time to the booming, rhythmic sound that was suddenly pumping up behind them. The effect on an audience was phenomenal, and a performance that might have carried some aspects of a recital suddenly "cooked," rocking and rolling, in Joe Turner's words, "like a big wheel through the Georgia cotton fields."[4] It didn't take long for Richmond to be able to improvise like a jazz soloist behind Rush ("Big Fat Woman") and Landrón ("Sweet Mama") on the Club 47 floor and later, fortunately, in a recording studio.

Live tapes in the Folk New England collection bear out the impression that Fritz Richmond never had "a bad night." Soon he was backing up almost every musician on the scene, and his mark remains on dozens of recordings. The same teenagers who were playing Chuck Berry's 45 rpm records at 33 to slow them down and learn the guitar notes became adept at *speeding up* Tom Rush records from 33 to 45, cranking up the bass setting, and listening to Fritz pop his running, Motown-like lines through the speakers. This might have been a hard thing to explain to your parents, but then, many things were.[5]

As far as can be determined from early twentieth-century recordings, makeshift instruments including the washtub bass, the jug (blown into with the tone modulated by the player's mouth), and the washboard (strummed snappily with thimbled fingers to create a tap dance effect) allowed poor Black performers to create a ragtime ensemble sound "down on the corner and out in the street" and later in recording studios. The appreciation of the jug band genre had been kept alive in America among jazz record collectors, and, incredibly, in postwar England, where discs brought to the United Kingdom by American GIs and picked up by Lonnie Donegan and others inspired hundreds of energetic teenagers to form pickup "skiffle bands." Most of these groups would be little noted and long forgotten, with the exception of a Liverpool outfit that called themselves the Quarrymen. Led by teenagers John Lennon and Paul McCartney, the group developed a repertoire that moved from the influence of Leadbelly's "Rock Island Line" to Carl Perkins's take on Blind Lemon Jefferson's "Matchbox," and then, in short order, on to self-penned compositions like "One After 909."

Jim Kweskin was the local master of the ragtime guitar, rolling out effortless solos that strutted along like a "darktown" piano rag, almost as if his notes were wearing spats. Bill Keith excelled at the banjo, studying it to the point where he would write the first tablature transcription of Earl Scruggs's collected solos, an accomplishment that, a bit later, would astonish no one more than it astonished Scruggs himself. Tom Rush created arrangements that made full use of his skills with the slide guitar, with open tunings, and with the rhythmic, percussive use of his trusty Epiphone Texan.

Master showman Jack Landrón has at times downplayed his guitar skills of yore, but archived live tapes from Club 47 reveal his mastery of the instrument on such songs as "I Hope She Finds Favor" and "Who's That Knockin'?" In general, ballad singers tended to concentrate on the vocal delivery of their antique narrative pieces, but Debbie Green's arrangements and Ed Freeman's lute-inspired guitar playing were both things of striking beauty. Among many other folk instrumentals, Tom Rush's take on Muldaur's "Mole's Moan," Mimi Fariña's solo on "The Falcon," Tim Hardin's opening picking on "Stackalee," Bill Keith's "Devil's Dream," the Kweskin Band's "Sadie Green," Peter Child's "Under the Double Eagle," and Mitch Greenhill's ragtime accompaniment at Newport with Jack Landrón on "Bill Bailey/Just Because" are among the many instrumental standouts of the period.[6]

Despite the rigors involved in mastering instrumentation, it was often the vocals that were the hardest to "get right." Clean-cut, popular, early '50s folk-style groups, who David Wilson once referred to collectively as "the Tollbooth Men," had put a premium on delivering ample quantities of earnest gusto to their foot-stomping campus audiences. A bit later on, though, the performance dynamic tended to involve barely postadolescent singers moving from the privacy of practicing in a dorm room to standing, socially naked, in a small and silent coffeehouse before a jury of their peers. Artists as talented as Joan Baez or Phil Ochs could be stricken with serious stage fright; it was a malady that could inflict anyone, even when it just came in the form of mild preperformance anxiety.

In addition to hours of practice, there were two major sources of balm to be found in the folk music Gilead of the day. The first were the voices, perhaps heard only on scratchy old 78s, of early performers whose lives might have been long gone but whose inspiration, through the medium of traditional songs playing on a turntable, bore enduring witness to the content of their hearts and their souls. On the one hand, there was something endearing about a young New Englander singing a song about a "boxcah daw" or a "clippah ship." On the other, near-miss approximations of an African American sound by white singers seemed in danger of venturing into the complex and questionable territory later referred to as "love and theft." Bob Dylan's approach was probably the simplest: he often succeeded in sounding neither white nor Black, but just plain *old*. In other cases, perhaps Geoff Muldaur's being the most noteworthy, the distance from heart to voice seemed to be effortless and inspired. We all had to find our way.

The second safety net on the high wire of public performance was the sense of devotion and mission that was being shared in what began to be experienced as "the folk community." We were all passengers on an underground railroad, we were all wayfaring pilgrims traveling through a worrisome land. In the process of making it up as we went along, reading ancient tea leaves, trying to make sense out of yellowed, oddly written manuscripts with pages missing, or with an "f" where there should be an "s," we knew that sometimes any one of us, maybe all of us, might wander or stumble. We were all trying to discover our voices across the borderlines of a self-made new frontier.

Coffeehouses continued to spring up: the Loft in 1960 on Charles Street, the Unicorn on Boylston soon thereafter, and then the King's Rook up in Marblehead, and later Ipswich. Club 47 was bringing in an impressive array of traditional musicians such as Roscoe Holcomb and Almeda Riddle, and the Unicorn was booking nationally known folk names including Dave Van Ronk and the Clancy Brothers. The amount of talent both in residence and traveling through Cambridge and Boston was increasing, and it became difficult to know who was in town and where they were performing.

David Wilson was an Arlington native, MIT student, and Air Force reservist with a love of folk music and an apartment that backed up, conveniently, to the rear entrance of the Unicorn Coffee House. To help folks keep track of the scene, in March 1962, David and a group of stalwart volunteers began printing a dynamic coffeehouse magazine that they named *Broadside*. (Coincidentally, two other folk music publications with the same name were launched that same spring: in New

York, by Agnes "Sis" Cunningham, and in Los Angeles, by Ed Pearl.) Soon to grow to a couple of dozen pages, the Boston paper came out every other week and included a treasure trove of schedules for all the coffeehouses and folk concerts in the region.[7]

The pace of musical exploration, discovery, and invention accelerated through the streets of Boston and Cambridge. The absence of media attention, the rarity of recording contracts, and the long lag time between studio sessions and the production of albums meant that the whole scene was self-contained and could function as a kind of teeming, organic terrarium. Every week brought new insights and skills, every weekend of parties brought new collaborations, and every month brought new schedules of local and visiting artists to David Wilson's *Broadside*. To really grasp it at all, you had to jump in and let yourself become a part of it; in Boston and Cambridge, you just had to be there.

There was no model for "alternative media" at the time, and the local and regional press largely ignored the folk music scene. When the *Boston Globe,* the *Herald-Traveler,* or the *Record-American* did pay attention, it was often to lampoon the artsy "beard and sandals crowd" as harmless deviants, best kept in line by hassles from the licensing board and the random application of muscle by cops on the beat. Because the explosion of progressive thinking fueled by activist political movements was to a great degree missed or misinterpreted by the national press, the influence of a publication like the *Broadside* was enormous. While circulation seems to have topped out at about five thousand, there were indications that the average issue was passed around much more widely among friends, classmates, and the patrons of local coffeehouses.

Broadside provided some of the only accurate access that many young white people in Boston could have regarding the street-level progress of the American Civil Rights Movement. As late as the mid-1960s, the mainstream press was still making regular references to "the Negro problem" or "racial strife" rather than to coverage of national progress toward our commitment to liberty and justice for all. "Are the Negroes Moving Too Fast?" was the sort of headline regularly seen in many Northern newspapers and magazines, not just in segregationist propaganda. Folk music publications such as *Broadside* and New York's folk music magazine *Sing Out!* opened doors into the Movement for young, middle-class, white suburban students who began to bear witness at civil rights rallies and to attend the Boston Freedom Folk Festivals of the mid-1960s.

Broadside played a considerable educational role in the community, since many of its readers were quite young, and almost all had been brought up within the narrow frames of reference of postwar suburbia. The basic rubric of folk song lore was suddenly being made accessible: Child ballads, spirituals, old-timey music, blues, bluegrass, "topical" songs, and other categories were being defined, contextualized, and explored in ways that allowed young people to absorb their American musical inheritance and to develop their tastes and interests in a natural and individualized manner. Figures as disparate, for example, as balladeer Jean Ritchie, bluesman Son House, folk composers Mimi and Richard Fariña, and "protest singer" Phil Ochs were treated as important parts of an integrated whole.

Broadside editor Wilson took pains to avoid "tilting" in favor of any of the many coffeehouses on the scene. When he took on the management of the Cafe Yana in 1964, David handed the editorial reins to Jill Henderson, who, together with Sandi Mandeville and Lynn Musgrave, were key participants in the rich life of *Broadside* and the whole burgeoning folk scene. The layout of the magazine was crisp and attractive; it was far more presentable than most of the underground publications that followed in the late 1960s. Columns were written by Wilson, Peter Stampfel, Pete Seeger, and Ed Freeman, the latter of whom contributed his insights into the hybrid mixtures of traditional music that he referred to as "Elizabethan ragtime." *Broadside* published a songwriter's column in every issue, including the works of Phil Ochs, Tom Paxton, Richard Fariña, and Dayle Stanley, among others. Many of the cover photographs were provided by Rick Sullo, a local teenager who took riveting black-and-white pictures in coffeehouses and at festivals. Like many of the local folk performers, he was an untrained young amateur in the process of discovering that, indeed, he had a gift.

Sullo's interest in music had begun a few years before at a neighborhood hangout in mid-'50s Medford. He and several teenage friends put together a street-corner doo-wop singing group that eventually caught the attention of local rock 'n' roll disc jockey Arnie Ginsburg. Calling themselves the Aladdins, they appeared at WMEX record hops all around Boston. By the early 1960s, many working-class white kids were experiencing an expansion of their rock 'n' roll loyalties to include folk music; after all, the young love expressed by the Fleetwoods was not that much different from the kind Bonnie Dobson was singing about. So Rick Sullo and his friends went on to form a folk group that featured a banjo, guitar, and washtub bass. Calling themselves the Hillside Singers, they would eventually open in Amherst for blues singer Taj Mahal and play in Cambridge at Club 47 hootenanny nights.[8]

Taj Mahal's musical journey had begun with his birth in Harlem and his early childhood in Springfield, Massachusetts, where, from his home's short-wave radio speakers, he absorbed the music of the Caribbean, as well as jazz and popular tunes. He began taking guitar lessons at the age of thirteen from Lynwood Perry, a friend of his step-father's and the nephew of bluesman Arthur Crudup (who wrote "That's All Right, Mama," Elvis Presley's first hit). Three years later, Taj was milking cows on a nearby dairy farm and singing in a doo-wop group. He entered the Stockbridge School of Agriculture at the University of Massachusetts and became a member of the Future Farmers of America. While in Amherst, he also began fronting an R & B band called Taj Mahal and the Elektras, and, after graduation, he moved to California. There, he would team up with Ry Cooder and Jesse Ed Davis in a blues band they called the Rising Sons, recording tapes for Columbia that were not released until 1992.

Vanguard Records had signed Joan Baez to a contract in 1960, followed soon thereafter by Jack Landrón and Jim Kweskin and the Jug Band, who added their first recordings to that label's established library. It is hard to envision just how difficult it was, in those times, to make a record. Musicians were at the mercy of record companies who, then as now, were unwilling to invest in unknown talent, particularly of the sort that couldn't be characterized as "clean cut." The Charles River Valley Boys took recording plans into their own hands by traveling to London to make their *Bringin' in the Georgia Mail* record. In January 1963, Eric von Schmidt, Richard Fariña, Ethan Signer, and Bob Dylan all found themselves across the Atlantic, where they conspired to cut their own record at Dobell's Record Shop. A good time appeared to have been had by all, and an actual release eventually ensued, *Dick Fariña and Eric von Schmidt,* with backup credits to Ethan Signer and to "Blind Boy Grunt" (Bob Dylan) and to Eric von Schmidt for cover art.[9]

Dylan's meteoric rise during this time presents a bit of a core sample of how "the folk scene," as it came to be called, evolved between 1961 and 1963. After arriving in Greenwich Village from Minnesota in January 1961, Bob slept on couches, lived on soup, and hung out with people like Jim Kweskin in the cluster of coffeehouses that lay scattered around the intersection of Bleeker and MacDougal Streets in New York City.

On May 6 of that year, after the end of a harsh winter, Bob drifted up to Brantford, Connecticut, the site of the Indian Neck Folk Festival, where he first met Mark Spoelstra and Robert L. Jones. Jones suggested that Bob should come to Boston and meet his brother-in-law, blues singer Eric von Schmidt, which Dylan did the following month. Back in the Village, Dylan met Texas folk singer Carolyn Hester (who had once recorded with Buddy Holly) and her husband, Dick Fariña, and they invited Bob to come up to Cambridge, where Carolyn was headlining at Club 47 Mount Auburn in August. Once there, Bob auditioned for club manager Paula Kelley, who quickly decided that this particular ragamuffin was not ready for *her* stage.[10]

Bob Dylan, of course, persisted, in his hybrid Charlie Chaplin / James Dean sort of way. He played harmonica on Hester's first album, cut in September 1961, and made the trip back to Cambridge several times that fall. On November 20 and 22, Bob entered the Columbia studios at 799 Seventh Avenue in New York and recorded seventeen songs for his own debut album, *Bob Dylan*. By the following spring, inspired by the political activism of his sweetheart, Suze Rotolo, he was writing songs nonstop and began the long process of creating his *Freewheelin'* album. Over the course of a year, he would put down not only multiple cuts of the twelve songs that were to be featured on that record but also two dozen other original songs that went unreleased at the time.

In the spring of 1963, as Bob's ability and reputation were rapidly advancing, he was booked into an appearance at the Brandeis Folk Festival. At the April 21 hootenanny at Club 47 Mount Auburn, he was invited onto the stage by Eric von Schmidt, and the two swashbuckled their way through "When I Lay My Burden Down," "Overseas Stomp," and "Cocaine" before Bob played a few of his own songs to a rapt audience. Within a night or two, Bob agreed to make a "surprise" appearance at the Cafe Yana on Kenmore Square and to allow the performance to be broadcast live under the condition that his new manager, Albert Grossman, not be told about either the gig or the radio show. Bob also made a brief stop at the *Broadside* offices, quietly thumbing through the collection of past issues that were collected there.

Later that summer, on July 28, he made a momentous appearance at the Sunday night culmination of the Newport Folk Festival, introducing his "Blowin' in the Wind" to the world. A bit later that year, he and Joan Baez (by then a couple) dropped in while Ray Pong was singing at Club 47, and Ray invited Bob to come up on stage for a few numbers.

Thereafter, Bob would be seen in public in Boston only in packed concert halls and heard primarily on his records, which became indispensable talismans of folk music in New England and around the world.[11]

There had been some thought given to the idea of a Mount Auburn Record company for artists associated with Club 47, and, eventually, one album was cut on that label by the Charles River Valley Boys. In 1963, Paul Rothchild succeeded in persuading jazz-oriented Prestige Records to rerelease the CRVB album on a label that he named Prestige/ Folklore. Over the course of two years, Rothchild recorded a stable of Boston and Cambridge coffeehouse regulars and visitors that included the Charles River Valley Boys, Keith & Rooney, Tom Rush, Eric von Schmidt, the Holy Modal Rounders, Mitch Greenhill, Geoff Muldaur, Bonnie Dobson, Jack Elliott, Dave Van Ronk, Jesse Fuller, and Reverend Gary Davis. By the end of 1964, Prestige/Folklore had put together a remarkable collection of nearly three dozen records, all distinctively marked with a deep green label and a stylized banjo logo. These remain the best recorded collection of the Boston-Cambridge Folk Revival, and some are quite rare today.

Although scholars and ideologues were striving to establish strict definitions of what was and was not worthy in musical expression, young musicians and record buyers were straddling several frames of reference. Rock 'n' roll singer Dion's *Runaround Sue* album and Tom Rush's *Got a Mind to Ramble* were released around the same timeframe of 1962–63, and those two very different albums could be found together in record collections all around Boston. Rock 'n' roll and folk music were two very different idioms, but they had a good deal in common: youthful nonconformity, innocence, romanticism, and high energy were all integral components of both forms. Young people began to grow into an understanding and an embrace of adopted folk traditions, and a Top 40 song like "Will You Still Love Me Tomorrow?" and a new folk tune like "The First Time Ever I Saw Your Face" could move the hearts of the same audience. It was a good time to be young.

Local folk radio shows helped to fuel youthful transformations. As late as 1964, Boston's Sunday airwaves still broadcast as many as twelve different nationality-themed radio programs, including Italian, German, and Polish variety hours, *The Jewish Hour,* and *Greece Speaks.* Boston folk shows began broadcasting over college radio stations: WHRB's *Hillbillies at Harvard* and *Balladeers* with Tom Rush, as well as MIT's folk show on WTBS with David Wilson were among the most popular. Robert J. Lurtsema got his start on the air with his *Folk City USA* program, which was broadcast on WCRB from 11:15 p.m. to 1 a.m. on Friday nights. In addition to playing records, Lurtsema brought live performers to his studio after the last sets and encores of their coffeehouse gigs and concert appearances, still exhilarated and still eager to sing after coming offstage. Lurtsema also served as art director of *Broadside,* whose "look" and "feel" owed much to the wealth of old engravings that he unearthed, of the same sort that Cafe Yana and Club 47 were also using in their posters.[12]

Club 47's strategies for survival were largely the product of Byron Linardos of Cambridge, the local entrepreneur hired by the club's board of directors in 1962 to manage the Mount Auburn Street coffeehouse. The operation of a coffeehouse in that place and time had to be conducted on a completely different level of pragmatism and business sense than most folkies could begin to muster. In addition to enforcing the laws of the commonwealth and its cities, some licensing boards and local police felt empowered to "lean on" nonconformist types, and the combination of innocence, weirdness, and radical politics left folk music establishments on either side of the Charles wide open to a broad spectrum of official harassment.

Linardos was more than capable of arm wrestling with the local gumshoes, bureaucrats, and bluenoses. The son of Greek immigrants, Byron brought a combination of street smarts and bottom-line acumen to the world of ballads, brotherhood, and banjoes. Underneath his tough exterior beat the heart of a genuine Renaissance man and a true patron of the arts. His devotion to creativity approached religious dimensions; in his hands, Club 47 became something of a temple to the homespun muses. Byron was a unique and a larger-than-life character whose talents and energy ensured not only that the trains ran on time but that the fares were being collected. He was a great American artistic entrepreneur, plain and simple.

The concept of "if" seemed firmly replaced by "how" in Linardo's repertoire. He had a business side, of course, but he was also a *mensch,* whose encouragement made it possible for stage-struck musical pioneers to get back up in front of a microphone after experiencing the equivalent of a folk music rodeo fall. The great heart of Byron Linardos became a defining force in the lives and the artistic development of many young folk artists, including Jim Rooney, Tom Rush, Jack Landrón, and Geoff Muldaur.

Soon after he took over the management of Club 47, Byron began to design a series of beautiful monthly calendars that reflected his creativity, energy, and love for art and life. Among his daughter Felice's earliest memories is the sight of her dad at work at the kitchen table, poring over his collection of wooden antique printer's blocks and matching a month's worth of folk musicians' names with old-timey images of buffalos, freight trains, fetching maidens, clipper ships, whales, and circus performers. Printed on fragile, brittle paper stock, Byron's Club 47 calendars are an iconic chronicle of the times.[13]

Managing a club meant balancing egos, dealing with licensing hassles, and organizing the scheduled performances; at Club 47, these were all handled by Byron, Betsy Minot Siggins, and Jim Rooney. When Club 47's landlady on Mount Auburn Street decided in 1963 that she had had enough of beatniks, Betsy and Byron had to scramble to find a new location for their coffeehouse, eventually settling in October in a vacant basement space on Palmer Street, to which they succeeded in affixing the familiar number 47. Before they could move in the stage, espresso machine, tables, and chairs, Linardos, Siggins, and a few friends had to lay the bricks on the new venue's dirt floor.

Soon, children's concerts were held on Saturday afternoons, and on Sundays, brunch was served there with the *New York Times*. On other days, the club showed old movies, hosted plays, featured classical music, and pushed the chairs back for contra dances. Robert L. Jones continued to emcee Monday night hootenannies at the new space, open-microphone opportunities where both folk music amateurs and accomplished pros could try out their craft in front of a living, breathing, reacting audience. Don MacSorley, Ray Pong, and others also led Club 47 "hoots," while the Yana, the Unicorn, and the Moon Cusser were also hosting their own lively open-mike events.

Coffeehouse fare tended toward the sweet and the caffeinated. American, espresso, mocha, Viennese, or cappuccino coffee would run you between twenty-five and fifty cents a cup; orange pekoe, Lapsang souchong or Earl Grey tea around forty cents. A slice of Camembert or something similar, a piece of pastry (baklava in the house of Linardos), and some form of colorful fruit drink rounded out the choices. Coffee beans were ground between sets, and at least one old coffeehouse tape exists of a young Bob Dylan launching into the old slave song "No More Auction Block" accompanied by the whine of an espresso machine being fired up in the background as he begins the first verse.

Although Club 47 and the Unicorn are remembered as the most prominent of the local coffeehouses, dozens of smaller venues were also in business at the time and are listed in the schedule pages of *Broadside*. The Orleans had opened in May 1958 at 13 Charles Street, a few steps below street level near the corner of Beacon, not far from the Boston Common; it featured a well-lit room with black-and-white linoleum flooring and a huge, gleaming, silver espresso machine set up next to a small stage. On any given weeknight, a dozen or so young people would drift in and take seats at small tables in the room, sipping coffee, conversing, or reading paperback books, perhaps one of the volumes of Tolkien's *The Lord of the Rings* or James Agee's *Let Us Now Praise Famous Men*. Sometime around 7:00 p.m., the front door would open, and the evening's performer would appear carrying a guitar or, in some cases, a twelve-string guitar or even a banjo.

In the smaller coffeehouses of Boston, there was little room for formality. A performer threaded his way around the tables to a tiny stage, greeted audience members as he entered, threw his coat over a chair, unsnapped his guitar case, turned on a microphone, and conducted a sound-check with a brief, "Hello there! Can you hear me? Thanks for coming out tonight!" The wide range of New England's outdoor temperatures and the increasing ambient warmth of a small room meant that a stringed instrument would need to be tuned constantly throughout the course of the two or three sets that a folk artist might play as an evening progressed.

Some musicians were known by their chosen specialties: blues singers, bluegrass players, "topical songwriters," and the like, but many drew from a broad inheritance of folk song styles that had come from across the country and around the globe over the years. A performer like Peter Childs might open with a song like "Abilene," which his audience would know from popular records, then move on to "Springfield Mountain," the eighteenth-century Vermont tale of a youth killed by a rattlesnake while mowing hay on a hillside meadow. Next might come an old blues tune like "Nobody Knows You When You're Down and Out," then the English racehorse song "Stewball" spliced to the account of a murder in a St. Louis bar by a bad, bad man named "Stackalee." This could be followed by Flatt & Scruggs's bluegrass piece "Jimmy Brown the Newsboy," then "The Golden Vanity," a Child ballad from the seventeenth century, the set closing with a rousing Irish highwayman song like "Whiskey in the Jar."

In smaller houses like the Turk's Head and the Orleans, the performer would take his breaks between sets in the same room with his audience. A fifteen-year-old in a sport coat and penny-loafers might sit down with the performer and ask about chords, keys, tunings, song sources, or "how you made the B string stretch there" on a blues tune. When, fifty years later, Peter Childs was reminded of his responses to such youthful questioning, he reacted emphatically, "That's what I should have done! That's what it was all about! Look, Pete Seeger was there for me and whole lot of others when we were young, and it was just our turn to pass it all along."[14]

In September 1963, WGBH began taping an unprecedented set of televised coffeehouse shows called *Folk Music USA*, hosted by country music journeyman Dusty Rhodes. Boston coffeehouse performers began to appear on airwaves that were otherwise filled with "the vast wasteland" of stale, conventional network programming. At the time, the show's producer, David Sloss, stated that "the idea was to provide a chance for 'authentic' folk music of all kinds to be heard on the air. To provide that chance, we meant to allow performers to display their own styles without control or censorship of any kind. At last, there would be a forum for the controversial: for the less popular, if not the downright unpopular."[15]

The exposure of suburban teenagers to singers Phil Ochs, Bonnie Dobson, Dave Van Ronk, Buffy Sainte-Marie, the Holy Modal Rounders, and the like presented a radicalizing prospect that was unique to Boston. About the same time, on radio, Jefferson Kaye's *Hootenanny* brought the recordings of local coffeehouse singers to WBZ's clear-channel AM station. This eclectic show was broadcast every Sunday night, and songs by Boston folk artists Dayle Stanley, Jim Kweskin, and Jack Landrón were played shoulder-to-shoulder with more widely known national performers. For the first time in at least a century, Boston was setting a good deal of the course for a national artistic movement.

In the Folk New England archive of live coffeehouse performance tapes at the Special Collections at the University of Massachusetts Amherst, the latter-day listener is struck by the camaraderie, the sense of conversation, really, between artist and audience in those times. Any public performance is likely to involve a degree of ego, but the fact that so many in the audience were attempting to play the guitar, the banjo, or the dulcimer and learning to sing folk songs (or trying to) lent a considerably leveling factor to the dynamic between the person on the stage and the listeners sitting at tables in the flickering candlelight.

Very often, performers felt compelled to describe where they picked up a song, citing such authorities as Flanders, Sharp, or Child, and describing encounters along the lines of "I learned this from Bonnie Dobson when I shared a bill with her at Gerde's Folk City" or telling a story about a source, as in "This one's from an old 78 that I found at a flea market in Watertown."

Lapses in performance were accepted as a matter of course. In repertoires made up of lengthy ballads that were often new additions to the evening's playlists, memory and concentration sometimes faltered. In the course of one Club 47 tape from the period, Dayle Stanley can be heard drawing a complete blank on the words to the last verse of a long English ballad, and then simply saying, "This is *such* a good song. Please, come back next Wednesday night, and I'll know it better!" A bond of hope and affection for the music grafted artist and audience closely in kinship. As Dayle remembered recently, "We were adamant about kindness in those days."[16]

Tom Rush, who was as integral a part of the folk community as anyone, recalls the point when he realized just how unique the Cambridge scene had become, almost to the point of being magical: "I remember walking in Harvard Square one day and suddenly having it hit me, that there was something unusual going on here; that this was something that was *really special.* I mean, I knew from time to time, in history, that artists congregated in a certain place and helped move each other to a high point of creativity, and I suddenly thought, well . . . here we are. It's happening right here."[17]

Musicians and audiences held a joint commitment to learn tradition, to honor it, and to carry it forward with heart and soul. A boyish Jim Rooney sometimes could not contain his enthusiasm while introducing one of his favorite Bill Monroe tunes, as if he were not quite able to believe that he was actually up there on stage, singing all the songs he had learned to love as a teenager. Jack Landrón was telling nothing but the whole truth when he walked out to a microphone and lit his audience up with, "Oh, babe, it ain't no lie, this life I'm livin' is mighty high!" A shy Dayle Stanley introduced "The Years" with the sudden realization that she had started writing her own songs while she was still in high school. On more than one occasion, Ed Freeman would bring the verses to a seventeenth-century ballad to a close and perfect silence would ensue, the audience unwilling to depart from the place of emotion and imagination that he had brought them to. The more formal settings of the larger venues often precluded that sort of personal transformation, but, at least at the outset, community was more important than celebrity at the heart of the Folk Revival.

Within the shelter of the coffeehouse, kindred souls could feel a sense of refuge from a modern, straight world that ran on convention and on conditional, calculated relationships. Once you became emotionally connected to traditional music, the new, modern America began to feel a whole lot weirder than all the old ones. If you were attempting to forge an identity free of your family and culture of origin, if you felt concerned about issues of peace and justice, and if you were not interested in the prospect of becoming a cog in the corporate economy, here in a small room full of music you could find camaraderie, spontaneity, and even a sense of mission. It was a time to take chances, to do what came naturally, and, above all, to make a joyful noise among friends.

FIGURE 8.
Fiddler Ed Larkin at the Tunbridge (VT) World's Fair, 1941.
Photo by Jack Delano, Library of Congress, Prints & Photographs Division,
FSA/OWI Collection, LC-USF33–021186-M1.

CHAPTER EIGHT

THE LAY OF THE LAND

Folk Music from across
the New England Countryside

IN THE BEGINNING, BEFORE conventions and categorizations began
to assert themselves, the act of becoming a folk music enthusiast was
often an ecumenical exercise in the appreciation of all forms of traditional, indigenous music. Coffeehouse schedules included a broad mix
of performance styles that reflected the folk traditions of many lands
and cultures. The first performers to gain entrance to coffeehouses such
as Tulla's in Cambridge or the Turk's Head on Charles Street in the 1950s
were classical guitarists and flamenco instrumentalists whose repertoires were both refined and unobtrusive. When folk singers actually
got enough access to begin to construct performance sets, many took
their cues from Pete Seeger's brand of artistic eclecticism. Those who
weren't specializing in bluegrass or the blues often felt compelled to
master "the songs of many lands" as an expression of faith in America's
diversity and international brotherhood.

Some, of course, succeeded at this better than others. Early coffeehouse tapes reveal tunes including "They Call the Wind Maria," "Scarlet
Ribbons for Her Hair," and "Abilene," all folk-style veterans of pop radio,
mixed in with sturdy summer-camp sing-along favorites such as "This
Little Light of Mine" and "Go Tell Aunt Rhody." But, very quickly, young
singers began to be motivated by a search for "authenticity," songs that
could be traced directly to "ethnic" folk sources, the older, the better.
There was an acceptance of a kind of magic afoot in the verses of those

old songs, and they seemed to carry passwords that gained entry into ancient truths and plenary indulgences that could shrive listeners from the stains of modern corruption.

A certificate of authenticity in recordings came in the form of pamphlets that accompanied every record released on the Folkways label, each secure in its own cardboard divider. Sources, places, and dates were listed, some of the tunes coming from old recordings and some directly sourced from tapes or transcriptions of an aging rural singer in some remote four-corners or seaport town. In this context, the works of Leadbelly and of Woody Guthrie became talismans. Pete Seeger routinely traced his repertoire to original sources, as did the New Lost City Ramblers when they took up the guitar, banjo, and fiddle in the late 1950s.

Young Bonnie Dobson was studying her craft under the guidance of folklorist Kenneth Goldstein, who had played a seminal role in assisting the work of Alan Lomax, cofounded the Philadelphia Folk Festival, and collected songs for the Smithsonian Institution (he would also serve as the chair of the Department of Folklore and Folklife at the University of Pennsylvania). His liner notes on Bonnie's first albums were illustrative of the devotion to authentic sources and to the breadth of material that was available to young folk musicians in the early 1960s.

Young New Englanders discovered that the music not only came from sources over in Scotland or down in Mississippi, they were also from living places like Roxbury, Keene, and White River Junction. As the music collector Eloise Linscott had written in 1934, "It has been said that the 'stamping ground of American balladry is in the state of Maine.' Here, richly preserved, is the music of the deep woods, the sea, and the home."[1] Regional folk singers were suddenly realizing that they had a three-hundred-year inheritance in their home states.

Ballads and Songs

The Anglo-Celtic traditions of ballad and song were portals into a rich historical past. Songs such as "Barbara Allen" and "Captain Kidd" became popular with budding young folk singers, who delved into Francis James Child's old volumes in search of ancient texts. Many folkies were surprised to learn that these old traditions had been living in the hills of Maine, New Hampshire, and Vermont before they were encountered in Appalachia by scholars Cecil Sharp and Maud Karpeles. In the early twentieth century, for example, Eloise Linscott collected a version of "Barbara Allen" in Cambridge, Massachusetts, from Mrs. Mary E. Harmon, whose family had kept the song alive through the generations since her immigrant ancestor arrived in Salem on the ship *Truelove* in 1637. In Waldoboro, Maine, Linscott collected a version of "In Good Old Colony Times," and in Somerville, Massachusetts, a variant of the old seafaring broadside "Captain Kidd." These are among the scores of songs she eventually published in 1937, decades before versions of these ballads would be sung in Boston's coffeehouses.[2]

In the isolated districts of New England, many of the old songs were sung a cappella. These were often framed in long, dramatic recitations of stories-in-songs that listeners were expected to envision while the singer intoned the verses. New England traditions seemed to lack, by and large, the fascination with "the murdered girl" theme that developed in the South. In Yankee culture, young mortality was more likely to be encountered by drowning off a fishing boat or through the fatal fall of a tree while yarding logs in the north woods. In the case of "Springfield Mountain," it was a rattlesnake bite in an upland hayfield above the Connecticut River that became immortalized in verse.

Some of the oldest tunes in New England were products of rich French Canadian traditions brought down from Quebec over the years and transplanted in farm villages and factory towns like Saint Johnsbury, Chicopee, and Woonsocket, Rhode Island. French Canadian fiddlers seemed right at home playing at speeds that would have been considered "way over the red line" by most standards. In logging camps, a virtuoso Quebecois might pick his spot after the younger men had blown off a little steam and proceed to put on a one-man tour de force of full-bore fiddling, singing, and clogging on a sturdy planked floor, his staccato steps accented by the frantic bobbing of a long scarlet sash that he wore around his neck. After finally taking a seat by the wood stove, he might be heard to shrug and say to his applauding audience, "Well, now, boys, I used to play a little bit, but . . . when one gets old . . ."[3]

In the 1940s, at places like the Tunbridge World's Fair in Vermont, traditional ballad singers could still be encountered wearing swallowtail coats and top hats and intoning old-time musical recitations that came from previous centuries. By then, of course, at the same time, radio had become a factor in home life, and sing-alongs in living rooms (and, later, in the family automobile) included the songs "I've Been Working on the Railroad" and "When the Red-Red Robin Comes Bob-Bob-Bobbin' Along." Veterans of the old Victorian and vaudeville days continued to make their appearances, such as "When You and I Were Young, Maggie," and "Heart of My Heart," with its often-harmonized refrain of "Oh, a tear would glisten, if once more I could listen, to that gang that sang 'Heart of My Heart.'"

In the course of the Folk Revival, old ballads that could be traced back to the 1600s found well-crafted expression in the singing and intricate guitar playing of Ed Freeman. Ed returned to his native Boston after studying the lute at Oberlin, followed by a stint in Europe, performing ballads at the Shakespeare Room in London. By the mid-1960s, college professors were referring their English literature students to Freeman's gigs at the Orleans and the Turk's Head on Charles Street, where, by candlelight in an old brick room, they could hear the closest thing to authentic Elizabethan music to be found on the streets of Boston after the passing of the last clipper ships.

Songs of the Yankee Coast

A rich maritime tradition had its beginnings in the 1600s in places like the old A. D. Story shipyard in Essex, Massachusetts, where hundreds of schooners were launched into the sea in search of cod, haddock, and halibut for the Boston and Gloucester markets. Over the salty course of three hundred years, Yankee, Swede, French Canadian, Cape Verdean, and Portuguese men plied the foggy waters between Cape Ann and Nova Scotia in small dories, setting out long lines of baited hooks, hauling in their catches, and then rowing back to the relative safety of the schooner. Thousands of sea shanties including "Haul Away, Joe," "Leave Her, Johnny, Leave Her," and "The Jolly Roving Tar" made their rollicking way back and forth across the ocean, and then up long rivers winding toward the scattered logging camps and the brawling, raw saloons of distant northern New England.

Because it was common for dorymen to become lost in fog banks and for whole crews to perish in the worst of the nor'easters that scourged the fishing grounds every year, fishermen's songs were often mournful dirges that matched the rowing cadence of spruce and ash oars.

> I pray you pay attention, and listen unto me
> Concerning all those noble men who drownded in the sea.
> A hundred twenty-nine brave men who lately left the land
> Now they sleep on George's Bank in the rough and shifting sand.[4]

Here and there on Cape Ann, the remains of a few of the fast and able old Essex wooden schooners could still be seen in the early 1960s, slowly moldering into the eelgrass and mudflats, not far from the shipyard ways where they had been launched years before.

Offshore traditions mingled wharfside with blue-water songs of the Yankee whaling fleets that sailed out of New Bedford and Nantucket in the 1800s on cruises that might last for several years. Their voyages were long and tedious, punctuated by the sudden sighting of a whale, pursuit in rowboats over the open sea, and the stabbing of a thrashing leviathan that was up to forty feet long and might "go" 130,000 pounds. The working calculation was simple: "a dead whale or a stove boat," as the sailors put it. Long days of greasy work followed the kill, as men, stripped to the waist, cut the carcass into chunks and melted ("tried") the oil out in smoky cauldrons and brick ovens that flickered and roiled into the night.

This hard work spawned its own tradition of songs of the very kind hand-lined and recorded by the New Bedford folklorist and singer Paul Clayton and then sung at Club 47, in Greenwich Village coffeehouses, and at the Newport Folk Festival. Later, Gordon Bok of Camden, Maine, also took up the tradition of maritime Yankee song, reviving the old tunes and writing songs of his own that were as spare and evocative as an Andrew Wyeth painting. The last New Bedford whaler was tossed up on the rocks in a gale off Cuttyhunk in 1924, yet the salty remnants of Yankee maritime culture are still to be found all along the coast where sea shanties are sung every summer, from Mystic and the Westport Point docks up to Machias.[5]

Irish Music in Boston

Irish music made landfall in New England early in the colonial period in the forms of songs, fife airs, and fiddle tunes. Folklorist Frank Warner, who had discovered the ballad "Tom Dooley" in the 1930s, later met an elderly woman named Lena Bourne Fish on a field trip to East Jaffrey,

New Hampshire, and from "Granny Fish," he collected the rousing Irish highwayman ballad called "Gilgarry Mountain" (or "Whiskey in the Jar"). The old song soon passed into the welcome hands of Peter Childs, the Highwaymen, and, eventually, Jerry Garcia, among others. Ireland's history of poverty, rebellion, and exile resonated with much of the American experience, a legacy as long on tunes and tales as it was short on titles and lands, and Boston was as good a place as any to attempt to understand the contradictions of American life. Irish culture in Boston was a crazy mix of bland, wannabe conformity, and devil-may-care impulse: one minute, cap in hand, bowing and scraping to the Yankee Republican whose lawn or septic system was being tended to, and, in the next instant, ready to take a hockey stick to a bank window just for the hell of it.

The Irish had long occupied an uneasy position in Boston, arriving as they did without the middle-class respectability that Protestant Huguenots had enjoyed under the sponsorship of well-to-do merchant Peter Faneuil. As late as 1834, the Catholic Ursuline convent in Charlestown was burned by a bigoted mob of nativists, and throughout the nineteenth century, unemployed Irish immigrants were confronted by storefront business windows in Boston that posted job openings with signs that read "No Irish Need Apply." Soon enough, the Irish came to be associated with the urban ills of poverty, overcrowding, illegitimacy, disease, and "drink." Circumstances forced them into crowded slum tenements where the community was often held together by a matriarchy of "sainted women."

But by the twentieth century, third-generation Irish were achieving majority status at the polls. The process of "pulling themselves up by their bootstraps" accelerated as Irishmen began to take over Massachusetts city halls, and steady jobs as policemen and firemen replaced day labor as ditch diggers, teamsters, or stevedores. Cultural assimilation is a hard row to hoe, and spirited and resilient people have always had to depend on their native ways to sustain themselves in their search to feel truly at home in a competitive and often bigoted society. In Boston neighborhoods, traditional Irish tales and Irish tunes continued to flourish in parlors, taverns, weddings, wakes, funerals, and everywhere the Hibernian faithful congregated for a "do."

In the 1920s, Justus DeWitt moved his family's business, a combined Irish music store and travel agency, from New York City to 51 Warren Street in the Roxbury section of Boston. There he began putting out traditional Irish music on records featuring reels such as "Jenny Picking Cockles," "Drowsy Maggie," and "Fitzgerald's Hornpipe," recorded by groups including the Flanagan Brothers, Murty Babbitt and His Gaelic Band, and accordionist Joe Derrane on labels such as O'Byrne DeWitt's Irish Records, All-Ireland Records, and, later, Copley Records. Well into the 1960s, the O'Byrne DeWitt Travel Agency sponsored radio programs of traditional Irish music on WMEX, encouraging misty-eyed listeners to "pick up the phone" and book a flight "back to the dear old Emerald Isle" that the vast majority of them had never set foot on. In many a lace-curtained household in South Boston, Charlestown, or West Roxbury, the day came to its close with *The Irish Hour* on WBOS, broadcast every weeknight between 8:30 and 9:25.[6]

Given the popularity of Irish music in Boston, Manny Greenhill arranged for the Clancy Brothers and Tommy Makem to appear in his early Folklore Concerts Series. Later on, the boys sang to a mixture of folkies and townies who packed themselves into the Unicorn Coffee House at its cellar site on Boylston Street. Ireland had sent hundreds of irresistible tunes out into the world of the sort that beguiled young folk song writers. Soon enough, the strains of "Brennan on the Moor," "The Leaving of Liverpool," and "Johnny, We Hardly Knew Ye" were being fitted out with brand new lyrics, a number of them written in support of leftist political causes that would not have been terribly popular in the alphabet streets of Southie or up on Savin Hill in Dorchester.

Swing and Salvation in Roxbury

In the old seaport towns of Portsmouth, Gloucester, and New Bedford, enclaves of people of color had long mixed in with Yankees, Canadians, Portuguese, and Swedes. But by the twentieth century, the largest concentration of African American culture in New England was to be found in the Roxbury section of Boston, where a vibrant community thrived in the heart of the city. The Athens of America had always been rife with racial contradictions; for example, the abolitionist movement had flourished in the same streets where the public schools were segregated by law until 1855 and by custom long thereafter. Outright racism as well as "anomalies in the shadows" persisted until challenged by the Civil Rights Movement of the 1950s, led locally by Roxbury's Ruth Batson, the leader in the cause of equality in education in Boston. The city's de facto segregation was as effective a separation of the races as the Berlin wall; Black people worked in downtown businesses and as "domestics" in the kitchens and living rooms of white neighborhoods every day, but very few white people ever ventured into what were genteelly termed "disadvantaged" or "depressed" areas.

Those who lived in "the Negro sections" of Roxbury and West Medford saw very little evidence of depression. Roxbury was a lively community in the postwar period, poor but proud, much like the other ethnic sections of Boston. Many people owned their own homes, and small businesses thrived throughout neighborhoods that later would be devastated by the twin scourges of gentrifying urban renewal and back-alley drug addiction. Small-time hoods, gamblers, and hustlers were as active as their white counterparts in Southie, Revere, or Winter Hill, but the Black church was a powerful force in the culture of the community, and serious crime was largely kept in line.

In the relative dearth of conventional wealth, music and style were the coins of the realm. As a young Black hustler from Omaha (who would someday become known as Malcolm X) recalled his first glimpse of Roxbury in the 1940s, "I didn't know the world contained as many Negroes as I saw thronging downtown Roxbury at night especially on Saturdays. Neon lights, nightclubs, pool halls, bars, the cars they drove! Restaurants made the streets smell rich-greasy, down-home Black cooking. Jukeboxes blared Erskine Hawkins, Duke Ellington, Cootie Williams, dozens of others."[7] To this rocking landscape of jazz and bebop music was added the burgeoning world of what became known in the 1950s as rhythm and blues, as performers such as Ray Charles, B. B. King, the Drifters, Lowell Fulson, and Big Maybelle made their way to the Northern terminus of the "chitlin' circuit."

Jim's Shanty Lounge, Basin Street South, and Louie's Lounge were among the joints that were jumping up and down "Mass Ave" in those days. Jazz clubs flourished around Copley Square, where George Wein's Storyville was located, and where performers such as Billie Holiday, Ella Fitzgerald, Sarah Vaughan, Louis Armstrong, Duke Ellington, Charlie Parker, and Dave Brubeck performed during the club's ten-year life. On radio station WBMS, "Symphony Sid" Torin played records by the new doo-wop groups, and Black-owned WILD broadcast from the Sherry-Biltmore Hotel.

At 1820 Washington Street, at Skippy White's Mass Records ("The Home of the Blues") you could find thousands of 45s and LPs of

African American music. White, whose given name was Fred LeBlanc, has long been one of the most dynamic personalities in the Boston music scene. In 1953, the sound of the Orioles singing "Crying in the Chapel" turned his life around, and by 1958, he had become the only disc jockey of French Canadian descent on the airwaves of WILD. He opened his record store in 1961, and it quickly became a nerve center for the Black community as well as a mecca for young pilgrims like Geoff Muldaur and Fritz Richmond. He ran his business and kept the faith at a number of locations in Roxbury over the course of nearly sixty years, finally retiring in 2020. He never ceased to be an inspired catalyst as well as a businessman. "If you wanted to find out what was happening, the latest in what was going on, you went to the record store," White remembered.[8]

Boston has had a regrettable reputation as an unfriendly place for musicians of color, but, fortunately, there was at least one exception. In the fall of 1964, Ray Charles was arrested at Boston's Logan Airport with a duffle bag full of heroin. It was the singer's third arrest for narcotics possession, and by statute, this meant mandatory hard time in federal prison. Charles retained the Tremont Street attorney Paul Redmond, who undertook a vigorous defense (including a word with Tip O'Neil's congressional office) that ultimately resulted in U.S. District Judge George Sweeny approving a fine, probation, and Charles's hospitalization in a private rehabilitation facility in Los Angeles. "I have to tell you—just as a fellow human being—," Sweeney wrote in a letter delivered posthumously to the judge who replaced him for Charles's sentencing, "that society would be better off with Ray Charles free, serving as a good example of a guy who kicked drugs, rather than being put away in prison."[9]

For the young and mostly white folk music crowd, Boston's living Black culture and modern R & B music scene presented a bit of a dilemma. Old folk blues performers such as Jesse Fuller and Reverend Gary Davis might have been icons in Cambridge, but they were anachronisms on Roxbury's lively Columbus Avenue, where the sounds of Jackie Wilson, Solomon Burke, Martha and the Vandellas, and the hundreds of singers who followed Sam Cooke into the world of sweet soul music issued forth out of screen windows at street level. The Back Bay Theatre (one of whose ushers in the early '60s was a young white boy named Peter Guralnick) is now airspace over the Massachusetts Turnpike, but during this time it was the scene of incredible touring soul revues. Folk and soul found their common ground in gospel music and in the persons of local performers such as the Silver Leaf Gospel Singers from Roxbury and visiting groups including the Clara Ward Singers and Roebuck, Cleotha, Mavis, Pervis, and Yvonne Staples of the incredible Staples Singers.

In hundreds of Roxbury homes, morning broke to the sounds of *Walk through the Valley* followed by *The Old Ship of Zion*, both hour-long gospel shows on WILD radio and hosted by Buddy Lowe and Jimmy Byrd, respectively. To call the gospel music of Roxbury "inspiring" was a pallid understatement; it was music that was created to move souls toward salvation, and it did just that. Folkies learned the truth in the old saying, "White folks go to church and never crack a smile, while Black folks go to church, and you can hear them off a mile!" Returning to academia or to the suburbs after taking part in Sunday services in Roxbury, young white folkies might well have concluded that it was they who were living in "a depressed area."

Country and Eastern Music

Late at night in New England, radio reception took on exotic super-powers, and the signals from powerful country music stations such as WWVA in Wheeling, West Virginia, and WSM in Nashville rolled loud and clear across the Berkshires, along the spines of the mountains on either side of the Connecticut River, and as far up as Aroostook County in Maine. In the "Deep North," between Houlton, Maine, and Essex Junction, Vermont, a rural culture had thrived for years before the Industrial Age and the Great Depression wiped out the Era of Home-spun. Thousands of up-country French Canadians and Yankees were displaced from their family farms and their native, land-based cultures. Women and men had to leave behind them the world of creamery and cupboard and were forced to take jobs in shoe factories and woolen mills along the dammed waterways of the Kennebec, the Androscoggin, and the Winooski, spending their days indoors, tending machines instead of flocks of chickens and teams of work horses on the sturdy old homesteads of the rural north.

Proud farming people were reduced to being the punch-clock servants of the Industrial Age. In the North Country, there was no middle class to aspire to, even if folks up there had "had a mind" to do so, which, by and large, they did not. Fortuitously, when *The Grand*

Ole Opry and *The WWVA Jamboree* came booming into the parlor radio from the South, they spoke in rural working-class voices, and they introduced music of a vitality and emotional intensity not to be found in the stiff-shirt formalities of most Boston radio stations. Advertisements broadcast on Southern country music shows touted chicken feed and other grain products for farm and home that were put up in one-hundred-pound bags of gaily printed cotton, which rural women used to make clothing or tablecloths, and country singers were "signed up" to pitch various brands of feed and flour. Flatt & Scruggs, for example, promoted the Martha White brand, while Hank Williams was a Mother's Best man.[10]

In the Deep North, Southern musical programming went from being a curiosity to being a point of personal allegiance. When radio announcers in Boston touted a sale in men's business suits at Jordan Marsh, folks who were dressed in coveralls up in Aroostook County might start to feel a whole lot closer to the streets of Wheeling, West Virginia, than they did to the Back Bay. People in the New England hinterlands developed a strong radio connection to the rural culture of the South and found an emotional foster home in its country and western music. With the additional influence of western movies after the 1930s, musical New Englanders up north began putting scores of country and western bands together that "appeared" on stations in places such as Laconia, Keene, and Montpelier. There, in tiny makeshift studios, Yankee groups spiffed up for the radio in embroidered western shirts, fringed skirts, and cowboy hats, gathered around huge metal microphones and crooned sentiments like, "There is no reason, my dahlin', for us to drift apa-a-aht. . ." The music wafted hopefully out of radio towers high above nearby sugar maples and whispering pines; undoubtedly all the relatives within radio range were thrilled.[11]

Northerners continued to revere the sound of the fiddle, but when dancers hit the floor in town halls and VFWs in the mid-twentieth century, the men were wearing not the old-fashioned swallowtail coats and top hats but western-style checkered shirts and Stetsons instead. Here and there throughout New England, roadside places like Clyde and Willie Mae Joy's Circle 9 Ranch Campground featured square dances, while larger places like the Lone Star Ranch in Reed's Ferry, New Hampshire, attracted performers ranging from locals Elton Britt, Georgia Mae, and Gene LaVerne to Nashville performers such as Webb Pierce and Johnny Cash. WCOP in Boston began broadcasting its popular *Hayloft Jamboree* around late 1951, with announcer Nelson Bragg ("the merry mayor of Milo, Maine") declaring that the program spread "from coast to coast, from Revere to Nantasket," while covering much of the rest of New England with a Jamboree Tour schedule. Featured performers included Cal Stuart, Muriel White, and the Bayou Boys: Buzz Busby, Scotty Stoneman, and Jack Clement. A bit later on, Rex Trailer and his palomino began patrolling the old Middlesex Fells trail, singing Gene Autry songs out among the hardwoods. When Jimmie Rodgers sang that "Portland, Maine, is just the same as sunny Tennessee," he knew what he was talking about.

Before Nashville became the place where country musicians came *from,* it was the place where country musicians went *to* from all the other parts of the nation.[12] Maine singers Harold Breau (self-styled as "Hal Lone Pine") of Pea Cove, Maine and his wife, Betty Cody (née Rita Coté), a native of Sherbrooke, Quebec, began touring in the 1940s, playing on local stations such as WCOU in Lewiston. Eventually, they recorded for RCA and appeared as regulars on the Wheeling Jamboree in West Virginia. After their marriage broke up, Cody was approached by Colonel Tom Parker (Elvis Presley's manager) with the idea of pursuing a national solo career, but she declined, citing her desire to raise her children back in Maine.

Another Mainer, the deep-voiced country singer Dick Curless, was from Fort Fairfield, up in Aroostook County. Dick's career began after his service in Korea, where he sang as "the Rice Paddy Ranger." On his return to the States, he appeared on the nationally syndicated Arthur Godfrey program in 1953. Hoping to follow up on this national exposure, Curless focused on a local recording studio in Westbrook, Maine, just outside of Portland, as a likely spot to make a 45 record.

Event Studios in Westbrook got its name when owner Al Hawkes attempted to gain his wife's support for the idea of starting a record business. After he listed off the names of the caliber of artists he hoped to attract, she answered, "If you can do that, it would be quite an event." As a young man in the late 1940s, Al had teamed up with African American guitar player Alton Myers to form the only integrated bluegrass duo in Maine, the Cumberland Ridge Runners, who played on the radio and on tour until both young men were drafted.[13] After serving in the U.S. Army in the early 1950s, Al returned to Maine and opened his home recording studio, where three things happened when the "record" button was pressed: a red light went on, the microphones and recording equipment sprang to life, and the oil furnace was shut down to avoid any ambient basement noise. After a few takes, Al remembered, the room could get a little chilly.[14]

Working well with what he had, Al Hawkes became a pioneer of New England country music, starting Dick Curless off by recording the old cowboy song "The Streets of Laredo." Later, his "Tombstone Every Mile" became a regional hit, and bars throughout New England echoed with Dick's warnings about the hazards of driving on ice-covered U.S. Route 2 in the Haynesville Woods southwest of Houlton, Maine.[15] Hawkes recorded scores of country singers before eventually settling for the steadier income of a TV repair business, but he always kept his hand in music. Among the recording artists that Al cherished the most were transplanted brothers from West Virginia living in Boston named Everett and Bea Lilly, who eventually went on to play the Hillbilly Ranch and Club 47 and became mainstays of the Boston-Cambridge scene.

The music of the Lilly Brothers, like that of the Charles River Valley Boys, lived out on the border between old-time string bands of the Appalachian Highlands and the hard-driving idiom called bluegrass that Kentucky's Bill Monroe invented in the 1940s. Monroe brought fiddle, guitar, bass, and banjo together with his mandolin to create an exhilarating and unique ensemble sound, yet one that could be readily replicated by talented and inspired country musicians. Dozens of players served apprenticeships with Monroe, including Lester Flatt, Earl Scruggs, Mac Wiseman, Kenny Baker, Del McCoury, and Boston's own Bill Keith and Peter Rowan. The Charles River Valley Boys became New England's leading bluegrass band, and the high harmony of Joe Val, their mandolin player, is still commemorated by the dozens of bands who flock every May to the bluegrass festival held in his name annually in the Boston area.

Ragtime

In the decades before World War I, before the twentieth century began to veer back and forth between war and depression, ragtime burst out of the border states and reigned supreme in an America on the move. It was a time of unbridled vitality and unalloyed optimism, qualities that were reflected in ragtime's unique blend of music and dance. Dance steps like the Eagle Rock, the Buzzard Lope, and the Shimmy sprang up in Black neighborhoods and spread between the races and across the country. It was almost impossible to sit still under the influence of this music, and a whole generation of Americans began to define itself by its embrace of syncopated rhythm. Through touring bands and recordings, ragtime was the first African American music since the Caribbean slave immigration of the 1700s to enter the New England region on its own vital terms rather than through the ludicrous blackface of the minstrel show era or the often highly sentimentalized form of reconstituted spirituals.

Millions of white teenagers discovered African American dance music in the Charleston and the Lindy Hop craze of the 1920s, and, a bit later on, in the jazz and swing music that sprang into fashion before and during World War II. Throughout New England, in dozens of places like Irwin's Gardens on Lake Winnipesaukee in New Hampshire and the Totem Pole Ballroom on the banks of the Charles, outfits like Duke Ellington's touring orchestra and Count Basie's group presided on the bandstand while hundreds of young couples jitterbugged across the floor and out onto patios illuminated by long strings of bobbing, multi-colored Japanese lanterns. In some instances, this youthful trend toward integrated music became a matter of controversy. For example, in the spring of 1941, about a year before enlisting in the U.S. Navy as a pilot, one young Middlebury student was forcibly escorted off the Totem Pole dance floor in Newton, Massachusetts, by local police, who evidently felt that his brand of "ballin' the jack" was just a little too rootsy.[16]

It was all a hell of a good time while it lasted. Fortunately for all concerned, when ragtime's practitioners began to die out, good old Folkways Records was there to step in and rescue the remnants of ragtime and "stride" piano playing on vinyl records. The sun may have begun to set on the British Empire, but it never seemed to go down on the global collecting of ethnic and traditional music accumulated by Moses Asch and Marian Distler. Bert Williams, Eubie Blake, and Joseph Lamb were among the many old-time ragtime piano and vocal masters whose work was rescued on the old blue-and-silver label. Around 1950, jazz critic Rudi Blesh and his partner Harriet Janis greatly advanced the tradition when they researched and wrote *They All Played Ragtime*, the definitive history of the era and its music. Reprinted in the 1960s by Folkway's Oak Publications, the book attracted the fervent attention of a group of young piano players who fell under the spell of the old ragtime ways in a new age.

Among them was Jeff Gutcheon, who at the age of twelve had dropped his classical piano lessons like a cold potato after he got hold of a Fats Waller record. He cultivated his musical skills while an under-graduate at Amherst College, then came eastward to begin graduate studies at MIT in 1962. At Club 47, he met Geoff and Maria Muldaur and the rest of Jim Kweskin's band, young musical soldiers of fortune who were already digging the ragtime music of Cannon's Jug Stompers, Minnie Douglas, the Memphis Jug Band, Fats Waller, Bessie Smith, and Frank Stokes. Soon thereafter, Gutcheon began appearing regularly as a solo at the Orleans, the only coffeehouse on Boston's Charles Street that sported a house piano. In the spirit of the old Leroy Carr/Scrapper Blackwell combo of the 1920s, Jeff started playing with ragtime guitarist Mitch Greenhill. A master ragtime piano player who truly "got it," Jeff Gutcheon's playing was indistinguishable from vintage recordings; his music lost nothing in translation.

Jack Landrón had been hearing and playing ragtime from the time he performed in Black variety shows as a little kid in Boston. His "Sweet Mama" and "Meet Me in the Bottom" were old tunes that he revived to good effect in performance with Fritz Richmond. Taj Mahal, a musician whose half century of work has included the mastery of a whole world's worth of styles, was also a key practitioner of ragtime; his "Cakewalk into Town" is still one of the most powerful musical images of the times. Having mastered the ragtime guitar styles of old-time bluesmen Reverend Gary Davis, Blind Boy Fuller, and Blind Blake, Dave Van Ronk came up from New York preaching the gospel of tunes such as "That'll Never Happen No More" and "The St. Louis Tickle." Soon enough, a young, lean Tom Rush was singing about a big, fat woman and letting everybody within earshot of Mount Auburn Street know that he was "feelin' so good, it scares the hell out of me."

Jim Kweskin has always been a walking encyclopedia of old-time music, and once he teamed up with Geoff Muldaur and Fritz Richmond in 1963, everybody in Cambridge started "doin' that rag." Like good bluegrass, good ragtime was complex music that took real skill to play well and with feeling. An old tune such as 1918's "Somebody Stole My Gal" was one that everybody's mother likely knew, but if a young folkie picked up a shiny new Harmony Sovereign guitar and actually tried to make it sound the way Jim Kweskin did with his Martin, well, all of a sudden he might get the urge to fall back into the familiar chug of "Freight Train."

Sixty years later, it is instructive to listen to live recordings of some of the old Newport Folk Festival performances, which for most

Boston-Cambridge artists were restricted to the small-time exposure of afternoon workshops. Among the few cuts in the Newport recordings where the audience is heard to leap from earnest applause to a spontaneous roar were the ragtime performances of Jack Landrón and Mitch Greenhill in 1963, combining "(Won't You Come Home) Bill Bailey" with "Just Because" and, a year later, of Jim Kweskin and the Jug Band boogying into "Sadie Green, the Vamp of New Orleans." From the audio evidence in both cases, you can just about picture them all hoofing it off stage as if they were vaudeville headliners leaving the Old Howard spotlight while the audience hollered out for more.[17]

In 2014, Rudi Blesh's grandson and musical heir, the late Carl Hultberg, digitized a copy of Mitch Greenhill, Jeff Gutcheon, Geoff Muldaur, and Fritz Richmond playing together on Greenhill's 1965 Prestige LP *Shepherd of the Highways*. He had this to say about the music: "The Cambridge crowd flunked out at being deadbeat beatniks. Instead, they excelled in authentic overachiever reproductions of earlier music styles and attitudes. . . . It was the Cambridge Folk Scene. My grandfather would have loved this record. It is full of the Blues/Jazz guitar and piano rhythms of the 1920s and 1930s. The real thing."[18]

Reform and Revival

The New England inclinations toward reform and revival are as old as the region's aptitudes for farming, fishing, and finance. The reformist strain of the Yankee character was one of the precipitating causes of both the American Revolution and the Civil War. And if not a cause of the Women's Suffrage Movement in the late nineteenth and early twentieth century, it was a key component. The post–World War II, media-induced American cultural emphasis on conformity, celebrity, and social homogenization was bound to stick like a fishbone in some segments of the old New England craw, and, indeed, it did.

In other parts of the country, particularly in New York, progressive causes tended to flow into expressions of political ideology. The Peoples' Songs movement, the organization of labor unions, and the repertoires of singers including Woody Guthrie, Pete Seeger, Leadbelly, and the Almanac Singers were all leftist in conviction and expression. Folkways Records and Oak Publications published songs of solidarity with liberation causes going back to the Spanish Civil War. From the beginning days of its publication in 1950, *Sing Out!* magazine embraced radical movements, with nearly every issue printing one or two incensed "cancel my subscription" letters.

New England was a different kettle. The bedrock twentieth-century expression of regional political activism had been the platform of Teddy Roosevelt's Bull Moose Party in 1912, an idiosyncratic mix of populist reform, trustbusting, women's rights, and the expansion of the U.S. Navy. Later on, when the antecedents of the New England Folk Revival began to stir, it was more as an expression of the tenets of Unitarian, Jewish, and Quaker thought than it was an alliance with any political organization. The late '40s denizens of Old Joe Clark's commune in Cambridge, by all accounts, were more likely to be AMC hikers, trout fishermen, and contra dancers than they were to be union organizers. Yet, when it came time, as it did in the 1950s, to react to the deployment of the Atomic Bomb, the struggle for civil rights, and the calculated political paranoia of the Joseph McCarthy period, Boston, Cambridge, and to a great degree the campuses and churches of the entire region moved toward the forefront of the reformist movement.

By the late 1950s, the old union song question "Which side are you on?" became an imperative component of self-examination as civil rights demonstrators began to take their stands in places such as Montgomery, Alabama; Greensboro, North Carolina; and Albany, Georgia. Civil rights had been a constant struggle in the South for people of color, but it had only been a matter of dormant history for most Northern whites until news arrived of the dramatic events in Montgomery and Little Rock. The cause of Southern integration quickly grew into a major force in New England, where it had to struggle with centuries of reflexive local bigotry and with the overwhelming postwar veneer of middle-class complacency. For liberal churchgoers, and especially for young people of college age, an old and distant bugle was calling once again for volunteers to respond to injustice in a new age.

Manny Greenhill's choice of artists for his "Midnight Owl" folk music concerts at the Hotel Ambassador and, later, the Boston YMCA, seems to be the instinctive calculations of a man on a mission as well as a person with deep musical interests. It should be remembered that, at the time Greenhill's Folklore Concerts Series began in 1957, African Americans were rarely seen on television, the Boston Red Sox was the only remaining segregated team in major-league baseball, and people of color in eastern Massachusetts were largely restricted to "Negro neighborhoods" in Roxbury and West Medford. All of a sudden, through

Greenhill's concerts, artists of color such as Odetta and Josh White were appearing not in the Black enclaves but in "polite" neighborhoods in the Back Bay and near Harvard Square.

In the 1960s, the dynamics of race had its own peculiar complications in the North. White people, even those with academic training and a commitment to brotherhood, had, almost without exception, been raised with a visceral tendency to confuse "otherness" with inferiority in regard to class, status, and wealth. In the world of logic (which was where liberal-minded folks were conditioned to think they lived), race prejudice was considered to be a wrong that needed to be stamped out immediately. But in the unexamined, acculturated realm of emotions (which governed how they actually behaved), most had inherited a hidden hitch in their step in regard to perceived social "inferiors."

The result was, not surprisingly, a set of profoundly mixed messages that was all too easily experienced by people of color in particular (and poor people in general) as paternalistic, conditional, and unreliable acceptance that required a burdensome and careful response. The answer to the combination of America's intentional bigotry and its acculturated, unconscious elitism might have been "blowing in the wind," but the cleansing and unburdening of hearts required a degree of cultural and personal self-examination and transformation that most in the majority were almost always too busy to tend to.

The events of the Civil Rights Movement and their coverage in national news media served as a flash point for the growing sense among young people that a number of other things were out of whack in America. In the early 1960s, the amount of cancer-inducing nuclear fallout wafting over Boston from open-air weapons tests in Nevada (ours) and the Soviet Union (theirs) was broadcast matter-of-factly on WBZ and WHDH television as if it were word of an impending thunderstorm or a wintry mix of slippery precipitation. People in the middle-class neighborhoods of places such as Lynnfield and Natick were paying to have fallout shelters installed underground in their yards in case of a nuclear attack. Politically minded folks in Cambridge were predicting that the growing military involvement in Vietnam was likely to become a quagmire without strategy or predictable outcome. In folk music circles, it became more and more difficult to see the status quo as defensible or, possibly, even as survivable.

Americans have always struggled for independence, for democracy, and for equality. Amid the old rigors and the new hopes of the frontier, we came to the realization that we would have to reject both hierarchy and greed if we were to evolve civilization in human as well as in economic terms. Benjamin Franklin, a native Bostonian, brought his enormous influence to bear in the construction of a new model of life and governance that combined the roots of Iroquois confederacy and democracy with Quaker self-reliance, equality, and self-examination. His generation bequeathed a legacy of freedom to the new nation that would belong to posterity as long as it was cared for. In the ensuing years, despite the clarity of the founding documents and the sacrifices of our political reformation, we have all too often tended to backslide into behavioral patterns of elitism and oppression that we had gone to great lengths to reject in the Revolution.

At its heart, the Folk Revival of Boston and Cambridge was an attempt to reclaim our moral birthright. Our movement toward a new traditionalism was fueled by the growing conviction that American civilization had taken enough cumulative wrong turns to warrant an ardent look back to our cultural roots for inspiration and direction. Henry Thoreau's assertion that in "wildness" was the preservation of the world and that defiance of the natural order would lead to catastrophe took on a new urgency in modern times that were being defined by indulgence and self-destruction. In the Folk Revival, traditional music was called on to act as a transformative and redemptive force that could inspire us to envision, and then to embark on, a pilgrimage toward a new and a safer day. If we couldn't drive the money changers from the temple of prevailing American culture, then it was time for us to seek out benediction and salvation in older testaments.

FIGURE 9.

Club 47 schedule poster by Byron Linardos, May 1963.
Department of Special Collections, W. E. B. Du Bois Library,
University of Massachusetts Amherst.

CHAPTER NINE

THE HOUR THAT
THE SHIP COMES IN

Boston and Cambridge, 1963–1964

JOAN BAEZ WAS A first-semester dropout from Boston University who went from auditioning at Tulla's Coffee Grinder in 1958 to packing the house at the Golden Vanity and Club 47 Mount Auburn in 1959, and, a year later, to a national recording contract. She happened to come into public attention in what seems like an act of perfect timing. Largely through television, 1950s American popular culture had fallen to wretched depths that would not be reached again until after the invention of the Internet; the country was hungry for substance and integrity. Joan's art was remarkable in its combination of refinement and roots; in many ways, it was the sort of fusion that had been demonstrated in the concert halls of the 1880s by the Fiske Jubilee Singers. Soon after her portrait appeared on the cover of *Time* magazine in November 1962, Baez would march through Selma, Alabama, with Reverend Dr. Martin Luther King, Jr., and would go on to become a leading and a lifelong force in world peace.

Bob Dylan was a first-semester dropout from the University of Minnesota who arrived in New York in the bitter weeks of January 1961 and drifted up to Boston now and then that year to hang out. In the printed program for his first concert at New York's Carnegie Chapter Hall that November, Bob listed "Peter Stampfel, Jim Queskin [*sic*] and Eric von Schmidt" among his primary influences. When he played the Cafe Yana on April 19, 1963, and the Brandeis Folk Festival in Waltham on May 10, about a month before the release of "Blowin' in the Wind" onto the airwaves, he was standing on the brink of notoriety and a career that would help change the face of popular music and would culminate in 2016 with a Nobel Prize for literature.

The names of Joan Baez and Bob Dylan have remained prominent for generations, but they were only two of scores of talented folk singers who led the national folk revival. Buffy Sainte-Marie was born on a Cree Indian reservation in Saskatchewan, was later adopted by a family of Micmac extraction, and came to live with them in Wakefield, Massachusetts. While in high school, she learned to play guitar and sang in the green gazebo in the park on the south end of Lake Quannapowitt. Thus, she entered a time of personal reinvention, growing beyond the conventional expectations for women in the 1950s and into a strong sense of self, art, and mission.

At the University of Massachusetts in Amherst, she majored in education and Oriental philosophy, began performing on stage, and wrote a number of songs, including "Now That the Buffalo's Gone." After college, she journeyed back to Canada to reconnect to her roots in the Cree Nation and then went on to sing at coffeehouses in Toronto's Yorkville and Greenwich Village in New York City. By the time she returned to perform in Boston in 1964, she had released *It's My Way* on Vanguard Records and had established herself as one of the most powerful writers and performers in the folk revival.

Buffy Sainte-Marie had started out in much the same way as several hundred other musicians who made their way across the New England landscape during this period. Each played on dim stages in the more than three dozen coffeehouses that sprang up between the Boar's Head in Kennebunkport, Maine, the Moon Cusser out on Martha's Vineyard, and the Saladin in Amherst. Some artists, such as Mississippi John Hurt, Dock Boggs, and Almeda Riddle, found honor in New England at the sunset of long musical careers; others, such as Judy Collins, Tom Paxton, Taj Mahal, Maria Muldaur, the Staples Singers, and the Lovin' Spoonful, became nationally prominent musicians. Local performers Tom Rush, Jack Landrón, Geoff Muldaur, Jim Kweskin, Fritz Richmond, Eric von Schmidt, the Charles River Valley Boys, and Mimi and Richard Fariña gained legendary status in New England.

Many other outstanding musicians kept faith with the traditions that called to them, including the less-well-known local artists Sylvia Mars, Ed Freeman, Peter Childs, Leonda, Jim Rooney, Bill Keith, Debbie Green, Joe Val, Mitch Greenhill, Dayle Stanley, Jerry Corbett, Ray Pong, Nancy Michaels, Carl Watanabe, and Jeff Gutcheon, among many others. Some performers either lived for a time in the area or were there so frequently that they became part of the local family; Bonnie Dobson, Judy Roderick,

Dave Van Ronk, Spider John Koerner, Lisa Kindred, Phil Ochs, and the singers of the Golden Ring seemed to fit into this category. All these musicians, and not just the most famous, were contributors to the glory of those times and wove rich and colorful filaments into the tapestry of community folk music that enlivened Boston and Cambridge. It was an incalculable gift to be able to sit within a dozen feet of Dayle Stanley or Mississippi John Hurt and watch them think and feel and sing their way through the songs that they clearly and deeply believed were in their care rather than their ownership. The dynamic between performer, tradition, creation, and audience was a living alchemy that transcended time, place, and a dominant American culture that seemed, otherwise, to have taken on the disturbing characteristics of an unidentified flying object.

Unity and community in music could be undercut at times by in-group dynamics, competition, one-upmanship, or all of the above. A hefty amount of academic left-brain analysis, theory, and criticism was often applied to the almost completely spontaneous, right-brain, creative, and expressive processes of traditional music making. Tempests brewed over what was "authentic" folk music and what was "too commercial," and in folk music publications many paragraphs and arch letters to the editor pitted the firmly held convictions of traditionalists against the eclectic tastes of the new folkies. Such vigorous arguments tended to overlook the reality that very little of what was being performed at the time was *truly* authentic and that anyone accepting money for a gig was engaging in a commercial act, regardless of how much cash was involved (they likely hadn't worried about such things back in the 1700s). Of all the many things that set Cambridge and Boston aside from other folk music scenes was an instinctive commitment to the visceral and the personal in music. Geoff Muldaur, Jim Kweskin, Jack Landrón, and Clay Jackson were no more likely to conform to critical opinions than they were to enroll in the Harvard Business School.[1]

On the traditional front, the Lilly Brothers, Bea and Everett, can be said to have brought bluegrass music "home" to New England when they arrived in the early 1950s. Seasoned musicians, they had been performing on the radio in their native West Virginia since 1938. Their influence was felt in Boston immediately; CRVB's Joe Val later remembered, "Those guys hit on like a bombshell. Nobody'd ever heard anything like that before."[2] The brothers sang out of the old Hillbilly Ranch in Park Square, a "country dive bar" that became a major port of call for long-haul truck drivers and homesick Southern sailors based at the Boston Naval Yard. Along with their fellow-musicians Don Stover and Tex Logan, the Lillys earned a sort of hazardous-duty pay at the bar, where a five-dollar bill often served as sufficient ID and altercations among the patrons were a regular part of the ambience, until, eventually, the barkeep might signal closing time by announcing, "You don't have to go home, but you can't stay here!" By 1963, after recording for Event Records, Folkways, and Prestige/ Folklore, the Lilly Brothers were playing regularly at Club 47, a couple of miles across the Charles River from the Hillbilly Ranch.[3]

For young people of college age and folky tastes, country music acted as a connection to bluegrass and its parent, "old-timey" string band music. Almeda Riddle, Dock Boggs, and Roscoe Holcomb were among the elder Southern singers who made the trip up to Cambridge. To the surprise of these musicians, Yankee youngsters were eager to sit at their feet and hear the old songs, or, in the case of folks like Jim Rooney, Bill Keith, and Bob Siggins, to add the older artists' influence to their own performances. Manny Greenhill brought Flatt & Scruggs to Jordan Hall in Boston, and other groups, including the Osborne Brothers, the Stanley Brothers, the Kentucky Colonels, and Bill Monroe and His Bluegrass Boys, all came to play bluegrass and Southern string band tunes amid the cups of espresso and mugs of cappuccino being served close by what Bob Dylan referred to as the "the green pastures of Harvard University."[4]

Arthel Lane "Doc" Watson was a young singer from Deep Gap, North Carolina, who came to Cambridge to appear at Club 47 in 1963. Born in 1923 and blind since boyhood, he nonetheless shared in the family's farm chores and bought his first guitar with money he earned chopping chestnut trees with his brother. He soon mastered the instrument, teaching himself to flat-pick fiddle tunes with speed and imagination. His first musical hero was Jimmie Rodgers, and Doc soon developed a playlist of his "blue yodels," augmented by songs learned from the Delmore Brothers, the Louvin Brothers, and Bill Monroe. By 1953, he had joined a country and western swing band whose repertoire included a broad variety of dance tunes.

In North Carolina in 1960, musicologist Ralph Rinzler rediscovered 1930s singer Clarence Ashley, some of whose early recordings had been included in the Harry Smith *Anthology of American Music*. Out of respect for Ashley's role as an important figure in old-timey folk music, Rinzler arranged for the singer to cut an album of traditional songs for Folkways Records. Ashley had brought along a friend, fiddler Gaither Carlton, to accompany him, and Carleton brought his son-in-law, Doc Watson, to join in as well. At the time, Watson was playing in a rockabilly band and did not own an acoustic instrument, but Ralph Rinzler encouraged Doc to play the folk material of his heritage, so Watson acquired a Martin D-18 guitar.

Doc then dusted off an old family repertoire of traditional songs and came north, where he quickly became a favorite of the local folk crowd at concerts, at Club 47, and at the Newport Folk Festival. A tape is preserved at the Folk New England archives of a magical winter night in Cambridge of Doc leading a sing-along of local folkies at Betsy and Bob Siggins's house, improvising new lyrics to Johnny Horton's "Springtime in Alaska," and singing "Whispering Pines" along with "Don't Let Your Deal Go Down," "The Tennessee Stud," and a collection of other traditional tunes. A genial and energetic performer with a rich baritone voice, Doc Watson soon became one of the leading proponents of traditional mountain music in New England's Folk Revival.[5]

Other pilgrims from the far corners of the country who came to sing in Boston and Cambridge included traditional Southern singers Almeda Riddle, Hobart Smith, and the bluegrass group the Osborne Brothers, all of whom appeared at Club 47 in the summer of 1963. "Granny Riddle" was an Arkansan in her sixties who sang unaccompanied ballads and songs, some of which had traveled through the centuries from England to New England on their way across the continent to her home in the Ozarks. Hobart Smith was a rural Virginian who had started a string band in 1915 and, in addition to many other audiences, had played before Eleanor Roosevelt at the White Top Folk Festival in 1936. While there, he and his sister, Texas Gladden, received an invitation to sing at the White House in Washington, DC, where they visited two years later.

At Club 47, Hobart Smith was joined on stage by the Charles River Valley Boys and by Jim Rooney, and soon thereafter he was featured on the cover of *Broadside*. Sonny and Bobby Osborne were Kentuckians who had started a bluegrass band after Bobby completed his service as a U.S. Marine in Korea. The brothers specialized in a hard-charging brand of bluegrass featuring no-holds-barred vocals, perhaps best displayed in their later hit "Rocky Top," which would sell 85,000 copies during the first two weeks of its release in December 1967.[6]

For all their commitment to inclusion, an audience of at least partially educated and, for the most part, financially comfortable children of suburbia had to learn to transcend their conditioned responses if they were to be able to appreciate authentic traditional music. Culturally speaking, for many young people it was a big jump from the performances of Peter, Paul, and Mary, say, or Odetta to the raw-sounding music of Bukka White or Frank Proffitt. In effect, many of the young city singers chose to become teachers of rural traditions, either explicitly, in live song introductions like those of Eric von Schmidt and Geoff Muldaur, or in liner notes to record albums such as Tom Rush's *Got a Mind to Ramble*. The blues and other African American musical expressions had already settled deep into young white hearts and souls through the magic of rock 'n' roll, but, with a few exceptions early on (including Jack Landrón, Sylvia Mars, Guitar Nubbit, and the Silver Leaf Gospel Singers), the local folk scene was mostly populated by young white singers. Blues enthusiasts including von Schmidt, Muldaur, Rush, Judy Roderick, John Koerner, and Lisa Kindred seemed to seek a personal connection with African American traditions as they sought to do more than drop the cursory inclusion of a few work songs and spirituals into their playlists.

Folkies treasured the old 78 rpm records of bluesmen who had recorded briefly in the 1920s and '30s and then disappeared back into rural anonymity, long presumed to be dead. In 1963, following clues of place names found in the old songs, a few Boston record collectors began to trace some of these musicians to locations in the rural South and then to bring them up to the Northern folk scene. Mississippi John Hurt, Skip James, Son House, and Bukka White all came to perform in Boston and Cambridge, where folk audiences received them as if they were resurrected royalty.

Mississippi John Hurt came north in 1963 at the age of seventy-one, four decades after he had recorded a few blues songs in a studio in New York. In the congregation of memorable personalities that gathered together in the national folk revival, John Hurt stood out like a kindly bishop; his impact is as profound in memory as it was in person. He was everything that a young person could hope to encounter in an elder during a time when it was easy for youth to feel cut off from age and experience. Wisdom, kindness, and a wry sense of humor were all his hallmarks; a laugh from this wonderful old man seemed to convey healing benediction to all those around him.

John Hurt appeared to be a diplomatic representative from a more benevolent and dignified world than most young white folks might ever have encountered. He was, like many other traditional artists, a perfect natural performer who had never sought "stardom" or seen himself as a "personality," even when he suddenly found himself transported from a Mississippi cotton field to a sea of faces at the Newport Folk Festival. Hurt played locally at the Unicorn, Club 47, the Moon Cusser, and the Turk's Head, and on tours that eventually took him to concert halls around the country.

At one point, Hurt sat for a portrait at the photography studio of folk guitarist Ed Freeman on Fallon Street in Cambridge. As he was preparing to take the old man's photograph, Freeman asked him, "You know, a year ago, you were working as a sharecropper for, like, $28 a month, and now you're making $2,000 a night, and everybody's applauding every note you play. It's incredible; your life is completely changed, you know? How does it feel?" The old singer responded by looking at him squarely in the eye and slowly replying, "Well, I guess it just don't make too much difference now, do it?"[7]

The folk revival in America coincided with both the national observance of the centennial of the Civil War and the maturation of the Civil Rights Movement in this country. By the 1950s, when young Black students began singing "freedom songs" and leading the fight for justice in the dime stores and bus stations of the South, the ugly reality of segregation in modern America had become undeniable to those who had previously felt able to overlook it. The country suddenly did not appear to be nearly as free as most white folks had assumed that it was. Even in the North, many white people grew to college age without ever meeting people of color, much less talking to or sharing friendship with them. Yet, since both African American culture and a belief in equality had been defining components of the national identity since the 1600s, the mounting evidence of persistent segregation was a flaw in the national character as deep and obvious as the crack in the Liberty Bell.

It is important to view the development of the "topical song" in the context of the times. From about 1959 to sometime in 1962, progressive tunes were very much "community property" in the Boston-Cambridge scene, often sung in group hoots led by singers such as Rolf Cahn. Boston's *Broadside* featured a regular singer-songwriter column, where Tom Paxton's "Ramblin' Boy" and Phil Ochs's "All the News That's Fit to Sing" columns appeared, along with songs by Dayle Stanley and Richard Fariña. Bob Dylan wrote "Blowin' in the Wind" in 1962, and by the time Peter, Paul, and Mary's version hit the airwaves and the Top 40 charts a year later, both the country and folk music had undergone a profound transformation.

"How many ears must one man have before he can hear people cry?" became a personal challenge to the hearts of millions of thoughtful young people throughout the nation. Even in the birthplace of abolition, in New England, no politicians were asking questions like that, but these were the concerns that resonated in the region's coffeehouses and concert halls. Freedom lyrics were being set to variations on the old slave tunes, and New York's *Broadside* and *Sing Out!* published riveting topical songs by Bonnie Dobson, Phil Ochs, Len Chandler, Tom Paxton, and many others. Led by Bernice Johnson, the Freedom Singers from Albany, Georgia, played to rapt audiences on a concert tour in early March 1963 that took them to Brandeis University, Club 47, the Concord Baptist Church, and the Community Church Arts Center in Boston. Between 1963 and 1966, more than a score of folk music benefit concerts for civil rights organizations were held in Boston.[8]

In the summer of 1963, thousands of middle-class youths experienced a sort of camp-meeting baptism in the Civil Rights Movement at the Newport Folk Festival. The Festival was the creation of Boston entrepreneur George Wein, a World War II veteran and Boston University graduate who owned Storyville, the jazz club in Kenmore Square that he named after the New Orleans red-light neighborhood where Louis Armstrong was born. In 1954, Wein was hired by tobacco heiress Elaine Lorillard to create a jazz event in Newport, held first at the Newport Casino and later at Freebody Park. In 1959, Wein enlisted help from the unlikely team of Albert Grossman and Pete Seeger in organizing a Newport Folk Festival, which in its first two years featured primarily old-line folk performers from New York such as Theodore Bikel, Oscar Brand, Cynthia Gooding, and Ed McCurdy.

A growing number of large outdoor folk music gatherings, including the Philadelphia Folk Festival and the Beers Family Festival (held south and west of Bennington, Vermont) dovetailed with the ebb and flow of the academic calendar and the traditional connection between summer camps and folk music. The atmosphere at these festivals was not unlike that of tourists gathering around a tent or a gazebo for a picnic: people sat on folding chairs or brought blankets to lie on and coolers full of sodas and sandwiches wrapped in wax paper and, eventually, some of the festivals created space for tents and camping. Newport, from the outset, attempted to balance the "big names" (Pete Seeger, Oscar Brand, and Odetta, for example) with traditional singers (such as Frank Proffitt and Almeda Riddle) and young, new performers. It was in that spirit, in 1959, that well-known singer Bob Gibson invited a very nervous Joan Baez to sing a few songs on stage with him in the appearance that brought her to national attention.[9]

Despite the fact that it was held within the borders of New England, the Newport Folk Festival seemed to tilt toward Manhattan in its board structure and in its performance hierarchy. Boston and Cambridge performers most often played the daytime workshops at Newport, while better-known (and more aggressively managed) New Yorkers were generally booked to headline the evening concerts. Nonetheless, Harvard Square and Charles Street were deserted on festival week, as everyone had headed down Route 1 to Rhode Island. When bluegrass patriarch Bill Monroe played Newport in 1963, Bay State–born banjo player Bill Keith had recently taken an honored place as one of his "Bluegrass Boys." The Cambridge crowd was overjoyed when the taciturn Monroe enthused on stage about Keith's facile banjo solo on "Devil's Dream," calling out, "What about that now? To hear that old-time playing, you'd a-thought he'd come from down South instead of Boston!"[10]

New leadership of the Newport Folk Festival in 1963, including its young board member Peter Yarrow (of Peter, Paul, and Mary), connected the rapidly progressing trajectories of the Civil Rights Movement, youthful interest in folk music, and the careers of both Joan Baez and Bob Dylan. Although there were many other memorable moments at Newport that year, a climax came on Sunday evening as an integrated group of performers—including the Freedom Singers; Peter, Paul, and Mary; Joan Baez; and Bob Dylan—took to the stage and led an audience of thousands in singing "Blowin' in the Wind" and "We Shall Overcome."[11] In the moment, it seemed as though the combination of artistic inspiration, folk tradition, and idealistic solidarity might actually bring peace and justice to the forefront of the national agenda.

Scores of young writers and singers took this crusade on as a personal calling, none with more impact than Bob Dylan. His gift was his ability to distill the sums and substances of American folk culture in his heart, and his craft was the ability to express his feelings in poetry through the framework of those homespun idioms. He was able, for example, to absorb the pathos he heard in Martin Carthy's version of the old British folk song "Lord Franklin's Dream," to apply the tune's patina of grief and loneliness to his own feelings of loss and longing, and then to write completely new and affecting lyrics to a song that he titled "Bob Dylan's Dream."

His songs were acts of creative genius, the inspired product of a devotional immersion in everything from Memphis Minnie to J. E. Mainer and his Mountaineers. Bob Dylan was a gifted, quirky, and ambitious member of a generation that sought to connect with authentic American cultural history and to draw on the birthright that it was discovering deep within its soul. Like him, many young folk musicians were becoming the students and curators of subjects that had never been taught in the schools and the defenders of causes that had languished for generations.

In what became known as "the folk process," borrowing from the body of traditional tunes was an accepted practice among performers, since few in the folk revival community had actually grown up listening to traditional music and nearly all playlists were developed either from old recordings or from other singers. The old songs in public domain were considered fair game. A cursory look at Bob Dylan's early output reveals about a dozen such melodies, including some probably gleaned from local singers Jack Landrón, Bonnie Dobson, Tom Rush, Paul Clayton, and Eric von Schmidt. Lifting arrangements was a bit more of a gray area; it was not encouraged, but it happened from time to time. Outright theft of original material was supposed to be verboten.[12]

The fundamental challenge involved in coming of age in America was (and probably still is) the surreal contradiction of living in a deeply flawed society that is, at the same time, firmly convinced of its own superiority and, even, its perfection. Conformity and superficiality were so well established that almost any form of creativity could qualify as strange. Yet, after a decade dominated by the fear of Communism, the idea that young people might express a patriotism that could be based on hope and faith, like that of the founding generations, was a very powerful notion. For many, the simple act of singing songs about whaling or chain gangs or wagon trains crossing the wide Missouri conjured up a sense of reverence and connection with the past while importing strong feelings of vitality and freedom to the present day. Photographs taken at the early Newport festivals show the faces of an audience looking downward or off to the distance, deep in thought rather than riveted on the presence of a performing "celebrity." There was a lot to think about.

The art of Joan Baez set a standard; the lyrics of Bob Dylan set a moral tone; and the well-crafted harmonies of Peter, Paul, and Mary provided a medium that would, for a time, elevate the substance as well as the style of American music to heights not achieved since the Civil War. In the course of a few years, traditional music had gone from being a neglected backwater to the source of anthems that accompanied the nationwide civil rights crusade sung in the voices of a generation of young people who saw clearly that bigotry was a form of treason. Events moved swiftly: exactly one month after the Sunday night fervor of the 1963 Newport Folk Festival, folk singers who had been playing in Kenmore and Harvard

Squares were now singing freedom songs on the National Mall following the immortal speech of Dr. Martin Luther King, Jr. The hope was abroad that, despite the fact that it had been a long time coming, peace and freedom might yet prevail in the American land.

THE IDEALISTIC PROMISE OF the summer of 1963 was shattered in gunfire, first when Medgar Evers, the NAACP Mississippi field director, was murdered by a sniper in Jackson, Mississippi, and a few months later when President John F. Kennedy was shot in the back by an unknown assailant in Dallas. Those who lived through that bitter fall and winter were seared by shock, grief, and depression. The prevailing innocence had been deeply traumatized, and fear and cynicism became coins of a new cultural realm. The only thing that seemed clear was that nothing was ever going to be the same.

When musical healing appeared a few months later, it seemed to come from far outside the folk world. On January 20, 1964, an album called *Meet the Beatles* was released in America, displacing *The Singing Nun* from the top of the charts. The response in the folk community to "the British invasion" was split, largely along lines of age and education. Older and more academically oriented people judged the new musical group to be yet another gimmicky pop confection being shoved into the "maws of the masses" by cynical commercial interests. But young people found beguiling magic in the new music that brought with it a saving grace and a release from national mourning.

In the early Beatles recordings, young folkies could hear the rhythm of acoustic Gibson guitars mingling with the borrowed harmonies of the Everly Brothers, Buddy Holly, and the African American "girl groups" of Detroit and Philadelphia. Folk singers who would never have dreamed of playing rock 'n' roll started singing Beatles songs at parties. It wasn't much of a surprise, years later, to learn that the Beatles had begun as a skiffle band (basically a ragtime jug band without a jug), and that they had been fans of Koerner, Ray, and Glover and Ramblin' Jack Elliott, as well as of Chuck Berry and Carl Perkins. June 1964 saw the arrival of another British group, the Animals, who suddenly launched a stunning version of the traditional song "House of the Rising Sun" onto the airways. American kids found themselves transfixed by a song on popular radio that, unbeknownst to them, had been written long before the Civil War. A new generation continued to be energized by vintage inspiration.[13]

Meanwhile, Bob Dylan appeared to be switching gears, running with an artsy crowd, and looking a whole lot less like Woody Guthrie and a whole lot more like Keith Richards. Bob was suddenly being referred to only by his last name, a sign that he was attaining iconic status like "Sinatra" or "Basie." To some, his *Another Side* record, released in August 1964, felt self-absorbed and detached, but people who had seen him at Newport that July were raving about a new song that he had reportedly written out on a wind-blown beach in the Cape Cod village of Cotuit. Rumors spread about the song all winter until his next album finally came out in March, featuring, surprisingly, electrically amplified instruments. The song, "Mr. Tambourine Man," seemed to infuse an entirely new artistic sensibility into the old folk traditions. Despite the youthful enthusiasm that followed this new direction, the powers that be at *Sing Out!* magazine and other folk traditionalists were not happy at all with young Bob's transition to an apolitical rock 'n' roll style, and resentment grew among old-line folk enthusiasts that would fester for months before exploding the following summer.

Bob Dylan's records were not the only ones that were being awaited with fervent anticipation. For decades, the staid Folkways catalog had featured obscure ethnic chants and foreign language collections along with the work of revered New York folk singers Pete Seeger and Dave Van Ronk. Suddenly, Prestige/Folklore, Vanguard, and Elektra were all putting out monthly releases with accompanied advertising aimed at an audience that was rapidly expanding throughout the entire country. In addition to college undergraduates, high school students began flocking into coffeehouses and concert halls, jamming into record stores such as Briggs and Briggs in Cambridge to sample records in listening booths before choosing their purchases.

Cambridge Common became something of a hangout, and Harvard Square was suddenly full of teenagers coming in from the suburbs on the weekends, dressed in suede and jeans and smoking Winstons. Kids read the *Broadside* cover to cover to absorb record reviews, to get a sense of the scene, and to see who was coming to town. Young people, particularly young women, began buying guitars and learning how to play them from the pages of *Sing Out!* and from Joan Baez and Bob Dylan songbooks.

Ownership of an acoustic guitar suddenly became more imperative than securing a driver's license. It was not an easy instrument to learn, and the process was made harder by the proliferation of cheap guitars that had "high action," that is, strings that lay so far above the fretboard that they defied the efforts of tender fingers to push them down. Although a low-cost Stella or Harmony Sovereign could see the owner through the "learner's permit" level of the *Folksinger's Guitar Guide,* at some point, an appetite might develop for a pricier and a higher-quality instrument.

The largest local selection of guitars could be found along the famed "wall of instruments" at the Folklore Center on 83 Mount Auburn Street, which was tucked between Harvard and Brattle Squares, next to a dry cleaner and a garage. The center had opened up in 1962, just as the "folk boom" began to hit its stride. Peter Walker owned the business, which was managed by folk singer Don West, assisted by Joy Kimball. Don described the center as "a place where the aficionado may come to learn the difference between a dulcimer and a balalaika, an oud or a lute: in short, a hub of all activity pertaining to folk music and its related fields." The center became the daytime hangout for many Cambridge folk singers, and it was not unusual to find Don West there trading guitar licks with Jim Kweskin, Eric von Schmidt, or Tim Hardin, who lived for a time in Cambridge while he was enrolled at the Longy School of Music on Garden Street. In August 1963, the center sponsored a three-day hootenanny for the benefit of the Boston Children's Hospital, featuring, among others, Peter Stampfel of the Holy Modal Rounders and Bob Siggins and John Cooke of the Charles River Valley Boys.[14]

For many, buying "a good guitar" became the motivation for securing a part-time job. Young folkies window-shopped at the Folklore Center or Briggs and Briggs in Cambridge or Jimmy Mosher Music in Lynn, seeking an instrument whose price might run to several hundred dollars, about the cost, at the time, of a road-worthy used car. Ownership of a Martin D-18, Gibson J-50, Epiphone Texan, or Guild F-47 marked you as a serious member of the folk tribe. Budding guitarists began to try to master Doc Watson's flat-picking techniques, the fingerpicking tablature for "Freight Train" that Ed Freeman taught, or Don West's engaging, rag-timey version of "Cocaine." For the more ambitious, Tom Rush's take on Geoff Muldaur's "Mole's Moan," Dick Rosmini's "Little Brown Dog," and Peter Childs's arrangement of "Under the Double Eagle" were major challenges. When John Fahey came onto the scene, he opened up a whole new universe of open tunings. It was a fine time to be learning to play a guitar.

The Kweskin Band was appearing on the Steve Allen Show on national TV! The Holy Modal Rounders were on educational television! Eric von Schmidt was illustrating children's books, including a compendium of folk tunes called *Come for to Sing!* Fritz Richmond was playing the washtub bass on every other record that came out of Cambridge! Jack Landrón, Tom Rush, Bonnie Dobson, and the Charles

River Valley Boys suddenly seemed to be playing at every high school gymnasium, B'nai B'rith, and Unitarian church located above high tide in the Commonwealth. It was wild.

There was hardly a New England college town that did not have at least one folk club or coffeehouse tucked into the landscape. The Boston-Cambridge Folk Revival had outposts that stretched from Orono to the Housatonic, with nerve centers in places like Amherst's Saladin and out on the Vineyard at the Moon Cusser. The roster of local performers on coffeehouse stages was augmented by visiting folk musicians who came to New England from all around the country. A loose touring network connected the Boston venues with Cafe Lena in Saratoga, New York (where, in 1960, Jack Landrón had been the charter performer), the burgeoning scene in New York City's Greenwich Village, the Second Fret in Philadelphia, and the Main Point in neighboring Bryn Mawr. From there, some performers launched themselves westward through Madison, Bloomington, and Ann Arbor to Denver's Folklore Center, the Ash Grove in LA, and the Cabale in Berkeley.

Dave Van Ronk, a regular visitor to Boston, kept the flame of traditional jazz burning through his curation of old numbers that ran from Buddy Bolden to Jelly Roll Morton. Like Eric von Schmidt, Dave was a larger-than-life figure, bluff, confident, and seasoned. Teri Thal, Dave's wife, was a crucial, respected figure behind the spotlight; she was Bob Dylan's first manager and an important, youthful "adult in the room" of the Village scene. Phil Ochs, another adopted New Yorker, combined the image of a prep school English teacher, the politics of the International Workers of the World, and the melodies of rock 'n' roll in an unforgettable presence. If ever there could be said to be a role model for patriotic leftists, it was Phil Ochs, and young listeners to songs such as "Links on the Chain" were transformed by his music and his enthusiasm. Judy Collins matched her pure voice with an eclectic and powerful repertoire of old and new songs. Her growing popularity, and that of other frequent visitors, such as Canadians Ian & Sylvia, filled the concert venues of Sanders Theatre in Cambridge and Jordan and Symphony Halls in downtown Boston.

As the solo artists defined and expanded their crafts, local groups evolved through changes in membership. Mel Lyman joined the Kweskin Jug Band in 1963, bringing with him a deep-seated devotion to traditional music and the ability to play both harmonica and banjo. The Charles River Valley Boys' roster, anchored by Bob Siggins, Ethan Signer, and Fritz Richmond, was augmented by mandolin player Joe Val and guitar player John Cooke. The CRVB were often joined by genial and accomplished fiddler Tex Logan, whose life credits included stints with the Lilly Brothers and Don Stover, a PhD in electrical engineering from MIT, and the authorship of the bluegrass standard "Christmas Time's A-Comin."

Out on Martha's Vineyard, a unique folk scene developed around the Moon Cusser, which David Lyman opened in 1963. Over the course of three memorable summers, the place attracted an impressive stable of performers who were often there as much to have a good time as they were to play a gig. Bonnie Dobson and the Charles River Valley Boys were among the first performers at the venue, which soon attracted a number of young musicians to take up temporary residence on the Vineyard, including bluegrass guitarist Peter Rowan and banjo picker Lowell Levinger (aka "Banana"). Levinger became part of the business operation known as "The Island String Shop" that opened up in back of the Moon Cusser, where, they say, nickel bags were dispensed and, from time to time, a few instruments were repaired. Hootenanny night at the Moon Cusser was a lively event, with local amateurs including the Simon Sisters (Carly and Lucy), Peter Cohon (now known as Peter Coyote), and a young James Taylor taking turns at the microphone.[15]

Nearly every weekend in Cambridge, there were after-hours parties, and you might be invited over to Nancy Sweezy's house, for example, or to the apartment shared by Helen and Eric von Schmidt and Betsy and Bob Siggins to sing and play until sunrise. Helen remembers the phone ringing at an ungodly early hour on a Sunday morning after a long night of music had come to an end near dawn. Stepping over a rug full of musical instruments and empty wine bottles, she answered it. On the line was a medium-known folk performer from New York who had been at the house the previous evening. "Uh, Helen," he said, "if there were any tapes made at the party last night, could you destroy them? My manager doesn't want anything circulating out there that might cut into the sales of my new record album." After asking him if this couldn't have waited until a civilized hour of the afternoon, she hung the phone up and went back to bed. "But," she remembers, "I knew that something had changed."[16]

THE BROADSIDE

ÓF BÓSTÓN

| Volume III, No. 8 | Cambridge, Massachusetts | June 10, 1964 |

FÓLK MÚSIC AND CÓFFEE HÓUSE NEWS ⅔ TEN CENTS

FIGURE 10.
Broadside cover, June 10, 1964. Department of Special Collections,
W. E. B. Du Bois Library, University of Massachusetts Amherst.

CHAPTER TEN

THE CHORDS OF FAME

Boston and Cambridge, 1965–1966

LATE IN 1964, CAMBRIDGE folk producer Paul Rothchild received a phone call from a man named Jac Holzman, the head of Elektra Records in Manhattan, who asked him what it would take to get him to work for Elektra. As it turned out, it would take double the amount he had been making at his present job, a share of record royalties, and a new car. With Rothchild's subsequent departure, the role of Prestige /Folklore Records in the Folk Revival came to a halt, ending a major local recording resource for the Boston-Cambridge community. Folk music was suddenly big business, and the Charles River had begun to flow into the Hudson.

Elektra was a well-established and well-capitalized company that already had Judy Collins, Bob Gibson, Phil Ochs, Oscar Brand, Josh White, and Theodore Bikel on its roster. It also had probably the best art director of any folk label in William Harvey. Through Rothchild, the New York–based label signed up Tom Rush, who cut a masterful set of albums that expanded on his broad repertoire of blues, ballads, and folk songs. Tom became the de facto roving ambassador of the Boston-Cambridge Folk Revival by virtue of his personality, his talent, and the rich material he chose to record. In 1964 and '65, Elektra called on a range of Boston and Cambridge musicians to join in on its set of five folk "project" albums, two of which were graced with covers painted by Eric von Schmidt.[1]

The first of these albums, named *The Blues Project,* featured Geoff Muldaur singing the old Memphis rag "Downtown Blues," joined by Fritz Richmond on bass, John Sebastian on harmonica, and a manic

149

single-piano combo of Eric von Schmidt on the high ivories and "Bob Landy," otherwise known by his friends as Bob Dylan, on the low keys. Muldaur's voice transcended time, style, and place, and it could be said that this cut was among the first recorded mergers of authentic folk music and rock 'n' roll. Of Muldaur's delivery, the *Little Sandy Review* said, "It's a style that is influenced by jug bands and city bluesmen as well as country blues; it's sort of a blend of Sleepy John Estes and Little Junior Parker. He uses a bold vibrato and caresses his notes till they squirm. It's crazy, but it has more and more effect every time you hear it."[2]

Calls for authenticity increased in fervor among some of the folk faithful in reaction to the proliferation of big names and the promotion of standing-room-only concerts. Up in Huntington, Vermont, Sandy and Caroline Paton founded Folk Legacy Records, a small label that became a haven for lesser-known artists who were attempting to keep faith with the original sources of traditional folk music. Working with the Patons, a group of amateur singers calling themselves the Golden Ring (including George and Gerry Armstrong, Ruth Meyer, Howie Mitchell, Herb Nudelman, Shannon Smith, Win Stracke, Ed Trickett, and Steve White) came together to sing old folk songs in the old-fashioned way: in the living room, among friends who had no aspirations other than to make good music. Their 1964 record is still one of the finest examples of the spirit of the American folk revival and is as clear an illustration as can be found of the distinction between "making music" and "making it." Caroline Paton later recalled that the goal of the company was not to achieve popularity but to celebrate the capacity of friends to make spontaneous music that was "simple and honest, and with a lack of guile."[3]

It may have been a further move toward "roots music" that led Bob Siggins, Clay Jackson, Jon Shahn, and Bob Mamis to convene a wonderful short-lived string band called the Mother Bay State Entertainers. Drawing on material from the 1920s and '30s that was even more obscure than the usual repertoire of the Charles River Valley Boys, the Entertainers featured rapid-fire instrumentation on mandolin, fiddle, harmonica, and banjo along with the singing of Jackson and Siggins. Clay Jackson's voice was and still is one of the most evocative icons of the Boston-Cambridge Folk Revival; he was, as Jim Rooney has said, "the real deal." In their one recording, a few outtakes, and a cut or two in Elektra's *String Band Project* record, the Entertainers can still bring listeners back to the days of the earliest encounters between farmers and city slickers, back when a country boy snookered by a fast crowd might, as in the title of one of their songs, "wish I'd bought me a half a pint and stayed in the wagon yard."[4] The sound and feel of the Mother Bay State Entertainers presaged both the repertoire and focus of the Old Crow Medicine Show, one of the best of the groups to emerge, fifty years later, in the roots revival of the new century.

Kathy Larisch and Carol McComb are folk musicians from Vista, California, who, as teenagers, created one of the most memorable recordings of the folk revival period. Kathy and Carol came to the attention of John Cohen while he was playing with the New Lost City Ramblers at Ed Pearl's Ash Grove in Los Angeles; on an afternoon break, John went over to Huntington Beach, where he was stunned to hear Elizabethan ballads floating oceanside in Everly Brothers harmony. The source was two teenage girls on a beach blanket, singing. Cohen brought the duo to the Ash Grove and then to the attention of former Cambridge folkie Paul Rothchild, still with Elektra but now on the West Coast. Rothchild, in turn, brought the young women to a studio in Burbank, where they cut twenty-three songs, a dozen of which were released on their album *Kathy & Carol* early in 1965, which has become among the most treasured gems of the folk revival.[5]

Their sound was utterly unique and their voices angelic. Entirely self-taught, the women sang Child ballads and Carter Family tunes from the 1920s with equal fervor, interchanging melody and harmony, sometimes singing in unison, then swapping parts. When the pair came east to appear at the Newport Folk Festival in July 1965, their unac-companied version of Richard Fariña's "A Swallow Song" stunned the enchanted audience. When they played at Club 47 the following week, long lines stretched from the club entrance up and around the block onto Church Street. From Cambridge, they returned to California and regular performances at the Ash Grove. At one point, Linda Ronstadt opened for them there; on another occasion they opened for Bill Monroe. Soon thereafter, Paul Rothchild shifted his attention to the production of the Doors, leaving Larisch and McComb to perform sporadically. They pursued separate careers into adulthood, and in 2010 they made a wonderful reunion record called *Keepsake,* an unforgetable expression of their unique talents.

Richard Fariña and his new wife, Mimi (the younger sister of Joan Baez), had begun singing and playing at Club 47 in 1964, and they soon came to personify a new wave of hope, grace, and artistry in local folk music. As they gained confidence and expanded their repertoire, they became mainstays of the Boston-Cambridge scene, playing the Unicorn, the King's Rook, the Moon Cusser on Martha's Vineyard, and the Loft on Charles Street, the site of their longest residency. Their first record, the magical *Celebrations for a Grey Day*, was released early in 1965 to much acclaim and enthusiasm; record reviewer Ed Freeman's reaction in *Broadside* was simply to say that the performances were extraordinarily beautiful. In late July of that year, Mimi and Richard played several sets at the Newport Folk Festival, where they were joined by Jean Ritchie, Peter Yarrow, Bruce Langhorne, Al Kooper, and Fritz Richmond. They played in the fondly remembered "thunderstorm set," when they ignored a sudden summer downpour and continued to play "Hard Lovin' Loser," "Reno, Nevada," and "Pack Up Your Sorrows" to a delighted and soaking-wet audience.

Also featured at Newport that year was the group of musicians and contra dancers from New Hampshire that eventually came to be known as the Canterbury Country Dance Orchestra. They had been scouted the previous year by Newport trustee Ralph Rinzler at a traditional music gathering in Northfield, Vermont. Their leader, Dudley Laufman, agreed to come down to the festival to perform at a small afternoon workshop and an evening concert. Laufman, who had been a high school hockey player in Arlington, Massachusetts, before going off to agricultural school, had begun calling dances in 1947 and by 1965 was legendary throughout New England as a tireless and charismatic advocate of folk dance. For a time, he served as activity director at the New Hampshire State Hospital, where he hired a teenager named Tom Rush to play for the patients. Laufman's knowledge of dance was encyclopedic, his ability to engage an audience unfailing, and his personality, as one woman put it, "swoon-worthy." The invitation from Rinzler was perfectly timed, since Laufman had convened a group of first-class musicians to cut a record, with appearances planned at venues that included Club 47 and the Beers Family Festival.

The group did not know what to expect of their afternoon workshop, which was to be followed by an appearance on the main stage that would open the evening concert. The fiddlers, flautist, accordion players, and pianist had just launched into an ancient tune and the dancers had just begun swinging around to the eighteenth-century calls when a horde of people suddenly swarmed the stage. It was the crowd that had been cut loose from Bob Dylan and the Paul Butterfield Blues Band's abbreviated set, and, hearing the high fiddle notes, they had run down to investigate. "The whole thing turned into a rip-roaring old-time square dance" is how Laufman remembered it decades later. The group's evening concert was another tour de force, during which Joan Baez began dancing in the aisles to the strains of "Petronella" and both Pete Seeger and Theodore Bikel were beguiled. Moments like this were when Newport was at its magical best: spontaneous, unpretentious, and communal.[6]

Much, possibly overmuch, has been made of the use of amplified instruments at Newport that day in 1965, when, in a phrase that long ago sailed over the boundaries of cliché, "Dylan went electric." On its own, the Paul Butterfield Blues Band performance had been overwhelmingly strong and well received, but the three-song set during which the group backed Bob Dylan was brief, underrehearsed, and tentative. It was neither a shocking betrayal of folk music nor the lightning bolt of "rock" innovation that would take form on the Dylan/Hawks tours later that year; it was simply a mediocre, experimental public performance cut short by the artists. A few people booed, a lot of them didn't, and it was all over quickly. Like state troopers catching a longhair out in a speed trap without an inspection sticker, New York ideologues who had been lurking in wait for a year turned on their rhetorical sirens and indignant blue lights and demanded proof of acoustic integrity, as if to say, "All right, buddy, empty the car—what have you done with the real Bob Dylan?"

In 1962, it would not have been unusual for a young folkie to say to him- or herself, "I really ought to write a song against war." By 1965, it was easier to complain, "Man, Dylan ought to write a song against the war," as if anyone could hit a G chord and cause troop ships to fill up with GIs and depart from Cam Ranh Bay. As fodder for hyperbole and instant mythology by political activists and rock critics, the myth of Newport 1965 has proven to be an irresistible chestnut over the years, a sort of counterculture equivalent of George Washington chopping down the cherry tree. An enormous amount of change and confusion was in play in all aspects of American life and culture in 1965; to conclude that it all hinged on Bob Dylan and ten minutes with a Fender guitar may have been a distortion of events. A whole lot more was going on.[7]

The lyrics of many folk songs referred to aspects of preindustrial, rural life, from "boilin' them cabbage down" to "roundin' up them little dogies," but most singers of traditional songs fell somewhat short of actual acquaintance with country skills and lifestyles. In an attempt to represent folk culture more broadly, exhibits of folk crafts including quilt making, pottery, toy building, and instrument construction began to appear alongside the sound stages at Newport and other venues. For some, the preservation of cultural folkways became an even higher calling than a sole concentration on the music.

This growing interest in all forms of traditional folk culture would quietly become a major force throughout the remaining decades of the twentieth century. Post-and-beam house construction, boatbuilding, foodways, traditional hand tool use, furniture and instrument making, blacksmithing, animal husbandry, gardening, and even the home brewing of beer all became the focal points of their own folk revivals, many of which still remain vibrant today. Some young enthusiasts went on to become practitioners. Jeff Gutcheon developed a keen interest in traditional quilting and eventually served as chairman of the board of the Haystack Mountain School of Crafts on Deer Isle in Maine. Others became professional folklorists, documenting all aspects of traditional culture and helping to preserve the old ways of countryside, farm, and field.[8] At Old Sturbridge Village in central Massachusetts, where the New England Village of the period between 1790 and 1830 is celebrated, Paul Clayton and Bill Balcomb organized folk music weekends that included performances by Pete Seeger and Tom Paxton.

No one was more important to this broadening of the Folk Revival's larger mission than Nancy Sweezy, a Cambridge potter and educator who had become involved with Club 47 in the early 1960s, helping to manage it, housing many of its performers, and serving as its board chair. Together with Ralph Rinzler and the traditional Scottish weaver and balladeer Norman Kennedy, she established Country Roads, a retail store carrying crafts from areas where some of the traditional music originated, which operated at 134 Mount Auburn Street from 1966 to 1968. After Rinzler left New England to help establish the Smithsonian Folklife Festival on the Mall in Washington, DC, and to archive its Folkways Records collection, Nancy pursued her commitment to preserving handmade crafts by moving south in 1968 to revive traditional pottery in the Seagrove, North Carolina, settlement called Jugtown. A renaissance in the era of homespun and hand crafts began to take shape that has matured and continued over the course of the ensuing decades.[9]

The opening of Sweezy's Country Roads store featured a performance by Bill Monroe and His Bluegrass Boys, who were in Cambridge for a gig at Club 47. At that time, Monroe's band included the Wayland, Massachusetts, native Peter Rowan, who had previously played with Joe Val and with Jim Rooney and Bill Keith. When word went out that the Bluegrass Boys needed a singer and guitar player, Peter had jumped at the chance and joined the group at a gig in Vermont. Rowan was an integral part of Monroe's group during his two and one half years of touring, recording, and songwriting with the bluegrass master. At one point, while driving to a gig, Bill signaled him to pull over to the side of the road in order to listen to a musical lick that had suddenly come to him, and he asked the young man to commit it to memory. A short time later, Rowan wrote words to this tune, called "The Walls of Time," which would become one of the Monroe group's strongest and most haunting numbers.

Bluegrass was only one of many compelling musical strains to be heard along the banks of the Charles River. By 1965, it was possible to go to a party and hear the soundtrack to the Beatles' *Help* mixed in with Spider John Koerner's "Rent Party Rag," the Temptations' "Ain't Too Proud to Beg," Tom Rush's "Panama Limited," and the long-anticipated "Mr. Tambourine Man." Channeling the old medicine-show roots of ragtime, Jim Kweskin and the Jug Band went into the studio to cut "Sadie Green, the Vamp of New Orleans," vaudeville's snappy "Somebody Stole My Gal," Leiber and Stoller's classic "I'm a Woman," and Chuck Berry's rock 'n 'roll "Memphis," marinating these improbable ingredients all together in a wonderful album simply titled *Jug Band Music*. On any given night, with sufficient cash, caffeine, leg strength, and subway tokens, you could catch bluesman Taj Mahal at Club 47, drop in on Jeff Gutcheon's barrelhouse piano over at the Orleans, and then grab Jesse Colin Young's last set down at the Unicorn. You might have to sleep through a study hall or two next day, but it was more than worth it.

When Tom Rush put together the playlists for his first two Elektra albums, he gathered in the work of Robert Johnson, Bo Diddley, Bukka White, Buddy Holly, and Woody Guthrie. In his third, he introduced the first recorded compositions of unknown writers Joni Mitchell, Jackson Browne, and James Taylor. "Love's Made a Fool of You," "Sugar Babe," and "The Urge for Going" were among the songs Tom recorded that were graced by the incandescent, firefly guitar notes of Bruce Langhorne. Jack Landrón made several memorable albums, including a live performance at Club 47 that featured his account of teaching at Freedom Schools in Mississippi. Buffy Sainte-Marie released remarkable records on Vanguard, among them *Little Wheel Spin and Spin* and the uniquely arranged *Fire & Fleet & Candlelight.* In the summer of 1966, Mitch Greenhill reeled in Geoff Muldaur, Fritz Richmond, and Jeff Gutcheon like gang-tackled bluefish to help create his second album, *Shepherd of the Highways,* an engaging snapshot of the sorts of things that went on around the streets of Cambridge, out on the Vineyard, or up at von Schmidt's place in Henniker on a pretty good day.

The Charles River Valley Boys underwent some shifts in personnel: by 1966, John Cooke, Ethan Signer, and Fritz Richmond had left the group, their places taken by Jim Field on guitar and Everett Allen Lilly (son of the Lilly Brother's Everett Lilly) on bass. Overcoming the misgivings of their mandolin player Joe Val, the group cut a demo tape of "I've Just Seen a Face" and "What Goes On," Beatles songs done up in bluegrass fashion. Elektra Records impresario Jac Holzman heard the tape and promptly flew to London to gain permission from Messrs. Lennon and McCartney for the CRVB to cut an entire album of Beatles material. Soon the Club 47 mainstays were setting up shop in a Tennessee studio with "Nashville cats" Buddy Spicher on fiddle, Craig Winfield on dobro, and Eric Thompson on lead guitar. The twelve songs that were released on the ensuing *Beatle Country* album (including "Norwegian Wood," "And Your Bird Can Sing," and "Baby's in Black") seemed unlikely choices for bluegrass renditions, but the result was an engaging album that became the group's most popular release.

Jesse Colin Young put out a superb debut album called *Soul of a City Boy*, following it up with a strong second entry titled *Young Blood*, accompanied by Boston's Peter Childs on dobro and his friend John Sebastian on harp. New Yorker Dave Van Ronk cut what might have been his strongest collection, *Just Dave Van Ronk*, for a record label that somehow managed to use a photograph of someone else in the promotional campaign. Mississippi John Hurt released an album titled *Today*, his first recording for a major label since 1928, with Ed Freeman's stark and sensitive portrait of the artist as its cover (see page 172).

For all its other progressive attributes, the folk revival predated the Women's Movement in both time and awareness. The role of many women at parties and festivals was relegated to preparing and serving food while men tuned instruments and sang competitively. The folk singer Ethel Raim once asked Helen von Schmidt if she ever got tired of that sort of role. Helen remembers shrugging the question off and then being told, "Helen, you're furious and you don't even know it!"[10]

The reality was that women often got short shrift in opportunity and recognition. In some cases, business managers made contractual decisions for their women clients without their knowledge or approval. Joan Baez, Judy Collins, and Buffy Sainte-Marie gained prominence through talent and sheer force of will, but other prospective women folk singers were often dismissed by club owners with "We already got a chick singer." Critics were quick to typecast and dismiss women folk singers: Dayle Stanley, a striking performer of her own material in her own right, was once too often referred to in a review as "a Joan Baez type," which led her to cut her hair short to define her individuality. It took years for women performers to be taken seriously and then to take the fore in the folk realm as leading singer-songwriters.

It was often easier to imagine a better world in the abstract than it was to try to make that goal into reality, especially through the quality of one's personal relationships. There was a fundamental imbalance in a social and musical landscape where young women were seeking "true love" in relationships with men who "had ramblin' on their mind" and who could often rationalize their inconstant wanderings with a shoulder-shrugging "that's what you get for lovin' me." In the scene largely populated by Woody Guthrie's inheritors, many men seemed conditioned to script their romantic fantasies with an easy exit on a convenient railroad train in mind. (The latter-day observer is left with the impression that if someone offered ten dollars a mile to male writers of folk-type songs for the cumulative distance that they could prove that they actually rode in freight trains during the course of the ramblin' '60s, the money might well go unclaimed.)

Jack Landrón had risen to the heights of folk music popularity in Boston and Cambridge, filling the seats of not only Club 47 but also Boston's Jordan Hall. Blessed with talent, energy, and a magnetic personality, Jack had been among the most respected performers on the Boston scene. Yet, as one of the few persons of color in the room, he was carrying more than the average folkie's burden of hard travelin'. Despite its overwhelming sympathy for integration and a generalized social justice, the Boston-Cambridge Folk Revival was largely the province of white people in general and white men in particular. By the latter part of the 1960s, the role Jack seemed asked to play was feeling constrained and artificial.

He left Boston to join the Civil Rights Movement in the South, where he taught at Freedom Schools in Mississippi and eventually became the personal assistant of Reverend Dr. Martin Luther King, Jr. Afterward, he moved to New York and, later, California, pursuing a distinguished career in theater, announcing, and music under his given name of Jack Landrón. He had added much to the life of his native Boston, and the years have brought a clearer sense of the real cost of his contributions to the Folk Revival, as well as their value. In appreciation of Jack's impact, it comes to mind that "thanks" might not be as good a word to offer as "much obliged."[11]

In 1962, Bob Dylan had asked how many seas a white dove had to sail before she could sleep in the sand, and by 1966 it was becoming clear that there would be no easy answer to that question. Radical leftists had been warning for some time that the creeping involvement in Vietnam would morph into another Korea-type quagmire, but, secure in their student deferments, many young people dismissed such pronouncements as alarmist and doctrinaire. Increasingly, however, White House press conferences were promoting an undeclared war through white-board marketing jargon including "pacification," "search and destroy," and "perimeter securing." All of this would have enormous implications for the young men in the coffeehouses and campuses of Boston and Cambridge, where many a wallet held a driver's license; a draft card; and a Club 47 membership pass signed by Betsy Siggins, Jim Rooney, or Byron Linardos.

If they were asked why they were attracted to folk music, many young people of the day would have answered, "Because I want to help to make a better world." As the 1960s wore on, the pursuit of that goal became increasingly difficult against a backdrop of burned-out urban streets, scorched Vietnam jungles, and constant scenes of murder and calamity. The question "What are you going to do about the draft?" became the most pressing issue of the day. War resistance was a growing response in Boston, with the American Friends Service Committee being one of the few resources open to young men who suddenly had some very hard decisions to make.

At the same time that the war in Vietnam was escalating, it was becoming clear that the battle against bigotry would involve a long siege in the North as well as dramatic marches in the South. Resentment grew as young African American radicals began to perceive that the sympathies expressed by their white counterparts often proved superficial when the chips were down. The course of events appeared to push the Civil Rights Movement toward disintegration. Well-intended brotherhood and effective political alliances fell by the wayside. People let themselves get angry, people let themselves get hurt, and then people got tired of doing the work. Somewhere in the distance, a bugle called retreat.

The course of the Boston-Cambridge Folk Revival seemed to be simultaneously accelerating and losing altitude, and, in consequence, doubt began to replace optimism as the prevailing tone. For many in New England, Mimi and Richard Fariña seemed to embody the best hope for the direction that traditional music might take in the future. By the time they released their *Celebrations for a Grey Day*, Mimi had developed into a remarkable singer and a facile guitar player, and Richard's musical art was rapidly catching up to the promise of his talent and the considerable drive of his ambition. If ever there could have been an opportunity for creative magic like that of the Beatles to intersect with the roots of folk music, it might have found form in the evolving art of the Fariñas. But that potential came to a tragic end on the evening of April 30, 1966, when Richard was killed in a motorcycle accident at Big Sur on the very day that his first book, *Been Down So Long, It Looks Like Up to Me,* was published. His death was a shock and a body blow to the entire folk community.

In retrospect, Fariña's impulsive decision at a party to jump onto the back of a motorcycle driven by a total stranger seems consistent with the kinds of risky choices that, at times, led to mayhem and tragedy out along the borderlines of late youth. The sort of swashbuckling alcohol consumption that had once seemed like the life of the party was, for some people, proving to be exactly the opposite. When heedless license was applied to personal relationships, people began to see just what careless love could do. And as opportunities for material success in the music business increased, it was tempting to detour around factors like actual inspiration and artistic discipline on the way to the fortune and fame that seemed to be waiting right out there, just beyond the Berkshire toll booths of the Massachusetts Turnpike.

Into this thicket came the popular introduction of recreational drugs. Pot had long been part and parcel of the city scene. Many musicians partook regularly or quietly dealt a few bags, and the venerable bluesmen up from the rural South turned out to be old hands at weed consumption. Young people who were trying out grass for the first time tended to be amazed at its benign effects; accidents and mayhem often followed alcohol abuse, but the worst that could happen after smoking a few joints might be the sudden urge to consume an entire can of chocolate frosting. The more gullible and, then, the more needy soon extrapolated the harmlessness of illegal pot into the reckless use of chemical substances that really *were* risky.

What had come to life as a cohesive community was devolving into the breakup of a group home, whiplashed by a mixture of random drug use, free-range ambition, and cutthroat competition. The imagined pastoral landscape of revival and renewal was turning into what Stephen Stills described in music as "a field day for the heat." The mass media began to fawn and obsess over famous "folk personalities," and as "folk-rock" began to flood the airwaves from California, it was becoming very hard to find one folk singer in a hundred with anything like "a satisfied mind."

FIGURE 11.

Final Club 47 schedule poster, Byron Linardos, April 1968.
Department of Special Collections, W. E. B. Du Bois Library,
University of Massachusetts Amherst.

CHAPTER ELEVEN

STAYED AROUND
THIS OLD TOWN TOO LONG

The Revival Passes Along, 1967–1968

THERE HAS BEEN A tendency to interpret the latter part of the 1960s as a liberating period, but in large part those times were as confusing, contradictory, and dangerous as they were exciting. Two major public figures (Martin Luther King, Jr., and Robert F. Kennedy) were shot in America during the run-up to the election of 1968. Cities were being reduced to smoldering ruins, and American lives were being lost by the thousands in an undeclared and seemingly aimless war in Southeast Asia. The country was splintering into roughly four groups: the "crusading" left; the "patriotic" right; a vast underclass of color; and an enormous and complacent middle class. Meanwhile, the hopeful movement of idealistic young people that had begun in the late 1950s started to morph into a freak show. All of this became a recipe for chaos, and, in many cases, that's exactly what ensued.

Urban neighborhoods throughout the nation erupted in fire and violence following the assassination of Dr. King on April 4, 1968. Many people believe that Boston was spared when soul singer James Brown agreed to have his Boston Garden concert, which was scheduled for the following night, televised for free instead over educational station WGBH. Brown and Boston's mayor, Kevin White, were successful in persuading Boston's African American citizens to stay at home and watch the show on their television sets. The hope of a "better day to come," so fervently anticipated in the early days of the Folk Revival, had been reduced to a sense of relief that Boston had not burned down to the waterline overnight in a riot.

Young idealists began to retreat and to regroup; for some, the search for folk roots would lead them on a pilgrimage to a different sort of freedom summer. A movement "back to the land" began to sprout up as small groups of folk pioneers ventured into the rural countryside of New England in search of the kind of homespun lives they had been singing about in traditional songs. Abandoned farmsteads out on overgrown dirt roads became places where hopes, convictions, and new skills could be tested out, and where local old-timers found amusement in the sight of hard-working young homestead women dressed in 1940s thrift shop hibiscus-print blouses and newly bearded young men in jeans trying, often clumsily, to learn the old ways.

For some, rural living proved only to be a temporary experiment, while, for others, the rigors of what Helen and Scott Nearing had called "the good life" turned out to be their way home. The back-to-the-land movement in New England drew much of its inspiration from the Folk Revival that preceded it; many of those who sought a connection to "the old ways" stepped through gates of a rural lifestyle that had originally been opened to them by traditional folk music. Young people carried the folk tunes that they had heard in coffeehouses back to the eastern frontiers they had originated from long before, to be sung anew on front porches at sundown and played on yard-sale turntables hooked up to truck batteries with jumper cables. On remote hillsides and in lonesome valleys, in the company of wood stoves and kerosene lamps, homestead families raised their children, tended to farm chores, and strove to keep the faith as best they could.[1]

Out in the hinterlands, liberal-minded folk singers might also discover that roadside bars were the only places they could sing in public. The prevailing audiences in such venues were far more interested in country and western music than they were in coffeehouse fare, much more likely to be familiar with Johnny Cash's records, say, than with the repertoire of Leonard Cohen. Transplanted city folk suddenly found that the concept of "cultural diversity" took on entirely new dimensions when it required interaction with factory workers, people who lived in trailers, and parents whose children were stationed on active duty in Vietnam. If the new homesteaders wanted to think of themselves as having clear hearts and open minds, it became apparent that their own city prejudice against "ignorant rednecks" was a knife that could cut from the left as handily as it could slice from the right. Respect was something that needed to be earned in action rather than presumed by virtue of education, privileged opinions, or good intentions.

Senior participants in the Boston-Cambridge Folk Revival such as Almeda Riddle and Mississippi John Hurt were extraordinary souls as well as being cultural treasures; over the next decade, young back-to-the-landers were fortunate to encounter common people in the rural districts of New England who were just as saintly, just as engaging, and just as conversant with the magic of rural America. A few of them might even have been Republicans. During a time when the country was splintering into political factions, the music of Cash, Charley Pride, and Bill Monroe, and tunes from the roots albums of Merle Haggard were received enthusiastically in the bars and beer parlors of the northern countryside.[2]

Across the Berkshires, in West Saugerties, New York, Bob Dylan had withdrawn from rock superstardom. By 1967, he was holed up with his band in a pink ranch house out under whispering pines off Stoll Road, teaching them folk songs such as "The Bonnie Ship the Diamond," "Four Strong Winds," "Five Hundred Miles," and Eric von Schmidt's "Joshua Gone Barbados." The resulting "basement tapes" appeared surreptitiously on bootleg records that were treasured for years. That October, Bob boarded a train to Nashville, where he recorded the album *John Wesley Harding*. Almost completely acoustic and traditional in form, its songs could have been echoes from the brick walls of Club 47 or the Turk's Head.

Back in Boston and Cambridge, the Folk Revival was running out the decade much as the Red Sox had finished most of their seasons in the 1950s: a talented and endearing group of players put some memorable games together, but, as the summer turned to fall, the local team was eventually outmaneuvered by New York muscle and big-time contracts. At one point, the Cambridge folk-entrepreneur Byron Linardos was summoned to Manhattan and asked if he would be interested in moving to the Big Apple. He declined, citing his desire to stay close to his wife and daughters, but others were not as reluctant to make a move. The candles had begun to flicker out in the tabletop wine bottles of the old Bay State.

The New York folk scene was concentrated in Greenwich Village, and its development from the late 1950s onward had paralleled that of Boston and Cambridge on a much more ambitious scale and self-promotional style. Venues such as the Kettle of Fish, Gerde's Folk City, and the Gaslight Cafe went from being spots where tourists gawked at beatniks to becoming the centers of a vibrant folk scene presided over by Dave Van Ronk and populated by Bob Dylan, Phil Ochs, Tom Paxton, Karen Dalton, Fred Neil, and dozens of other performers. New York's *Broadside*, Moe Asch's Oak Publications, *Sing Out!* magazine, and Izzy Young's Folklore Center all came together to constitute a folky equivalent to Tin Pan Alley, and the Village became the wheelhouse for the national popularity of traditional and topical acoustic music. Later on, as more than one musician recalls, the appearance of Andy Warhol and his entourage in lower Manhattan led members of the folk community to conclude that it was high time to get out of Dodge.

In Boston, audiences increasingly hungered after the sort of famous "national acts" that only big night clubs could afford. Motivated more by mission than by money, small coffeehouses began to fall by the wayside. Club 47 gamely forged on, booking big names such as the Muddy Waters Blues Band and the Paul Butterfield Blues Band, but by late 1967, the venue had fallen more than ten thousand dollars into debt, a tremendous burden for a hundred-seat club to consider recouping with a cover charge of $1.50. The Charles River Valley Boys and Tom Rush kicked in for a series of benefits that brought income, but in reality the club's nonbusiness model was no longer viable. When manager Jim Rooney left to take on a leadership role at the Newport Folk Festival, Byron Linardos returned to the helm for a final four months, and then, after heartfelt farewell reunions of the faithful held on April 26 and 27, 1968, Club 47 closed its doors.[3]

The *Broadside*, too, had fallen on difficult times. If people were not digging folk music anymore, then it followed that there would not be much of a market for folk music news. In October 1967, the publication changed in format and focus and became a large, newspaper-sized magazine taking rock music, alternative culture, and politics into its purview. Eventually, it would join forces with the *Boston Free Press* and, later on, with the *Avatar*. The coffeehouse schedules remained, but both the feel and the content were considerably altered. About that time, at the King's Rook in Ipswich, where talents as impressive as the Fariñas, Judy Collins, and Mississippi John Hurt had previously appeared on its stage, the schedule in *Broadside* read simply, "King's Rook A-Go-Go Dancers" five nights a week. What emanated from some of the performance stages began to seem like not much more than a whole lot of sound effects.

A beloved period was coming to a close in loss and confusion. In light of the traumatic character of other political events of the day, the closing of Club 47 and the departure of many of its stalwarts from the valley of the Charles could hardly be seen as a tragedy. But for the participants and the emotional stakeholders, something dear to the heart was passing, and there seemed to be very little that anyone could do about it. A long, lonesome valley lay up ahead, and the members of the folk community were coming to the realization that they were all going to have to walk it by themselves.

The 1968 Newport Folk Festival would prove to be a watershed event, reprising the distance that the folk revival had traversed and predicting the forces that its legacy would have to reckon with in the decades to come. The reporter from the *Harvard Crimson* observed that "with Dylan's return to grace, many unhappy *aficionados* spent a good portion of this year's festival waiting for and speculating on the possibility of his appearance. . . . A feeling of waiting and speculation permeated all the concerts, however, and this feeling made it difficult to enjoy or appreciate what actually was happening on the stage. The reason for this was partly due to the audience, its great impatience and at times actual rudeness . . . the vast numbers in attendance were just so many witnesses to the end of an era and the demise of an institution."[4] But lost in the melee of that hot July weekend was Big Brother and the Holding Company's dedication of the traditional song "The Cuckoo" to Buell Kazee, a traditional performer from Kentucky who had recorded the song in the 1920s. A small gesture, perhaps, but evidence that folk music was still influencing the new music coming out of the West Coast, as it had done since Rolf Cahn and Debbie Green first opened the Cabale in Berkeley back in 1963.

The New York critic and rock 'n' roll historian Ed Ward once listed the four most influential groups of the 1960s as the Beatles, the Rolling Stones, the Byrds, and Jim Kweskin and the Jug Band.[5] The Kweskin group's first record and their subsequent West Coast appearances had an enormous influence on the San Francisco scene. In 1964, Palo Alto high school sophomore Bob Weir and a friend hitchhiked to Berkeley to see the Jug Band play, and the very next night they set out to put together their own folk group (local banjo player Jerry Garcia joined up within a few days). The earliest tape of Mother McCree's Uptown Jug Champions, precursor of the Grateful Dead, includes seven songs drawn from the first Kweskin album, and even a cursory listening makes it clear just how much Jerry Garcia was trying to sound like Geoff Muldaur. Other folk revival songs that were included in the repertoire of the early Grateful Dead were Bonnie Dobson's "Morning Dew," folk songs "Whiskey in the Jar" and "Oh, Babe, It Ain't No Lie," and a version of "I Know You Rider" that may have been sourced from Bonnie Dobson's friend and roommate, the blues singer Judy Roderick.

If one portion of the legacy of Boston and Cambridge went across the great divide to California, another was crossing the Hudson at Rhinebeck and taking root closer to home, in Woodstock, New York. Many of the displaced coffeehouse faithful found echoes of the old-time folk music religion in the group that had backed up Bob Dylan on his international tours of 1966. Even as the glitz and flash of the psychedelic craze was taking hold, the members of this brotherhood were putting their musical trousers on one leg at a time, writing songs conceived and recorded on living room rugs and in basements. Their lead guitar licks rang like a mandolin, and their drumheads were set so loose they could have been stretched on a frame in a wigwam. With piano chords striding along like an energetic spinster at a Grange Hall dance and a churchy organ that seemed ready for the Resurrection, their music channeled the listener into some very old American stories. Syncopated by a loping, Motown bass line from an unfretted fingerboard, the music of the Band conveyed the sense that, despite evidence to the contrary, our lives would probably turn out fine.

Jim Rooney had been called in to oversee the construction of the Bearsville Recording Studio in Woodstock by Albert Grossman, who was managing both the Band and Bob Dylan. Before long, Bill Keith and Geoff and Maria Muldaur joined the scene. The New England contingent began a process of musical cross-pollination, jamming with New York folkies Happy and Artie Traum, and, at times, Rick Danko and Garth Hudson of the Band. Impromptu sessions were joined sporadically by Eric von Schmidt, who made the run over the Berkshires from Henniker, New Hampshire, and by Paul Butterfield, who also convened a band called Paul Butterfield's Better Days. Under the shadow of Overlook Mountain, a number of Cambridge folkies became key elements in the group called Woodstock Mountain Review, which played on a landscape bounded, on the east, by a pink ranch house where homespun tapes were being made in the basement and, on the west, by the Ashokan Reservoir, the inspiration for the theme to Ken Burns's PBS series "The Civil War."

Further afield, the Boston-Cambridge influence would find a welcome home on the banks of the Cumberland River in Nashville, Tennessee, where the Grand Ole Opry had been holding court since 1925. After Bob Dylan recorded *John Wesley Harding* on Nashville's Music Row in late 1967, folk musicians Ian & Sylvia, Buffy Sainte-Marie, Tracy Nelson, and Roger McGuinn all made pilgrimages to Nashville and recorded excellent albums with the local Nashville musicians. Johnny Cash began hosting a live television show at Nashville's Ryman Auditorium in 1969, where he introduced his country and western audience to Bob Dylan, Joni Mitchell, and Ramblin' Jack Elliott. Around the same time, Jim Rooney and Bill Keith's group, the Blue Velvet Band, added their contribution to the country music renaissance with an eponymous album enlivened by Eric von Schmidt's memorable graphics.[6]

Boston's roots in Nashville can be traced in good part back to the improbable career and irrepressible personality of the Tennessee native and country music producer Jack Clement. After serving in the U.S. Marine Corps, Jack began singing and playing guitar. By 1953, he was appearing in Boston at the Hillbilly Ranch in Park Square. Jack became a regular on WCOP's *Hayloft Jamboree* program, where he cut a song on a local label called Sheraton Records before returning south to attend college, briefly, in his native Memphis.

By 1956, Jack had left school and become an assistant to Sam Phillips, the owner of Sun Records in Memphis and discoverer of Elvis Presley, Carl Perkins, Johnny Cash, and young Roy Orbison. Jack Clement seemed to possess some of the same "good ear," and good luck, as his boss. One time, when Sam was on a business trip in Florida selling 45s out of his car trunk, Jack oversaw an audition in the Sun Studio for a teenage piano player whose father had driven him all the way up the Mississippi River from Ferriday, Louisiana, the result of which was Jack's production of "Whole Lotta Shakin' Going On," by then unknown Jerry Lee Lewis.[7]

Jack Clement became one of the most influential producers in Nashville, displaying an unconventional streak in a field where tradition had ruled the day. His production credits included records by country artists Dolly Parton, Jim Reeves, Hank Snow, Charley Pride, and Waylon Jennings and, eventually, U2 and B. B. King. Former Cambridge folkie Jim Rooney walked into Jack's studio in Nashville one day looking for work, and the resulting partnership became the stuff of musical history. Over the course of several decades, Clement and Rooney fostered the birth of what later became known as "Americana" music through the work of Nanci Griffith, Iris DeMent, Townes Van Zandt, and John Prine, among many others. Jim Rooney was given a Lifetime Achievement Award by the Americana Music Association in Nashville in 2009, for a career ably recounted in his book *In It for the Long Run,* published in 2014. Today, Jim remains one of the most highly regarded figures in Nashville.

Taj Mahal studied ethnomusicology at the University of Massachusetts and has steadily expanded his knowledge to embrace and to express a broad spectrum of music that stretches around the world. His body of work has always demonstrated that there was a lot more cultural vibrancy in the deep roots of international music than there was in whatever fashion was being promoted in the media of the moment. Over the years, he has brought delta blues, ragtime, calypso, reggae, jazz, and rhythm and blues together in an ever-growing musical whole. "I just play to the goddess of music," Taj once said, "and I know she's dancing."[8]

Back in New England, a new stable of acoustic performers began to make appearances, many of them creating their own compositions and grafting them onto the tried-and-true rootstocks of traditional music. In the forefront were singers James Taylor and Carly Simon, who had both performed at the Moon Cusser's coffeehouse hootenannies on Martha's Vineyard. By the end of the decade, these artists were writing their own songs, experimenting with new forms of acoustic music, and eventually winning audiences on a scale that would have seemed inconceivable for "folkies" a few years before.

Women musicians came to the vanguard of what eventually became known as the "singer-songwriter" movement in the 1970s and '80s, using traditional folk idioms as the setting for lyrics drawn from the landscape of relationships and emotions. As Dayle Stanley now remembers, "All the old folk songs were about pirates and sheriffs and people being murdered and thrown in the river. I wanted to sing about the things that were in my heart."[9] Years later, scores of women singers would follow her lead. In its final months of operation, Club 47 hosted a very young Joni Mitchell, who had come to Cambridge at the suggestion of Tom Rush and had stunned audiences with the strength of her writing and the magnetism of her performances.

Drawn to Boston by its folk and blues scene, an unknown singer and Radcliffe student by the name of Bonnie Raitt began appearing at local coffeehouses in the late 1960s. Other names came to town: Paul Geremia, Chris Smither, and Bill Staines, among them, playing the same rooms in which Nancy Michaels, Leonda, and Peter Childs had once performed. At the Sword in the Stone and the Turk's Head on Charles Street, young musicians continued to tune up and play the old music in the company of meager audiences and strong coffee. After a term as the McCarthy for President headquarters, the vacant second site of Club 47 on Palmer Street in Cambridge became the home of acoustic music once again when a new coffeehouse, Passim, began operating in 1969, led by the memorable personalities of Bob and Rae Anne Donlin for a quarter of a century.

Also in 1969, in a converted 1832 meetinghouse close by the University of New Hampshire, the Stone Church opened its doors in Newmarket to a folk music clientele whose tastes ran a bit more toward beer than espresso. Within a few years, Widdie and Jonathan Hall began a coffeehouse named the Folkway in Peterborough, New Hampshire, where Folk Revival veterans Tom Paxton and Bill Staines appeared occasionally, joined over time by David Mallett, Mary Chapin Carpenter, Shawn Colvin, Lui Collins, Suzanne Vega, Christine Lavin, and Guy Van Duser, among others. This succeeding generation of folk artists was chronicled by Kari Estrin in her publication *The Black Sheep Review,* a worthy successor to the old *Broadside* that covered the entire New England acoustic music scene. With a new name and new management, Club Passim opened at the old 47 Palmer Street address as a nonprofit after the retirement of the Donlins in the mid-1990s, and on that holy ground in the decades since, it has provided a venue and a vision for young folk artists from across the region and the country.

Out along the Connecticut River in Massachusetts, the Pioneer Valley Folklore Society has continued to thrive. In 1988, members Annie

Patterson and Peter Blood worked with Pete and Toshi Seeger to create a songbook called *Rise Up Singing,* which became the vehicle by which new generations would find their way to the inspiring music of roots and revival. The organization has had a nationwide impact in ways that were probably never dreamed of by its founding members Jim Rooney, Bill Keith, Buffy Sainte-Marie, and Taj Mahal.

With extraordinary vigor, the contra dance tradition rolled on through the Boston-Cambridge Folk Revival, picked up a certain amount of speed for a time, and then resumed steady flowage on its four-hundred-year-old course, undisturbed by concerns about authenticity, electricity, folk-rock, New York City, San Francisco, psychedelia, or, for that matter, disco. Prominent among the dozens of traditional dance groups active throughout New England, Dudley Laufman and his Canterbury Country Dance Orchestra made three outstanding record albums in the 1970s and '80s with stalwarts Sylvia Miskoe, Bob McQuillen, and Jack Sloanaker. Peter Colby, master of the autoharp, banjo, and harmonica; gifted fiddler April Limber; and Deanna Stiles, with her quicksilver flute, all brought their talents to a later edition of the group.

More than five decades after his Newport and Club 47 appearances, Dudley Laufman continues to inspire the followers and discoverers of traditional dance, and he and Bob McQuillen both earned recognition as National Heritage Fellows by the National Endowment for the Arts. In 2016, the Canterbury Country Dance Orchestra held a reunion recording session for a CD they titled *Welcome Here Again* in the same chapel at Concord Academy where they had gathered to make their first recording in 1972. A dozen veteran musicians in their sixties, seventies, and eighties were joined by four younger players who had been students of either Dudley or Bob McQuillen to produce twenty-eight songs with no rehearsals and only two retakes. Nineteen songs were released.[10]

Throughout New England, bluegrass, blues, string band, Celtic, country and western, and contra dance enthusiasts have continued to keep the faith in small groups gathered in modest venues. The music returned from the bailiwick of folk celebrities back into the unheralded hands of earnest amateurs, where, the case could be made, it had always truly belonged. Even now, a half century after the height of the Folk Revival of Boston and Cambridge, the Charles River continues to roll back and forth on the tides, through the lowlands, and out onto a long, island-studded coastline. If we listen for them, we can still hear the echoes of swashbuckle, chant, and quadrille; ragtime and reel; jug band rhythm; sea shanties; and the endless old voices of blues, ballads, and songs still coming forth from all the old familiar places of all of our roots and all of our revivals.

FIGURE 12.
Mississippi John Hurt in Cambridge, 1965.
Photograph © 2020 by Ed Freeman. All rights reserved. Used by permission.

WHERE DID YOU COME FROM, WHERE DO YOU GO?

Winning Back Our Own Hearts and Minds

SIXTY YEARS HAVE PASSED now, and more, since the first stirrings of the folk revival and the subsequent events of the 1960s played out on the American stage. In the interim, women's rights came to the fore, environmental concerns became a matter of immediate import across the entire nation, and technology advanced to a degree that no one would ever have predicted. In 2008, an African American was elected president of the United States, a man who seemed both capable and committed to guiding us forward as a unified people.

And, yet, nearly every aspect of "the better world" that was envisioned back in the days of the New Frontier feels as though it has morphed into its own shadow. Doubt, distrust, and fear are loose and rampant in the land of life, liberty, and the pursuit of happiness. The primacy of technology has been established in ways that IBM could never have envisioned in the 1950s; and even as American wealth reigns supreme around the globe, a host of unintended consequences loom like apocalyptic tornadoes on the rim of our horizon.

The nation that was born when ideals could move mountains and principles could stride across continents seems to have become steeped in the sort of aimless despair that haunted Steven Foster nearly two hundred years ago. We can hear echoes from the voices of all the regrets, displacements, and longings of our history: What have they done to the old home place? Why did they tear it down?

Now, in this time of confusion, we find ourselves asking where we are to go to find our way, and, indeed, how do we get back to where we once belonged?

AMERICA'S NEED FOR REVIVAL has been a recurring phenomenon ever since Europeans and Africans first came to these shores. Whenever we find ourselves removed from a sense of home and culture, we have felt the need to gather in community and to rekindle a sense of belief and belonging. The magnetic pull of the past, the personal, and the homespun has tended to increase in strength during bewildering periods of national uncertainty and rapid change. Time and time again, we keep coming back to try to locate the promised and often elusive land where we are delivered from evil and where our best intentions may come to fruition in identity, security, and sustenance. When we hear reference made to "roots revivals," we might ask ourselves, Which revivals? Over the course of more than four hundred years of American culture and history, we can count multiple occasions when a hearkening back to basics served to revive our capacity for common sense through our embrace of uncommon passion.

On the long national journey that has spanned pilgrimage, revolution, and nationhood, Americans have relied on a set of creative and cultural compass points that have led us toward renewal through the radical application of heritage. From Tom Paine's *Common Sense* to Henry Thoreau's *Walden,* the works of activist artists have served to refine and rekindle the basic ideals that inspire us to believe, once again, that we shall overcome. When Harriet Beecher Stowe wrote the words that helped inspire America to abolish slavery, Abraham Lincoln reportedly referred to her as the woman who started the war. One hundred years later, when Joan Baez took the stage at the Lincoln Memorial, she sang in a voice that would do much to end another one.

The Folk Revival that unfolded in Boston and Cambridge in the late 1950s and early '60s was a lucid interval in a delusional age. Imperfect as it was and as diverted as it became, it served for a time as a kind of covered bridge for young pilgrims to cross over from an embittered present toward hoped-for better days to come. The Revival occurred during a time of superficial prosperity that was belied by a whole litany of societal deficits and unrequited human desires:

The crime against life, the worst of all crimes, is *not* to feel. And there was never, perhaps, a civilization in which that crime, the crime of torpor, of lethargy, of apathy, the snake-like sin of coldness-at-the-heart, was commoner than in our technological civilization. . . . It is the modern painless death, this commercialized atrophy of the heart. None of us is safe from it.[1]

So wrote the poet Archibald MacLeish in Cambridge in 1960, when the powers that be in Boston were burrowing into fallout shelters underneath John Winthrop's City upon a Hill.

It was no wonder that young people along the Charles found themselves called on to embrace the old emotions, to rekindle the old songs, to master the old instruments, and to secure for themselves a sense of permanence and community in the midst of what was proving to be a dangerously delusional age. In short order, we were assured that Americans, at least the white ones, would be zipping around the landscape in personal hovercraft. Soon enough, disease and hunger would be eradicated from the planet, and, within a few years, nuclear power would surely produce so much electricity that there would be no point in charging money for it. The assumptions of "space-age" society seemed not only to be too good to be true, they seemed to be the expression of a hubris that was riddled with vulnerability.

Perhaps the most remarkable thing about the Boston-Cambridge Folk Revival was that it germinated out of ideals rather than from necessity. In the beginning, a creative strain of patriotic idealism was its guiding light. Hope, and not fear or anger, fueled a united progress, and neither angst nor impatience, but faith, kept it moving forward. Freedom songs that were played among friends in tiny coffeehouses somehow came to be broadcast from nearly every car radio, every living room record player, and every beach blanket transistor in the country, to be heeded, for a time at least, even in the halls of government.

The creed of nonviolence brought a quiet and unshakeable confidence to the cause. The dormant embers of old New England idealism that are always ready to ignite the dawning of a better day unleashed a moral force of dimension and power that had not been deployed since the Civil War. Everyone in the struggle for civil rights that came to be known as "the Movement" felt that as long as they kept the faith, kept moving in the direction of justice, and kept learning from differing viewpoints and cultures, the cause would not, could not, lose.

In its own serendipitous way, the Boston-Cambridge Folk Revival sought to connect our past times, our richest cultures, and our favorite stories through a music that knit us all together in community. We ventured out, more or less bravely, into the national fault lines of race, sectionalism, conformity, and greed (if not yet those of gender and class), and tried to rekindle an active sense of shared vision that had gone out of fashion in American life. The youthful crusades back toward new and old frontiers began bravely, achieved enormous early success, and taught us that transformation and redemption were not only still possible in the modern world, they were probably the basis of our integrity and, thus, our survival. It all felt right.

It wasn't perfect—it couldn't have been expected to be—but it was an enormous improvement on the racial segregation, economic elitism, and dumbed-down materialism of the dominant culture in the 1950s. Yet, other than in the cases of the bravest of the civil rights workers and the most dedicated Peace Corps and Vista volunteers, there was no boot camp where young people could learn to develop the skills and the character traits necessary to work effectively when the game got rough or struggled on into extra innings. As the unresolved, age-old "problems" of race and new allegations of deeply imbedded misogyny increasingly called the bluff of our lofty self-assumptions, it became easier, and more appealing, to focus on our individual feelings than on our collective fate. So, by the late 1960s, the crusade was coming to be supplanted by a carnival; maybe what we really wanted to do was to run away and join the circus, at least for the remaining summer months of youth. We backed away from the ramparts, we allowed ourselves to become distracted, and then we bought ourselves off.

Eventually, it seemed clear that it was high time for us to get down to the brass tacks of careers, marriage, and parenthood, self-satisfied in the belief that we had "changed the world." The bell-bottom jeans went up into the attic, "liberals" retreated to self-referential and superior contact with "their own kind," the unredeemed promissory notes of American possibility and peril went on a minimum-payment schedule, and, as we now know, the debts of history kept on compounding. Inevitably, the empire struck back.

Americans have now been jolted from a long sleep into what seems like a waking nightmare, in which the national soul, once again, is bleeding from compound fractures of gender, race, class, age, ill health, and sectionalism. A new Gilded Age has corrupted free enterprise and forced the economy into a distorted game of musical chairs. Our leadership conducts itself like a walking swindle while our media cashes in on our horrified fascination with the sideshows of nonstop crises. Technology, which promised so glibly to save the world in the late 1950s, has gone on to spawn a century of auto-addiction, leaving the populace adrift and chartless in a welter of gadgets, fandom, and quackery.

We seem to be wandering across the desert in our own tired tracks, stumbling over our own litter, exposed to more lies per day, perhaps, than any other human beings in history. We have, as Thoreau once put it, perfected a host of "improved means to an unimproved end,"[2] and for decades, we have pushed aside the disquieting feeling that a time of reckoning might be coming. Our first acculturated impulses (to assume superiority, to compete, and to consume) cannot serve to deliver us from the deficits that have accumulated in the ledgers of a profoundly short-sighted and perilously self-centered culture.

This book has been written over the course of six years in the hope that, when the time was right, it might prove to be a resource for anyone who felt called, once again, to bear witness to the truth, the beauty, the need for contrition, and the unrequited love that live together at the heart of American culture. In the final weeks before this manuscript was to be submitted to the University of Massachusetts Press, everyone in the country was suddenly pulled into isolation amid the onslaught of the coronavirus. It was not just the health of the nation that was compromised: the viability of modern culture itself was called into question.

Yet, even as a pandemic imperiled the safety and well-being of every soul on the planet, the disease was being treated as if it were an economic issue, a conundrum for the Dow-Jones Industrial Average instead of a mortal threat to our species. The popular press seemed intent on counting the days until the country could return to a weird combination of greed and narcissism than could not be considered "normal" in any sense of the word. The self-evident thesis that America was more in need than it has ever been for a spiritual and a cultural revival seemed to be playing out in what has come to be called "real time."

My first impulse was to rewrite this whole last chapter of this book (at least), not only in light of what was happening in 2020 but also what had happened in the Native American pandemic of 1617, the signs of comets and dark days in colonial times, and in the various scourges of diphtheria, malaria, Spanish influenza, and the polio epidemic that have occurred over the years. On reflection, I began to sense that either this work, as it is, has a role to play as a sort of visiting midwife at a forthcoming cultural rebirth . . . or it doesn't. So, other than this pause between ornaments here, I'm going to let this chapter stand, largely as I wrote it, weeks, months, and even years ago, and edit the bulk of this book under the present circumstances as part of my "essential work." I hope that you are all okay, I hope that you are still faithful, still hopeful, and that you still believe in the healing power of love. If this piece can be a help to you, it is all yours. By all means, run with it.

∾

New England's guiding role in the stewardship of the national soul receded generations ago. The region has gradually seen itself relegated from a position of visionary leadership to that of a quirky but relatively powerless subset of consumers crowded into a northeastern cul-de-sac, the sort of group that had, as the poet Archibald MacLeish once observed, "sold their souls, and not for necessities of life, but for its comforts, its amenities—for a mess of prosperity-on-credit."[3] Yet it was in this very place that the old poet Henry Longfellow had predicted that "in the hour of darkness and peril and need, the people would waken and listen to hear" a clarion call to community rebirth like the one that had heralded the national nativity. Over time, that call has come from the green at Lexington, from the wharves of Boston, from the lyceums of Concord, from campuses and pulpits on seacoast villages and upland hill towns, from the brick-walled coffeehouses of Cambridge, and from the steps of the Lincoln Memorial in a voice that called us to "let freedom ring from the mighty mountains of New Hampshire." If we are to have a national revival once again, let it begin here.

For we still need to attend to the unredeemed promises of our forebears, or we will surely continue to suffer from a host of accelerating and unsavory consequences. Our future is quite likely to depend on our clear-eyed ability to identify and understand the cultural forces that have shaped us as a people over the years, both for good and for ill. We need to demonstrate a willingness to learn equally from the triumphs and the shortcomings of our complicated family history and resolve to reform and to renew the national vows of purpose and unity. We need to be about the business, as editor and author Richard Todd once said, of winning back our own hearts and minds.[4]

We have the chance to carefully retrace our steps until we come to find landmarks that we remember. This is where we can recalibrate our moral compass points, regain our equilibrium, rediscover our direction, and rekindle our sense of promise. This is where the power of tradition and revival not only becomes relevant once again but also becomes the stuff of rebirth and redemption. This is where we rediscover our faith: in memory, in gratitude, and in celebration.

Time and time again, the perennial magic of traditional music has helped us find a place where we can truly understand and then redeem our national birthright. As composer and teacher Alice Parker has said, "Music, especially song, is the most human of the arts. It needs no materials or tools other than the ear and the throat—along with mind and heart."[5] Music continues to occupy a place where the North borders the South, where Black and white have the opportunity to earn trust in shared creation and fate, where town and country can find balance, and where female and male can learn to look at one another with unclouded eyes and resolve to live together in fairness and fruition. It could simply be that traditional music can help bring us back to a place where trust is possible, where the fix isn't in, where the books aren't cooked, where the lyrics aren't written down, and where the instruments don't always have to be in tune.

We have, each of us, deep in our bodies and souls, a birthright whose character and possibilities have been thousands of years in the making. Here, in the beloved landscape of New England, in the light of what we know about the course of human events over the past four hundred years, we can grasp a fairly good sense of the range of catastrophe and promise that balances on the fulcrum of our moment. We can rejoice in the heritage that has sustained us on our journey through a human landscape that remains rich with hope and love, and, yet, as we know, is always susceptible to a complacency that backslides into delusion, deceit, and fear.

Americans have been struggling to secure liberty and justice for all since the days when we first sought to find a home in this promised land. Today, we are further called by a hundred thousand old voices to heed the most traditional folk imperative of all: the impulse to survive. Our diverse American culture is the keystone of our birthright, the most basic source of our reason to believe in democracy, and the true location of our Promised Land. The times call us now to draw on our many gifts, to invoke the better angels of our traditions, and to embrace, once again, the hard work of forging a better world for ourselves and for our children.

The late Dr. Martin Luther King, Jr., once said, "If you can't fly, then run. If you can't run, then walk. And if you can't walk, then crawl. But whatever you do, you have to keep moving." Perhaps we should add to this: and if you can't sing, well, then, sing anyway.

VOICES

I don't know how many years later, maybe 1967, Geoff and Maria [Muldaur] had moved to Woodstock, and Dylan was there, the Band was there. Dylan picked me up, I think, at Muldaurs' house. Now, driving with Bob Dylan was an adventure, and it was snowing, and it had been snowing and snowing and snowing, and we were going to Rick Danko's for a party. Rick had an old piano in his beautiful cabin, and we got rip-roaring drunk. At sunrise, Rick Danko said, "Let's all go outside and sing 'Amazing Grace' to the sun coming up." So we went outside, and we stood facing the sun in a line of people, and we sang "Amazing Grace." It was the first time I had ever heard the song, and it was a whole bunch of drunks singing it, and, at the last note, we all fell straight back into the snow. It was . . . you couldn't have scripted it. It's a nice memory. It's an innocent memory.

—Betsy Siggins, personal conversation with the author, 2016

Find out what you love the most and hold to it like a loved one! Learn to play; play to learn. In learning to play any specific thing, there is a rule: know exactly what you want to play and never play anything faster than you can play it perfectly. That way, you make no mistakes. Consequently, things go directly into the memory bank without having to go through the checking and correction processes, and you learn much faster. Rules, of course are made to be broken! But this is a good one.

—Peter Childs, personal conversation with the author, 2016

Just do it! Make music! Singing's good for you. And it's something you can share when you're playing with other musicians. I mean, I'm still singing, and I'm seventy-three. I don't know why my voice has lasted all this time, but, you know, it has . . . and it's wonderful! It feels good! Singing is really good for you!

—Bonnie Dobson, personal conversation with the author, 2016

APPENDIX ONE

Coffeehouses in New England, 1955–1968

(Dates in parentheses are based on available information and subject to further research.)

Adam's Rib	Lynn, Mass. (1967)
Ballad and Banjo	Hyannis, Mass. (1962)
Ballad Room	near Copley Square, Boston (1958–60)
Big Toe	St. Mark's Church, Foxboro, Mass. (1967)
Blues Bag	120 Commercial Street, Provincetown, Mass. (by 1967)
Boar's Head	US Route 1A, Kennebunk Center, Maine (1964)
Damaged Angel	Arlington Street Church, Boston (opened 2/1966)
Cafe Yana	Beacon Street, Boston; then 50 Brookline Avenue, Kenmore Square (1958–64)
Cholmondeley's	413 South Street, Waltham, Mass., on Brandeis University campus (1960 onward)
Club 47	47 Mt. Auburn, Cambridge (2/1958); next at 47 Palmer St. (10/1963–4/1968)
Flying Lion	Fall River, Mass. (1966)
Golden Fleece	Zero Greendale Road, Boston (1967)
Golden Vanity	on Boston University campus (1960)
Green Frog	Kenmore Square, Boston (c. 1960; closed by 1962)
Hillbilly Ranch	Stuart Street, Boston (late 1950s)
Jolly Beaver	Cambridge (1962)
King Arthur's	Boston (1966)
King's Rook	4 South Main Street, Ipswich, Mass. (opened 4/1963)
King's Rook	12 State Street, Marblehead, Mass. (by 1963)
Loft	upstairs at 54 Charles Street, Boston (1960)
Moon Cusser	Circuit Avenue, Oak Bluffs, Martha's Vineyard (6/1963–9/1965)
Moondial	53 Berkley Street, Boston (1966)

Nameless	First Parish Unitarian Universalist Church in Harvard Square (1967–2015)
New World Gallery	47 Bow Street, Portsmouth, N.H. (c. 1964)
Odyssey	corner of Cambridge and Hancock Streets, Boston (10/1964–1/1966)
One-Eyed Jack's	Manchester, N.H. (c. 1965)
Orleans	13 Charles Street, Boston (3/1958–c. 1968, then Sword in the Stone)
Parable	Quincy, Mass. (1967)
Pesky Serpent	612 1/2 Page Boulevard, Springfield, Mass. (1966)
Potting Shed	Lenox, Mass. (1967)
Quest	140 Clarendon Street, Boston (1967)
Rose	122 Salem Street, Boston (1964)
Sachem's	Boston (1967)
Saladin	Amherst, Mass. (c. 1964)
Salamander	Huntington Avenue, Boston (c. 1961)
Saxon	39 Charles Street, Newport, R.I. (1967)
Seventh Circle	location unknown (opened in autumn 1965, operating in 1967)
Silver Vanity	640 Main Street, Worcester, Mass. (1963)
Sword in the Stone	See Orleans above
Tête-A-Tête	286 Thayer Street, Providence, R.I. (c. 1965)
This Is It	near Symphony Hall, Boston (1968)
Tulla's Coffee Grinder	30 Dunster Street, Cambridge (1955)
Turk's Head	71 1/2 Charles Street, Boston ("Boston's Oldest Coffeehouse," 7/1957)
Turk's Head	Orleans, Mass. (mid-1960s)
Turk's Head	Wellfleet, Mass. (c. 1966)
Unicorn	825 Boylston Street, Boston (c. 1960)
Unicorn II	Vineyard Haven, Mass. (1964)
Unicorn North	South Daniel Webster Highway, Nashua, N.H. (1967)
Where It's At	location unknown (from 2/1966 until at least 1967)
White Whale	Beverly, Mass. (c. 1967)
Y-Not	Worcester, Mass. (1967)

APPENDIX TWO

Music Recordings in the Folk New England Collection, 1948–1968

1948
Ralph Page and His New Hampshire Contradance Orchestra, *Ralph Page and His New Hampshire Contradance Orchestra*, 78 rpm (Disc Records)

1949
Allerton & Alton, *Black, White, and Bluegrass*, released in 2010 (Bear Family BCD 16559)

1950
Ralph Page and His Boston Boys, *Ralph Page and His Boston Boys*, 78 rpm (Folk Dancer)

1951
Various artists (including Jack Clement), *WCOP Hayloft Jamboree*, 3-record set, 78 rpm (Sheraton)

1955
Paul Clayton, *Bay State Ballads* (Folkways FA 2106)

1956
Paul Clayton, *Bloody Ballads* (Riverside RLP 12–615)
Paul Clayton, *Whaling and Sailing Songs* (Tradition TLP 1005)

1957
Paul Clayton, *Bobby Burns Merry Muses of Caledonia* (Elektra EKL 155)
Paul Clayton, *British Broadside Ballads* (Folkways FW 8708)
Paul Clayton, *Unholy Matrimony* (Elektra EKL 147)
Hal Lone Pine and Betty Cody, *The Coast of Maine and Other Favourites* (Arc A 600)
Alan Mills, *Songs of the Sea* (Folkways FA 2312)

1958

Joan Baez, *Joan Baez in San Francisco* (recorded, not released)
Paul Clayton, *Timber-r-r! Lumberjack Folksongs and Ballads*
(Riverside RLP 12–648)

1959

Paul Clayton and the Foc'sle Singers (Van Ronk, etc.), *Foc'sle Songs
and Shanties* (Folkways FA 2429)
Alan Mills, *Folksongs of the Maritimes* (Folkways FW 8744)
Shakers of Sabbathday Lake, *Early Shaker Spirituals* (Rounder 0078)
Various artists (Baez, Wood, Alevizos), *Folksingers 'round Harvard
Square* (Veritas XTV 62202–3)

1960

Joan Baez, *Vanguard* (VSD 2077)
Bonnie Dobson, *Dear Companion* (Prestige International PR 7801)
Bonnie Dobson, *She's Like a Swallow* (Prestige/Folklore FL 14015)
Pete Seeger, *Champlain Valley Songs* (Folkways FH 5210)
Various artists, *Evening Concerts at Newport 1959* (Vanguard)

1961

Rolf Cahn and Eric von Schmidt, *Rolf Cahn and Eric von Schmidt*
(Folkways FA 2417)
Charles River Valley Boys, *Bringin' in the Georgia Mail* (Folklore UK,
FL EUT-3)
Paul Clayton, *Home-Made Songs and Ballads* (Monument M4001)
Tony Saletan, *The Song Bag* (Western TV Records)
Various artists (Washington, Kindred, etc.), *New Folks* (Vanguard
VRS 9096)

1962

Joan Baez, *Joan Baez, Vol. 2* (Vanguard VRS 9094)
Joan Baez, *Joan Baez in Concert* (Vanguard VRS 9112)
Charles River Valley Boys, *Bluegrass and Old Timey Music* (Mount
Auburn Records MTA 1; later, Prestige International PR-
INT-13074; then Prestige/Folklore FL 14017)
Paul Clayton, *Dulcimer Songs* (Folkways FG 3571)
Helen Creighton, *Maritime Folk Songs* (Folkways FE 4307)
Bonnie Dobson, *Hootenanny at Folk City* (Prestige/Folklore FL
14018)
Bonnie Dobson, *Sings a Merry-Go-Round of Children's Songs*
(Prestige International INT 13064)

Knob Lick Upper 10,000 (including Peter Childs), *The Introduction
    of Knob Lick Upper 10,000* (Mercury SR 60780)
Jim Kweskin and the Jug Band, *Jim Kweskin and the Jug Band*
    (Vanguard VSD 2158)
Lilly Brothers and Don Stover, *Lilly Brothers and Don Stover*
    (Folkways FA 2433)
Sylvia Mars, *Blues Walk Right In* (Folk Lyric FL 124)
Tom Rush, *Tom Rush Live at the Unicorn* (Lycornu SA 70)
Jackie Washington, *Jackie Washington* (Vanguard VRS 9110)
Various artists (Washington, von Schmidt, Cahn, etc.), *Come for to
    Sing* (Pathways of Sound POS1033)
Various artists, *Hootenanny,* 1962 Philadelphia Folk Festival live
    (Prestige/Folklore FL 14020)

1963
Joan Baez, *Joan Baez in Concert, Part 2* (Vanguard VSD 2123)
Paul Clayton, *Whaling Songs and Ballads* (Stinson SLP 69)
Dick Fariña and Eric von Schmidt, *Dick Fariña and Eric von Schmidt*
    (Folklore/UK F-LEUT/7)
Keith & Rooney, *Livin' on the Mountain* (Prestige/Folklore FL 14002)
Knob Lick Upper 10,000 (including Peter Childs), *Workout!!!*
    (Mercury MG 20852)
Margaret MacArthur, *Folksongs of Vermont* (Folkways FH 5314)
Geoff Muldaur, *Sleepy Man Blues* (Prestige/Folklore FL 14004)
Tom Rush, *Got a Mind to Ramble* (Prestige/Folklore PL 14003)
Mark Spoelstra, *Live at the Club 47* (Folkways FG 3572)
Dayle Stanley, *Child of Hollow Times* (Squire SSQ 33002)
Eric von Schmidt, *Folk Blues of Eric von Schmidt* (Prestige/Folklore
    FL 14005)
Jackie Washington, *Jackie Washington 2* (Vanguard VRS 9141)

1964
Joan Baez, *Joan Baez 5* (Vanguard VRS 9160)
Charles River Valley Boys and Tex Logan, *Bluegrass Get Together*
    (Prestige/Folklore FL 14024)
Bonnie Dobson, *For the Love of Him* (Mercury MG 20987)
Holy Modal Rounders, *Holy Modal Rounders* (Prestige/Folklore PR
    7720)
The Golden Ring, *The Golden Ring* (Folk Legacy FSI 16)
Mitch Greenhill, *Pickin' the City Blues* (Prestige/Folklore FL 12046)
The Lilly Brothers, *Bluegrass Breakdown* (Prestige/Folklore FL 14010)

The Lilly Brothers, *The Country Songs* (Prestige/Folklore FL 14035)
Old Sturbridge Singers, *New England Harmony* (Folkways FA 2377)
Tom Rush, *Blues, Songs, and Ballads* (Prestige/Folklore PR 7374)
Buffy Sainte-Marie, *It's My Way* (Vanguard VRS 9142)
Dayle Stanley, *After the Snow* (Squire SQ 33006)
Various artists (Mississippi John Hurt, Van Ronk, etc.), *Blues at Newport* (Vanguard VS-79145
Various artists (Muldaur, von Schmidt, etc.), *The Blues Project* (Elektra EKL 264)
Various artists (New Lost City Ramblers, Tex Logan, etc.), *Country Music and Bluegrass at Newport* (Vanguard VSD-79146)
Various artists (Lisa Kindred, Bob Jones, etc.), *New Folks 2* (Vanguard VRS 9140)
Various artists (Baez, Ochs, Seeger, etc.), *Newport Broadside* (Vanguard VSD-79144)
Various artists, *Newport Festival 1963: Evening Concerts, Vols. 1 and 2* (Vanguard VRS 9148 and 9149)
Various artists (including Bob Siggins), *Old Time Banjo Project* (Elektra EKS 7276)
Various artists (Doc Watson, Tom Ashley, Maybelle Carter, etc.), *Old Time Music at Newport* (Vanguard VSD-79147)
Eric von Schmidt, *Eric Sings von Schmidt* (Prestige PR 7384)

1965
Joan Baez, *Farewell, Angelina* (Vanguard VSD 79200)
Gordon Bok, *Gordon Bok* (Verve/Folkways FT 3016)
Paul Clayton, *Folksinger!* (Monument MLP 8017)
Dick Curless, *Tombstone Every Mile* (Tower T5005)
Mimi and Richard Fariña, *Celebrations for a Grey Day* (Vanguard VRS 9174)
Mimi and Richard Fariña, *Reflections in a Crystal Wind* (Vanguard VSD 79204)
Jim Kweskin, *Relax Your Mind* (Vanguard VRS 9188)
Jim Kweskin and the Jug Band, *Jug Band Music* (Vanguard VRS 9163)
Mother Bay State Entertainers, *Mother Bay State Entertainers* (Riverboat RB-2)
Tom Rush, *Tom Rush* (Elektra EKL 288)
Buffy Sainte-Marie, *Many a Mile* (Vanguard VRS 9171)
Jackie Washington, *Jackie Washington at Club 47* (Vanguard VSD 79172)

Various artists, *Newport Festival 1964: Evening Concerts, Vols. 1 and 2*
     (Vanguard VRS-9184 and 9185)
Various artists (Richard Fariña, etc.), *Singer Songwriter Project*
     (Elektra EKL 299)
Various artists (Bob Siggins, Clay Jackson, Mother Bay State, etc.),
     String Band Project (Elektra EKS 7292)

1966

Joan Baez, *Noel* (Vanguard VSD 79230)
Charles River Valley Boys, *Beatle Country* (Elektra EKL 4086)
Jim Kweskin and the Jug Band, *See Reverse Side* (Vanguard VRS
     9234)
Tom Rush, *Take a Little Walk with Me* (Elektra EKS 7308)
Buffy Sainte-Marie, *Little Wheel Spin and Spin* (Vanguard VRS 9211)
Various artists (performing at Newport 1965), *Festival!* (Vanguard
     VRS 9225)

1967

Joan Baez, *Joan* (Vanguard VSD 79240)
Mitch Greenhill (with Muldaur, Gutcheon, and Richmond), *Shepherd
     of the Highways* (Prestige PR 7438)
Jim Kweskin, *Jump for Joy* (Vanguard VRS 9243)
Jim Kweskin and the Jug Band, *Garden of Joy* (Reprise RS 6266)
Buffy Sainte-Marie, *Fire & Fleet & Candlelight* (Vanguard VRS 9250)
Various artists (including Canterbury Country Dance Orchestra),
     Fox Hollow Folk Festival, 1967, Archive of Folk Culture,
     American Folklife Center, Library of Congress, Washington,
     D.C., AFC 1974/020)
Jackie Washington, *Morning Song* (Vanguard VRS 9254)

1968

Joan Baez, *Any Day Now* (Vanguard VSD 79306)
Joan Baez, *Baptism* (Vanguard VSD 79275)
Mimi and Richard Fariña, *Memories* (Vanguard VSD 79263)
Jim Kweskin and His Friends (Fritz Richmond and Maria Muldaur),
     Whatever Happened to Those Good Old Days at the 47
     (Vanguard VSD 79278)
Leonda, *Woman in the Sun* (Epic BN 26383)
Taj Mahal, *The Natch'l Blues* (Columbia CS 9698)
Taj Mahal, *Taj Mahal* (Columbia CS 9579)

Joni Mitchell, *Joni Mitchell Live at Club 47* (bootleg)
Geoff and Maria Muldaur, *Pottery Pie* (Reprise RS 6350)
Tom Rush, *The Circle Game* (Elektra EKS 74018)
Buffy Sainte-Marie, *I'm Gonna Be a Country Girl Again* (Vanguard
 VRS 9280)

APPENDIX THREE

A Sampler of Songs from the Folk Revival

(Some personal favorites in roughly chronological order, opening and closing with the cuts that Jefferson Kaye used every week on his WBZ show as he read the coffeehouse schedules from the latest issue of *Broadside*.)

1. Little Brown Dog—Dick Rosmini
2. The Trees They Do Grow High—Debbie Green
3. Who's Gonna Buy You Ribbons (When I'm Gone)—Paul Clayton
4. Ten Thousand Miles—Joan Baez
5. Buddy Bolden's Blues—Rolf Cahn
6. Shule Aroon—Bonnie Dobson
7. Bob Dylan's Dream—Bob Dylan
8. Blues Walk Right In—Sylvia Mars
9. From Boston Harbor—Joe Hickerson with Jeff and Gerret Warner and Tony Saletan
10. DeKalb Blues—Eric von Schmidt
11. Black and Blue—Jackie Washington
12. One Morning in May—Keith & Rooney
13. I Wonder How the Old Folks Are at Home—Lilly Brothers and Don Stover
14. Rolling Home to Old New England—The Golden Ring
15. Petronella—Canterbury Country Dance Orchestra
16. Northfield—The Good Old Plough
17. McPherson's Lament—Ed Freeman
18. I Wish I Had Stayed in the Wagon Yard—Mother Bay State Entertainers
19. Make Me a Pallet on Your Floor—Tom Rush
20. Nobody Knows That I Have a Name—Dayle Stanley
21. It Isn't Nice—Barbara Dane and the Chambers Brothers
22. One Man's Hands—Jackie Washington (Newport)

23. Won't You Come Home, Bill Bailey?—Jackie Washington and Mitch Greenhill (Newport)
24. Colby's Medley—Peter Colby
25. I Can't Help but Wonder Where I'm Bound—Tom Paxton
26. C. C. Rider—Mississippi John Hurt (Newport)
27. Wanderin'—Dave Van Ronk
28. Downtown Blues—Geoff Muldaur (from Elektra, *The Blues Project*)
29. Sadie Green, the Vamp of New Orleans—Jim Kweskin and the Jug Band
30. Greenland Whale Fisheries—Judy Collins and Theodore Bikel (Newport)
31. Devil's Dream—Bill Monroe and His Bluegrass Boys (Newport)
32. Joshua Gone Barbados—Tom Rush
33. The Falcon—Richard and Mimi Fariña
34. The Power and the Glory—Phil Ochs
35. Now That the Buffalo's Gone—Buffy Sainte-Marie
36. Broom of the Cowdenknows—Jean Redpath
37. House of the Rising Son—Doc and Merle Watson
38. Whiskey in the Jar—Peter Childs
39. Love's Made a Fool of You—Tom Rush
40. I've Just Seen a Face—Charles River Valley Boys
41. Doc Geiger—Jesse Colin Young
42. Pack Up Your Sorrows—Richard and Mimi Fariña
43. A Swallow Song—Kathy & Carol
44. Someday Soon—Ian & Sylvia
45. When I'm Gone—Phil Ochs
46. Both Sides Now—Joni Mitchell (Club 47)
47. The Urge for Going—Tom Rush
48. Somebody's Gonna Ask Me Who I Was—Leonda
49. I Shall Be Released—Bob Dylan and the Band (the Basement Tapes)
50. Mole's Moan—Tom Rush

APPENDIX FOUR

Contra Dance at Newport, 1965

"In the fall of 1964, Joe Ryan, Dave Fuller, Jack Sloanaker, and myself provided music for dancing and intermission entertainment during the Vermont Old Time Fiddlers' Contest at Goddard College. As we were getting ready to leave on Sunday night, a chap who introduced himself as Ralph Rinzler said he was a 'scout' for the Newport Folk Festival, and he would like to arrange for the four of us to come to Newport the following summer to conduct workshops on New England dance music. The ensuing months saw a lot of phone conversations and letters back and forth between Ralph and me. I tried to tell him that we should bring along Newt Tolman, our flute player from Nelson. Ralph had never heard of a flute being used with fiddles. In fact, he had a hard time believing that there was any traditional music at all in New England. (He may have been of the school that thought the only traditional music came from North Carolina and Kentucky.)

"Somehow he agreed to have Newt come along. Then he discovered that there actually was dancing done to the music and we eventually arranged to have twelve dancers and ten musicians (some ringers) with a large budget make the trip to Newport. We were billed as the New England Contra Dancers. What a time. They wined and dined us, putting us up in some of the estates. We did a workshop on Saturday afternoon. This was in 1965, the year Bob Dylan shocked everyone by going electric. He was doing a mini concert in the space just above our workshop, and it finished up before we were done. Throngs of groupies chased Dylan down the hill right by our stand, and many of them sort of syphoned off into our dance session. Contra dances fell off the program and the whole thing turned into a rip-roaring old-time square dance.

"That evening we opened the concert. Loring Puffer nearly threw up when we mounted the stage and faced sixteen thousand people. I asked Harvey Tolman to play a little of 'Money Musk' as a strathspey before we danced it as a reel. He borrowed Jack O'Connor's fiddle, found it not tuned to his liking, and said 'Shit' over the microphone. But we got going, and what fun we had on that stage to that great music. When we exited after thunderous ovation, we were greeted by Pete Seeger and Theo Bikel, who both said we sounded like a Handel concerto. Took a long time to come down from all that heady experience."

Introduction to the evening concert by Norman Kennedy. Tunes included "Sherbrooke Slide," "Petronella," "Ross's Reel," and "Money Musk."

Musicians: Dudley Laufman, Walter Loeb, Sylvia Miskoe, Nicholas Howe, Gus Ellicot, Dave Fuller, Jack O'Connor, Joseph Ryan, Jack Sloanaker, Newton F. Tolman, and Ellen Vaughan.

Dancers: Cynthia Laufman, Betty and Arthur Williams, Deborah and Loring Puffer, Hallie and Bob Robinson, Pam and Ethan Tolman, and Mr. and Mrs. Harvey Tolman.

Written account by Dudley Laufman. Used by permission.

SUGGESTIONS FOR FURTHER READING AND LISTENING

RESOURCES FOR THE SEVENTEENTH AND EIGHTEENTH CENTURIES
Those who want to gain a practical sense of what happened in the earliest days of European exploration and settlement can consult Charles E. Clark's *The Eastern Frontier* (New York: Knopf, 1970), a thorough and readable exploration of tidewater northern New England in early colonial times. Charles Knowles Bolton's *The Real Founders of New England* (Boston: F. W. Faxon, 1929) is an earlier companion piece. One of the most memorable books about this or any other period is *The Unredeemed Captive* (New York: Alfred Knopf, 1994) by John Demos, a powerful exploration of tragedy and hope in the frontier town of Deerfield, Massachusetts. Jared Ross Hardesty's *Black Lives, Native Lands, White Worlds* (Amherst, MA: Bright Leaf Press, 2019) breaks new ground in the chronicles of slavery in New England. Samuel Eliot Morison, who was the last Harvard faculty member to arrive on campus on horseback, created a masterpiece with his book *The Maritime History of Massachusetts* (Boston: Houghton Mifflin, 1921), as good a picture of Yankee enterprise as has ever been set to paper. *Paul Revere and the World He Lived In* (Boston: Houghton Mifflin, 1942) won Esther Forbes a well-deserved Pulitzer Prize during World War II; it is a broad and rich picture of the years before, during, and after the Revolution. Richard Ketchum's *Saratoga* (Norwalk, CT: Easton Press, 1997) tells the story of the war's climax in the North.

David R. Proper wrote a biography of America's first published African American songwriter, "Lucy Terry Prince: Singer of History," in *Contributions in Black Studies* 9 (1992): 187–214. Alan Clark Buechner's *Yankee Singing Schools and the Golden Age of Choral Music in New England, 1760–1800* (Boston: Dublin Seminar, 2003) is a thorough exploration of the age of the New England fuguing tunes, some of the most beautiful music of our history. Barbara Lambert edited two stunningly comprehensive volumes of *Music in Colonial Massachusetts, 1630–1820* (Boston: Colonial Society of Massachusetts, 1973 and 1985). Stephen

Mallory wrote a charming essay titled "The Folk Violin in New England, 1750–1850" in *New England Music: The Public Sphere*, Proceedings of the Dublin Seminar for New England Folklife 1996, ed. Peter Benes (Boston: Boston University, 1998). *Music in New Hampshire, 1623–1800* (New York: Columbia University Press, 1960) is Louis Pichierri's comprehensive look at the life and times of early American music.

Among my favorite recordings of the period, the absolute finest is *A Land of Pure Delight,* by Paul Hillier and His Majesties Clerkes, a brilliant collection of William Billings's works released on the Harmonia Mundi label (HCX 3957048). The Oregon State University Choir compiled a wonderful group of compositions by other early regional composers in *Make A Joyful Noise* on New World Records (80255–2). Available on Smithsonian Folkways (FA 2377) is the Old Sturbridge Singers' *New England Harmony,* the groundbreaking first modern recordings of the fuguing-tune era. *Kathy & Carol* (Elektra EKS7289, rereleased as Collector's Choice B00020QWRS) contains a mixture of old English and Carter Family tunes set in beatific harmony. In Appendix 2 of this book, recordings by Joan Baez, Paul Clayton, Bonnie Dobson, and Dayle Stanley include fine renditions of a number of the early Child ballads.

RESOURCES FOR THE NINETEENTH CENTURY
Jeremy Belknap's description of the New England village can be found in his *History of New Hampshire* (Philadelphia: Robert Aiken, 1784–92). The works of Eric Sloane, including *Seasons of America Past* (New York: Funk and Wagnalls, 1958), serve well as illustrated introductions to New England country life. *A Long Deep Furrow: Three Centuries of Farming in New England* (Hanover, NH: University Press of New England, 1976) is Howard Russell's comprehensive history of this topic. *Taylor's Guide to Heirloom Vegetables,* by Benjamin Watson (Boston: Houghton Mifflin, 1996), is a practical encyclopedia of early garden lore. Henry C. Kittredge's *Mooncussers of Cape Cod* (Boston: Houghton Mifflin, 1937) is an engaging chronicle of human nature on display in the realm between high and low tide. Washington Irving's "The Legend of Sleepy Hollow" (in *The Sketch Book*, Philadelphia: Franklin Library, 1993) is a masterful picture of village life, if you can afford the caloric intake. *Tall Trees, Tough Men* (New York: Norton, 1963), Robert Pike's saga of logging in New England, makes good reading by the fireplace on a January night. *The Flowering of New England* by Van Wyck Brooks

(New York: E. P. Dutton, 1936) is a fine account of the period's literature and won the author a Pulitzer Prize in 1937. David W. Blight's *Frederick Douglass* (New York: Simon and Schuster, 2018) is a new biography of one of the defining figures of the nineteenth century. *Old Home Day Addresses* (Concord: Rumford Press, 1900) by Frank Rollins is an inspired and prophetic set of celebratory and cautionary essays, written on the cusp of the twentieth century, by a state governor who had a remarkable appreciation of the value of traditional folk culture.

At the junction of music and literature, we begin with *The Country Dance Book* (New York: A. S. Barnes, 1937), written by Ralph Page and Beth Tolman, about the roots, branches, and culture of New England contra dance. George Jackson Pullen's *Spiritual Folk Songs of Early America* (New York: J. J. Augustin, 1939) connects Northern and Southern traditions, and Peter Benes's *New England Music: The Public Sphere, Proceedings of the 1996 Dublin Seminar for New England Folklife* (Boston: Boston University Press, 1998), covers the tradition of town "bands of music." *Doo-dah! Stephen Foster and the Rise of American Popular Culture* (New York: Simon and Schuster, 1997) is Ken Emerson's tour de force through the foundations of many of our musical traditions and assumptions. *Singing for Freedom: The Hutchinson Family Singers* (New Haven, CT: Yale Press, 2007) by Scott Gac is a recent examination of the historic impact of these important New Hampshire singers. W. E. B. Du Bois's *The Souls of Black Folk* (Grand Rapids, MI: The Candace Press, 1996) uncovered, as it still does, hidden dynamics that shed light on our family story.

Recorded resources for the period include the following works of the Canterbury Country Dance Orchestra: its eponymous first album (Farm and Wilderness Records, F-72-FW3, 1972), *Mistwold* (Farm and Wilderness Records, F74-FW-5, 1974), *Belle of the Contradance* (no recording company, 1986; rereleased by Dudley Laufman, CCDO#3, 2017), *Welcome Here Again* (no recording company, 2016), and the unreleased *Live at the Coffin Factory*, all of which reside at the Folk New England Archive at the University of Massachusetts Amherst. The New Hampshire singing group The Good Old Plough performs a heartfelt collection of hill-farm songs from the period 1790–1890 at various venues in New England. *Beautiful Dreamer* (American Roots, 591594-2, 2004) is a compilation of Stephen Foster songs performed by, among others, Mavis Staples and the late John Prine.

RESOURCES FOR THE TWENTIETH CENTURY

Major reference works include Robert M. W. Dixon and John Godrich's *Blues and Gospel Records, 1902–1943* (Essex, UK: Storyville Publications, 1982) and Tony Russell's *Country Music Records, 1921–1942* (New York: Oxford University Press, 2004). *They All Played Ragtime* (New York: Oak Publications, 1971) is Rudi Blesh and Harriet Janis's tribute to an age, a music, and a way of life. Paul Oliver picks up the saga in *The Story of the Blues* (Philadelphia: Chilton, 1969), and Samuel Charters carries it on in *The Bluesmakers* (New York: Da Capo, 1977). Barry Mazor's *Ralph Peer and the Making of Popular Roots Music* (Chicago: Chicago Review Press, 2015) establishes the role of commercial artist-and-repertoire men as key rural-music collectors in the 1920s and '30s. *Where Dead Voices Gather* (Boston: Little, Brown, 2001) is Nick Tosches's shoebox of cultural snapshots and news clippings from the tired twilight of black-face performance. Neil Rosenberg chronicles the roots and branches of Bill Monroe's "hillbilly music for the jet age" in *Bluegrass: A History* (Urbana: University of Illinois Press, 1993), a story that Clifford Murphy brings to the Deep North of New England in his work *Yankee Twang* (Urbana: University of Illinois, 2014). Peter Guralnick's *Sam Phillips, The Man Who Invented Rock 'n' Roll* (Boston: Little, Brown, 2014) makes good sense and true of what happened next, as do all his books. Jim Rooney and Eric von Schmidt take it from there in *Baby, Let Me Follow You Down* (Amherst: University of Massachusetts Press, 1979); Jim Rooney's *Bossmen* is an indispensable testament to the lives and art of Muddy Waters and Bill Monroe.

Appendix 1 lists many folk records that originated in New England during the Boston-Cambridge Folk Revival. A personal discography that stretches beyond the region would include works by the Band; Kenny Baker; the Blue Sky Boys; Solomon Burke; Gus Cannon; Hoagy Carmichael; Johnny Cash; the Chambers Brothers; the Clancy Brothers and Tommy Makem; Sam Cooke; Reverend Gary Davis; Bob Dylan; the Everly Brothers; Eddie Floyd; Jesse Fuller; Merle Haggard; Ramblin' Jack Elliott; John Fahey; Lester Flatt and Earl Scruggs; Aretha Franklin; Don Gibson; Emmylou Harris; Mississippi John Hurt; Muddy Waters; Ian & Sylvia; Kathy & Carol; Koerner, Ray, & Glover; the Memphis Jug Band; Memphis Minnie; Bill Monroe and (all) His Bluegrass Boys; Tracy Nelson; Phil Ochs; the Osborne Brothers; Carl Perkins; John Prine; Jean Redpath; Dick Rosmini; Sam & Dave; Pete Seeger; the Sons of the Pioneers; the Staples Singers; Frank Stokes; Bessie Smith; Sister

Rosetta Tharpe; Dave Van Ronk; Don Williams; Hank Williams; Bob Wills; and Jesse Colin Young, as well as a number of releases by County Sales of Floyd, Virginia.

Later recordings of personal note, particularly from the still-thriving "Roots and Americana" period, include the work of the Carolina Chocolate Drops, Shuney Crampsey, Jim Kweskin, David Mallett, Geoff Muldaur, Willie Nelson, the indomitable Old Crow Medicine Show, John Prine, Leon Redbone, Jim Rooney, Tom Rush, and the incredible rereleases put out by Old Hat Records of Raleigh, North Carolina.

FOLK NEW ENGLAND ARCHIVAL MATERIALS

During her years at Club 47, Betsy Siggins began collecting reel-to-reel tapes, photographs, sheet music, and ephemera associated with the renaissance in traditional music that sprang up on the banks of the Charles River during the early 1960s. In 2007, Betsy formally founded Folk New England, an organization whose mission was to preserve and to expand on her collections, including material that, over the years, she and others had donated to the Cambridge Historical Society. A small and intrepid group of volunteers led by Brian Quinn assisted her in the work, and in 2014 the combined collections of Folk New England were formally transferred to the Special Collections at the W. E. B. Du Bois Library at the University of Massachusetts Amherst. There, director Rob Cox and his archivist Aaron Rubinstein have supervised preserving and making accessible boxes of material brought to Amherst from throughout the region and across the continent. A large-scale project to digitize significant portions of the collection began with David Wilson's generous donation of the rights to *Broadside* magazine, which are now available online. Major gifts of material have been given by Jim Rooney, Bill Nowlin, Dayle Stanley, Peter Childs, Bob Siggins, Ethan Signer, Jim Kweskin, the late Mel Lyman, Tom Rush, Kari Estrin, and the families of Bill Keith, Eric von Schmidt, Byron Linardos, and Fritz Richmond. Additional, vital support has been provided by Mavis Staples, Judy Collins, Caitlin von Schmidt, Ed Freeman, and Geoff Muldaur. Before his passing in 2020, Rob Cox was a welcoming and an enthusiastic advocate for the collection, and he is sorely missed.

Scholars and other interested persons are encouraged to access the collections online at both the University of Massachusetts Special Collections and the Folk New England websites. As Tom Rush has written in support of the effort, "Music is all about connections—connecting the musician with the listener, connecting the listener with wisps of memory, flickerings of emotion. . . . Folk New England is a vital part of making that connection for new generations of voices, of making available to them the building blocks from the past that they can use to fashion their own vision, make their own connections with new audiences—connecting the past to the present, and to the future" (Tom Rush, "Our Mission and Collection Goals," Folk New England website, www.folknewengland.org).

THE REDEEMING ROLE OF NEW ENGLAND CULTURE

Much of the author's inspiration has been nurtured by a treasured body of work that keeps alive the faith in and hopes we have for New England culture. Henry Thoreau's *Walden* (1854) leads the pack here. Sarah Orne Jewett's *The Country of the Pointed Firs and Other Stories* (Boston: Houghton Mifflin, 1925) is an indispensable anchor to cultural windward. Robert Frost's iconic work is collected in *The Poetry of Robert Frost* (New York: Holt, Rinehart, and Winston, 1969). His friend Cornelius Weygandt's books on the old ways are also well worth reading, among them *November Rowan* (New York: Appleton Century, 1941). *The American Tradition* (New York: F. S. Crofts, 1941), edited by Louis B. Wright and H. T. Swedenborg, is an indispensable anthology. Ruth Moore's *Spoonhandle* (New York: William Morrow, 1946) is as visceral a picture of the assault of the twentieth century on New England culture as you'll find; there's one hell of a good story about a halibut in there, too. My late neighbor, Don Hall, wrote the wonderful *Seasons on Eagle Pond* (New York: Ticknor and Fields, 1987). Kathy Neustadt's *Clambake* (Amherst: University of Massachusetts Press, 1992) changed my life and could change yours. *The Thing Itself* (New York: Riverhead Books, 2008) is Richard Todd's thoughtful testimony to identity and place. Finally, with my most heartfelt recommendation, I give you Archibald MacLeish's play *Scratch* (Boston: Houghton Mifflin, 1971), the work he invited Bob Dylan to score in 1968.

I'll leave the last word here to music, with a chorus sung by Mississippi John Hurt from the Club 47 stage as nighttime fell over the city of Cambridge on May 15, 1966:

> Hold to His hand, to God's unchanging hand,
> Hold to His hand, to God's unchanging hand,
> Build your hopes on things eternal,
> Hold to God's unchanging hand.

NOTES

CHAPTER ONE: TO MAKE A BETTER WORLD

1. References here to traditional New England celebrations are from Kathy Neustadt's *Clambake: A History and Celebration of an American Tradition* (Amherst: University of Massachusetts Press, 1992), a deep examination of folkways in the Allen's Neck Quaker community of Dartmouth, Massachusetts.

CHAPTER TWO: WHEN FIRST UNTO THIS COUNTRY

1. Barry Lopez, *Horizon* (New York: Alfred A. Knopf, 2019), 343.
2. Charles Knowles Bolton, *The Real Founders of New England* (Boston: F. W. Faxon, 1929), 8.
3. Bolton, *Real Founders*, 21.
4. Rowland Parker, *The Common Stream* (New York: Holt, Rhinehart, and Winston, 1975), is a remarkable two-thousand-year account of the life of an English village.
5. As quoted in Louis Pichierri's *Music in New Hampshire, 1623–1800* (New York: Columbia University Press, 1960), 18, the original source being John Josselyn's *Two Voyages in New England* (in 1638 and 1663). The popular fiddler was named Scozway.
6. Charles E. Clark, *The Eastern Frontier: The Settlement of Northern New England, 1610–1763* (New York: Knopf, 1970), 22.
7. Everett S. Stackpole, *Old Kittery and her Families* (Lewiston, ME: Lewiston Journal, 1903).
8. Henry Howe, *Salt Rivers of the Massachusetts Shore* (New York: Rhinehart, 1951), 112.
9. Aaron S. Fogelman, "Slaves, Convicts, and Servants to Free Passengers: The Transformation of Immigration in the American Revolution," *Journal of American History* 85 (June 1998): 43–76.
10. Jared Ross Hardesty, *Black Lives, Native Lands, White Worlds* (Amherst, MA: Bright Leaf Press, 2019), 6.
11. David R. Proper, "Lucy Terry Prince: Singer of History," *Contributions in Black Studies* 9 (1992): article 15.
12. This is the author's speculative scenario but one that might explain the earliest presence of free Africans in New England seaport towns.
13. Shane White, "Pinkster: Afro-Dutch Syncretization in New York City and the Hudson Valley," *Journal of American Folklore* 102 (January–March 1989): 68–75.

14. Mark Sammons and Valerie Cunningham, *Black Portsmouth* (Durham: University of New Hampshire Press, 2004), 88–89.

15. Carleton Sprague Smith, "Broadsides and Their Music in Colonial America," *Music in Colonial Massachusetts, 1630–1820*, ed. Barbara Lambert (Boston: Colonial Society of Massachusetts, 1985), 1:157–367.

16. As sung by Ed Freeman at the Turk's Head Coffeehouse, 71½ Charles Street, Boston, in 1964.

17. "O, Come, Come Away" can be heard on Boston Camerata's *The American Vocalist: Spirituals and Folk Hymns, 1850–1870* (Erato CD 2292-45818-2, 1993).

18. Alan Clark Buechner, *Yankee Singing Schools and the Golden Age of Choral Music in New England, 1760–1800* (Boston: Dublin Seminar, 2003), 112 and throughout.

19. William Billings, *The Complete Works of William Billings* (Boston: The Colonial Society of Massachusetts, 1990), 4:29n42.

20. Robert J. Lurtsema, "On the Scene," *Broadside* 5, no. 6 (May 11, 1966): 8.

21. David P. McKay and Richard Crawford, *William Billings of Boston* (Princeton, NJ: Princeton University Press, 1975), 63–64.

22. Louis Albert Banks, *Immortal Songs of Camp and Field* (New York: Burrows, 1898), 42–43.

23. Pete Seeger, "The Riflemen of Bennington," *American Favorite Ballads*, vol. 5 (Folkways Records SFW 40154), band 27.

24. J. Philip McCarthy, "A Forgotten Naval Hero," *New England Magazine* 53 (October 1915): 264.

25. Stephen C. Mallory, "The Folk Violin in New England, 1750–1850," *New England Music, The Public Sphere, 1600–1900* (Proceedings of the Dublin Seminar for New England Folklife 1996), ed. Peter Benes (Boston: Boston University, 1998), 176–87.

26. Beth Tolman and Ralph Page, *The Country Dance Book* (New York: A. S. Barnes, 1937), 13. "Old Medford" refers to rum.

27. Henry David Thoreau, *Elevating Ourselves: Thoreau on Mountains*, ed. J. Parker Huber (Boston: Houghton, Mifflin, 1999), 71.

28. In *A Long Deep Furrow: Three Centuries of Farming in New England* (Hanover, NH: University Press of New England, 1976), 116, Howard Russell lists the cargo of mid–Connecticut River Valley products that set sail in the sloop *Fox* from New London bound for Saint Thomas in 1759: "10 bbls. [barrels] Pork; 8 bbls. Beef, 14 bbls. Fish; 14 casks Bread, 800 Staves [barrel staves]; 6500 ropes Onions, 55 Cheeses, 16 kegs Briskets, 50 bu. [bushels] Potatoes, 10 boxes Sope, 50 Shoats [piglets], 32 Gees, 7 Duz ½ of Fowls, 1 Duz Ducks, 47 Turkeys, 13 bbls. Apples."

29. Samuel Elliott Morison, *The Maritime History of Massachusetts* (Boston: Houghton Mifflin, 1941), 103.

30. For a long, but delightful, discussion of the different terms, see Joanna Colcord, *Songs of American Sailormen* (New York: W. W. Norton, 1938), 32–35.

31. "Boston Harbor," *Songs and Sounds of the Sea* (National Geographic Society:

NGC # 705, 1973), band #A3, as sung by Joe Hickerson with Jeff Warner, Gerret Warner, and Tony Saletan.

32. For Lincoln Colcord's stirring description of a clipper ship's return to its homeport of Boston, see the appendix in the post-1940 printings of Morison's *Maritime History*, 378–83.

33. Van Wyck Brooks, *The Flowering of New England* (New York: E. P. Dutton, 1936), 42.

CHAPTER THREE: THERE'S A GOOD TIME COMING

1. Van Wyck Brooks, *The Flowering of New England* (New York: E. P. Dutton, 1936), 41.

2. A fine essay on the connections between shape-note singing and modern folk music can be found in Sean Willentz's *Bob Dylan in America* (New York: Doubleday, 2010), 237–58.

3. George Pullen Jackson, *White and Negro Spirituals: Their Life Span and Kinship* (New York: J. J. Augustin, 1943), 69.

4. See Donald Towle, "New Hampshire, Birthplace of the Spiritual?," *Historical New Hampshire* 45, no. 4 (1990): 296–316; and also Joanna Brooks, "Six Hymns by Samson Occum," *Early American Literature* 38, no. 1 (2003): 67–87.

5. See Sandra Harbert Petrulionis, *To Set This World Right: The Antislavery Movement in Thoreau's Concord* (Ithaca, NY: Cornell University Press, 2014).

6. Parker was a Unitarian minister and reformer whose words would later be reflected in the speeches of Abraham Lincoln and Reverend Martin Luther King, Jr.

7. The Hutchinson Family, sheet music, "The Old Granite State" (New York: Firth and Hall, 1843).

8. William Lloyd Garrison, quoted in Scott Gac, *Singing for Freedom: The Hutchinson Family Singers* (New Haven, CT: Yale Press, 2007), 11.

9. From Frederick Douglass's introduction to John Walker Hutchinson's *The Story of the Hutchinson Family* (Boston: Lee and Shepherd, 1896), xvi–xvii.

10. Thomas Curren, *Old Home Day in New Hampshire* (Concord: Inherit New Hampshire, 1999).

11. Popular Grange song, "Stay on the Farm," written in 1891 by James L. Orr, in *Grange Melodies*, edited by Orr (Philadelphia: Geo. Ferguson, 1915), 120–21.

12. Frank Rollins, *Old Home Week Addresses* (Concord, NH: private printing, 1900), 52.

13. Francis James Child, *The English and Scottish Popular Ballads*, 5 vols. (Boston: Houghton, Mifflin, 1904).

14. Fannie Hardy Eckstorm, *The Minstrelsy of Maine* (Boston: Houghton, Mifflin, 1927).

15. Eloise Hubbard Linscott, *Folksongs of Old New England* (New York: Dover, 1993), 316 and viii.

16. Helen Hartness Flanders and George Brown, *Vermont Folk-Songs and Ballads* (Brattleboro, VT: Stephen Daye Press, 1932).

17. Thomas Curren, *A Bicentennial History of Bridgewater, New Hampshire* (Concord, NH: private printing, 1986). My neighbor, eighty-year-old logger Jim Burbank, spoke fondly of the good times he remembered having at barn dances in the 1920s up in the Gilpatric place on Hammond Hill Road.

CHAPTER FOUR: THE SOUND OF YOUNG AMERICA

1. Joanna C. Colcord, *Songs of American Sailormen* (New York: W. W. Norton, 1938), 169.
2. Ken Emerson, *Doo-Dah! Stephen Foster and the Rise of American Popular Culture* (New York: Simon and Schuster, 1997), 10, citing Archer Butler Hulbert's *Forty-Niners: The Chronicle of the California Trail* (Boston: Little, Brown, 1931), 260.
3. Emerson, *Doo-Dah!*, 21.
4. Mark Twain quoted in Emerson, *Doo-Dah!*, 91–92.
5. For detailed accounts of the great national tragedy in whose sequels we have been living for generations, see Shelby Foote's *The Civil War: A Narrative*, 3 vols. (New York: Random House, 1958, 1963, and 1974); Bruce Catton's *Army of the Potomac*, 3 vols. (New York: Doubleday & Company, 1951, 1952, and 1953), and Douglas Southall Freeman's *Lee's Lieutenants: A Study in Command* (New York: Scribner's, 1942).
6. Rudi Blesh and Harriet Janis, *They All Played Ragtime* (New York: Oak Publications, 1971).
7. Edward A. Berlin, *King of Ragtime* (London: Oxford University Press, 1994), 9.
8. Bean Blossom would later become the home of Bill Monroe's annual bluegrass festival.
9. According to his grandson Carl Hultberg, Rudi Blesh, the great jazz critic of the *San Francisco Chronicle* and the *New York Herald Tribune*, first heard ragtime around 1917 in a beer joint in Franklin, New Hampshire, while waiting for a train connection to Dartmouth College.
10. Paul Oliver, *The Story of the Blues* (Philadelphia: Chilton, 1969); and Samuel Charters, *The Bluesmakers* (New York: Da Capo, 1977).
11. Dennis McNally, *On Highway 61* (Berkeley: Counterpoint, 2014), 103–5. McNally lists several recorded instances of the "discovery" of the early blues in Mississippi around 1900. One of these was written by Harvard archaeologist Charles Peabody, who took note of the singing of Black employees he had hired to excavate Native American burial mounds near Clarksdale in 1901. An indelible image, that.
12. Bob Dylan on "Theme Time Radio Hour," as quoted in the liner note booklet for *Good for What Ails You: Music of the Medicine Shows, 1926–1937* (Old Hat Records, CD 1005, 2006): "If you want to hear some of the range of music that could be heard on medicine shows, there's a compilation called *Good for What Ails You*. I got nothing against downloads and MP3s, but getting this CD with all the pictures and liner notes, well, it's not as good as having it on the big 12" record, but at least there's a booklet there, and

believe it or not, folks, you can even read it in a power failure—as long as it's daytime."

CHAPTER FIVE: DOWN IN THE GROOVE

1. I am deeply indebted to the late Carl Hultberg for his dedication and persistence in discovering, restoring, and digitizing thousands of 78 rpm records and sharing them with me. Some of these he bought online or at yard sales, and others he retrieved at the last minute from dumpster oblivion at the Danbury, New Hampshire, dump. For the better part of a decade, Carl spent his time tinkering with various pieces of expensive sound equipment and producing CDs of superb quality that, in his curative hands, became anthologies of American music from the 1890s to the 1940s. Carl regularly made pronouncements about, say, the connection between Bert Williams and Hoagy Carmichael or between Dan Burley and the Beatles, and he would then back his theories up with the testimony of musical witnesses that ignored fashion, rejected fame, and transcended time. He was a promoter of the legacies of lost musicians. Like his grandfather, Rudi Blesh, Carl reveled in being behind his times; at his most optimistic, he could hope that he was ahead of them, as well.

2. Barry Mazor, *Ralph Peer and the Making of Popular Roots Music* (Chicago: Chicago Review Press, 2015).

3. Robert Dixon and John Godrich, *Blues and Gospel Records, 1902–1943* (Essex, UK: Storyville Publications, 1982); and Tony Russell, *Country Music Records, 1921–1942* (New York: Oxford University Press, 2004).

4. *Sing Out!* magazine issues from 1962 to 1968. From a distance, much of the leftist political use of folk music in the 1940s and '50s can seem both naive and misleading. The "solidarity" among academics, factory workers, "Negroes," and the rural white poor seems at times to have been fantasy or wishful thinking, based primarily on the ideologies of the times and the instincts, oratorical skills, and political success of Franklin D. Roosevelt, who did not play the banjo. But we might remember that, in a complacent society, the doctrinaire Left made the only organized response to what was going on in Germany prior to Pearl Harbor. They were at least paying attention, and if *Sing Out!* magazine's postwar allegiance to "people's movements" in places such as East Germany now seems forced and delusional, those tendencies were more than matched by the venality of the McCarthy era. All of which reinforces the view that, when it comes to art, politics sometimes giveth but eventually taketh away.

5. The documentary work of Holocaust archives such as Facing History and Ourselves enables the modern viewer to come to the realization that the same manipulative techniques that were crafted to single out and persecute the Jewish people have been used over the past eighty years to sell everything from fried chicken to computers. Goebbels's influence continues to this day; through the instantaneous and global use of the Internet, "the lies go marching on."

6. From Tracy Chapman's "Across the Lines," *Tracy Chapman*, recorded 1987–88, produced by David Kershenbaum, Electra 960774-1. In 2000, Tracy suggested to an NPR announcer that she may have decided to play the guitar after watching the country music show *Hee Haw* on television. As a Tufts student in the mid-1980s, she busked in the Harvard Square T Station and played at Passim on 47 Palmer Street in Cambridge.

7. Charles R. Townsend's *San Antonio Rose: The Life and Music of Bob Wills* (Urbana: University of Illinois Press, 1976) tells the story of the career of one of the most influential musicians of the twentieth century.

8. My boyhood journey into the realm of American history and music began with Fred Waring's patriotic box set *The Song of America* (Decca DL 8033), a copy of which I won at the age of seven in WBZ-TV's "What the Flag Means to Me" essay contest. Belafonte and the Kingston Trio came along right after that, and it was the Trio's 45 rpm version of "Where Have All the Flowers Gone?" that introduced me to Pete Seeger.

9. Dayle Stanley, interview by Baltimore radio station host, April 1963, digitized tape, Folk New England Archive, Special Collections of the University of Massachusetts Amherst.

10. The Kingston Trio's *The New Frontier* album was recorded in 1962 and released in November (produced by Voyle Gilmore, Capitol Records, T-1809). "The New Frontier" 45, on the flip side of "Green Back Dollar," which was a big hit, was released in January 1963 (Capitol Records: 4898).

CHAPTER SIX: ROLLING HOME TO OLD NEW ENGLAND

1. Dudley Laufman, Sylvia Miskoe, and Art Bryan, conversations with author, 2016–18. The Special Collections at the University of Massachusetts Amherst has an extensive collection of contra dance material in its Folk New England archive.

2. *Sing Out!* magazine issues from 1962 to 1965 include coverage of Seeger's contempt of Congress conviction and its eventual overturning by the courts.

3. David Wilson, conversation with author, 2016–20.

4. John Cohen, conversations with author, March 2018.

5. Betsy Siggins, conversations with author, 2016–20.

6. From a recorded interview with Sylvia Miskoe by Kathy Neustadt, January 17, 2017, for the New Hampshire State Arts Council / Traditional Arts Program (used by permission). Old Joe Clark's seems to have been the New England precursor of later, more celebrated artistic communes in Greenwich Village and San Francisco.

7. Jim Rooney and Eric von Schmidt, *Baby, Let Me Follow You Down* (Amherst: University of Massachusetts Press, 1979), the key resource for the Folk Revival.

8. Eric von Schmidt, *Who Knocked the Brains Out of the Sky?*, released 1969, unknown producer, Smash Records SRS 67124, with liner notes by Bob Dylan.

9. David Wilson, cover notes, *Broadside* 5, no. 10 (July 6, 1966): 1.

10. Peter Guralnick's *Sam Phillips, The Man Who Invented Rock n Roll* (Boston:

Little, Brown and Company, 2015) is a key source for the story of the birth of rock 'n' roll in and around Memphis. It is interesting to note that the *Charlotte* (North Carolina) *Observer's* issue of February 2, 1956, headlined an article on Elvis Presley with the title "Folk Singer Coming Here."

11. Rooney and von Schmidt, *Baby, Let Me,* 21, and Siggins conversations. The fast-paced events of the Boston-Cambridge Folk Revival overtook jazz and poetry in the early coffeehouse scene.

12. A digitization of this tape is in the Folk New England Archive at the Special Collections at the University of Massachusetts Amherst.

13. Siggins conversations; liner notes by the Charles River Valley Boys on their *Bringin' in the Georgia Mail.* Digitized tapes of the CRVB are in the Folk New England Archive at the Special Collections at the University of Massachusetts Amherst.

14. Rooney and von Schmidt, *Baby, Let Me,* 94.

15. Rooney and von Schmidt, *Baby, Let Me,* 96 and 99.

16. The digitization of a tape of Keith & Rooney is in the Folk New England Archive at the Special Collections at the University of Massachusetts Amherst.

17. Keith & Rooney, *Livin' on the Mountain,* released November 1963, produced by Paul A. Rothchild, Prestige/Folklore 14002.

18. Jack Landrón, conversations with author, 2016–17; digitized tapes of his performances are in the Folk New England Collection at the Special Collections at the University of Massachusetts Amherst.

19. Digitized tapes of Tom Rush in performance are in the Folk New England Archive at the Special Collections at the University of Massachusetts Amherst.

20. Richard Thompson, quoted in *The London Times:* "There are only three white blues singers, and Geoff Muldaur is at least two of them," from the Geoff Muldaur website.

21. Skippy White is a heroic figure in the history of Boston music; only he could have thought of his native city as "Bluestown," as he did when choosing a name for his homemade record label.

22. From liner notes to British Matchbox release *Bluesmaster Series* (MB 1201); and Wilson conversations. Skippy White's Mass Records was located at 2255 Washington Street; his motto: "Just hum it."

23. Dayle Stanley, conversations with author, 2017–20. Digitized tapes of Stanley's performances are in the Folk New England Archive at the Special Collections at the University of Massachusetts Amherst.

24. Bonnie Dobson, conversations with author, 2016.

25. John Cohen, conversation with author, March 2018.

CHAPTER SEVEN: TENTING TONIGHT ON THE BANKS OF THE CHARLES

1. Digitized tapes of Joan Baez's coffeehouse performances can be found in the Folk New England Collection at the Special Collections at the University of Massachusetts Amherst.

2. Interview with Joan Baez by Kurt Loder in *Rolling Stone,* no. 393, April 14, 1983, included in Sid Holt's *The Rolling Stone Interviews: The 1980s* (New York: St. Martin's Press, 1989), 89–90.

3. Jim Rooney and Eric von Schmidt, *Baby, Let Me Follow You Down* (Amherst: University of Massachusetts Press, 1979), 96–97.

4. Big Joe Turner, "Honey Hush," *Rock & Roll,* released 1957, unknown producer, Atlantic 8005. Others who have covered the song include Chuck Berry, Jerry Lee Lewis, George Jones, Paul McCartney, and Elvis Costello.

5. Digitized tapes of Fritz Richmond and others can be found in the Folk New England Archive at the Special Collections at the University of Massachusetts Amherst.

6. Jackie Washington (Jack Landrón), "Bill Bailey," *Evening Concerts at Newport 1963,* vol. 2, recorded July 1963, released 1964, no producer, Vanguard VRS 9149.

7. David Wilson, conversations with author, 2016–20.

8. Rick Sullo, conversations with author, 2017–20.

9. *Dick Fariña and Eric von Schmidt* (Folklore/UK F-LEUT/7); this record was largely an overlooked obscurity until people began collecting Bob Dylan minutiae in the late 1960s.

10. David Hajdu, *Positively Fourth Street* (New York: Farrar, Strauss, and Giroux), 87–88.

11. Betsy Siggins, Catherine Linardos, Felice Linardos, Jim Rooney, Tom Rush, and Geoff Muldaur, conversations with author, 2016–20.

12. Drawn from radio listings in *Broadside* magazine, vols. 2 and 3, 1963–64.

13. Catherine Linardos, Felice Silverman, and Betsy Siggins, conversations with author, 2016–20. The entire collection of Club 47 calendars was generously donated by the Linardos family to the Folk New England Archive at the Special Collections at the University of Massachusetts Amherst.

14. Author's memory of Orleans coffeehouse performances by Peter Childs; Peter Childs, interviews with author, 2016–17. Digitized tapes of his coffeehouse repertoire are in the Folk New England Archive at the Special Collections at the University of Massachusetts Amherst.

15. David Sloss, *Broadside* 3 (March 4, 1964): 6 and 17; conversation with author at WGBH, March 2016. *Folk Music USA* was the brainchild of WGBH veteran Fred Barzyk, who collaborated with David Wilson on the series, taping two sessions at the Museum of Science and the remainder at the WGBH studios. Since the artists were not paid, the musicians' union insisted that each tape be "wiped" after it aired.

16. Dayle Stanley, conversations with author, 2017–20.

17. Tom Rush, conversations with author, 2019.

CHAPTER EIGHT: THE LAY OF THE LAND

1. Eloise Hubbard Linscott, *Folk Songs of Old New England* (New York: Dover Publications, 1993), 154.

2. From Linscott's *Folk Songs:* "Barbara Allen," 163; "Colony Times," 213; and "Captain Kidd," 131.

3. Adapted from a story in Robert Pike's *Tall Trees, Tough Men* (New York: Norton, 1963), 96–97.

4. Gordon Bok, "Fifteen Ships on George's Bank," *Bay of Fundy* (Folk Legacy Records FSI-54, 1975), band 5. The old tune commemorated the loss that Gloucester suffered on February 24, 1862.

5. Paul Clayton's records included *Whaling and Sailing Songs* (Tradition TLP 1005, 1956) and *Foc'sle Songs and Shanties* (Folkways FA 2429, 1959), with a group called the Foc'sle Singers, which included an old tar named Dave Van Ronk.

6. Author's memories of radio shows and *Broadside* calendars.

7. Malcolm X and Alex Haley, *The Autobiography of Malcolm X* (1965; repr., New York: Ballantine Books, 1973), 41.

8. Christopher Gavin, "Skippy White Has Been Selling Records in Boston for Nearly Six Decades. But It's Time to Close Up Shop, He Says," *Boston Globe*, December 19, 2019, https://www.boston.com/news/local-news/2019/12/19/skippy-whites-records-closing.

9. Hank Bordowitz, "Saving Ray Charles," *Super Lawyers Magazine*, November 2005, https://www.superlawyers.com/massachusetts/article/saving-ray-charles/fe67801d-057d-4b2a-8f71-eb083e313f91.html; and Mike Evans, *Ray Charles: Birth of Soul* (New York: Omnibus Press, 2005).

10. Clifford Murphy, *Yankee Twang* (Urbana: University of Illinois, 2014).

11. As an example of this genre, Duke and the Swingbillies were led by Michael J. Pellilo of Graniteville, Vermont, whose parents were Italian immigrants. "Duke" played guitar, accompanied by an accordion player, two women singers, a fiddler, and a bass player. In the late 1940s, the group played in Kittery, Maine, and in Rye and Portsmouth, New Hampshire, and appeared on WHEB in Portsmouth, WLAW in Lawrence, and WMUR in Manchester.

12. For a moving account of this dynamic, see (or listen to) Lacy J. Dalton's recording of "Sixteenth Avenue." (*16th Avenue*, released 1982, produced by Billy Sherrill, Columbia FC 37975.

13. Allerton & Alton, *Black, White, and Bluegrass* (Bear Family BCD 16559, 2010).

14. See the DVD *The Eventful Life of Al Hawkes*, directed by Andrew Jawitz (Rockhouse Mountain Productions, 2010).

15. Dick Curless, *A Tombstone Every Mile*, originally recorded in 1965, was reissued by Sundazed Records in 2004 (SC 9001).

16. T. Holmes Moore, W. W. II *Kingfisher* pilot and headmaster of New Hampton School (New Hampton, New Hampshire), conversation with author, 1990.

17. *Evening Concerts at Newport 1963*, vol. 2 (Vanguard VRS 9149), band 4; and *Evening Concerts at Newport 1964*, vol. 1 (VRS-9184), band 15.

18. Carl Hultberg, from a note written to the author, 2016.

CHAPTER NINE: THE HOUR THAT THE SHIP COMES IN

1. In many instances, nothing much was revealed in national folk music criticism other than that the ego was even easier to play than the kazoo. There were relatively few critical gatekeepers along the Charles.

2. Quoted in Kurt Wolff and Orla Duane, *Country Music: The Rough Guide* (London: Rough Guides, 2000).

3. The first long-playing album by the Lilly Brothers (*Folk Songs from the Southern* Mountains, released in 1962, Folkways Records FA 2433) was produced by Mike Seeger, Pete's half brother.

4. In his introduction to "Baby Let Me Follow You Down" (*Bob Dylan*, recorded November 20, 1961, produced by John Hammond, Sr., Columbia Records CS8579), Dylan says, "I first heard this from Ric von Schmidt. He lives in Cambridge. Ric's a blues guitar player; I met him one day in the green pastures of Harvard University."

5. A digitized tape recording of a house party performance by Doc Watson is in the Folk New England Archive at the Special Collections at the University of Massachusetts Amherst.

6. For more, see "Almeda Riddle: Anglo-American Ballad Singer," *Masters of Traditional Arts: A Biographical Dictionary,* ed. Alan Grovenar (Santa Barbara, CA: ABC-Clio, 2001), 2:532–34.

7. Ed Freeman, conversation with author, 2016. Ed's portrait of John Hurt is among the greatest images of the Boston-Cambridge Folk Revival. His evocative folio "Fallon Place Portraits," of Hurt and a dozen other folk and blues artists, is available from his website (Ed Freeman Photography, "Portfolios: The Fallon Place Portraits," at www.edfreeman.com).

8. Among the civil rights benefit concerts held during the Boston-Cambridge Folk Revival were the March on Washington Benefit held at Harvard's Sander's Theatre in August 1963 (featuring Jack Landrón, the Silver Leaf Gospel Singers, Eric von Schmidt, Dayle Stanley, Mitch Greenhill, and Mark Spoelstra); the benefit in memory of Reverend James Reeb at the King's Rook in March 1965 (with Carl Watanabe, Dayle Stanley, Bill Staines, the Silver Leaf Gospel Singers, Debbie Green and Eric Anderson, Richard and Mimi Fariña, Jerry Corbitt, Lisa Kindred, John Updike, and Barry and the Remains); and the SNCC Benefit Folk Concerts held at the Charles Street Meetinghouse in May 1965 (with Jim Kweskin, Sylvia Mars, Ed Freeman, Don MacSorley, and Bob Gahtan.

9. *Folk Festival at Newport 1959,* vol. 2 (Vanguard Records VRS 9063), bands 5 and 6.

10. Bill Monroe, *Two Days at Newport* (Bear Family ACD 25001 AA), band 4.

11. *Evening Concerts at Newport 1963,* vol. 1 (Vanguard VRS 9148). In the author's view, this night was both Bob Dylan's first and his most "electric" performance at Newport.

12. In an unfortunate incident, Bonnie Dobson's "Walk Me Out in the Morning Dew," which was clearly her composition, was purloined by a New York–based

folk singer who decided to make minor adjustments and claim copyright. It took decades for the author to secure clear and rightful title to her own work.

13. "House of the Rising Sun" on *The Best of the Animals* (MGM SE 4324), band 5.

14. Don West, "Concept of a Crossroad," *Broadside* 3, (March 4, 1964): 4. He wrote, "I believe we here in Boston are a focal point for the entire New England area, and we should keep our enthusiasts and potential enthusiasts to the north, west, and south of us well informed of the delights of folk music. For folk music offers untold wealth to young and old, in the education of our American heritage as well as that of other countries. *Viva, la musica de la gente!*" Also author's conversation with Don West in 2018 about his years at the Folklore Center in Cambridge: Don is a true keeper of the flame.

15. See the Moon Cusser's schedule, 1963–65, on the Folk New England website (Folk New England, Archives, Coffee Houses, The Mooncusser at www. folknewengland.org.

16. Helen von Schmidt, conversations with author, 2017 and February 2020. Helen's bona fides in the Boston-Cambridge Folk Revival go back to when she waitressed at the Cafe Yana with Betsy Minot (Siggins) and have continued through years of marriage and motherhood and decades of friendships.

CHAPTER TEN: THE CHORDS OF FAME

1. Jac Holzman with Gavin Daws, *Follow the Music* (Santa Monica, CA: FirstMedia Books, 1998). Through the artistic choices of Jac Holzman and the graphic genius of William Harvey, you could spot an Elektra album cover a mile away.

2. Barry Hanson, review, *Little Sandy Review* 30 (Fall 1964): 16.

3. Caroline Paton, conversation with author, 2016.

4. From the Mother Bay State Entertainers' eponymous album (Riverboat Records RB-2, 1965), band 3.

5. *Kathy & Carol* (Elektra EKL 289, 1965).

6. From author's conversations with Jack Sloanaker, 2016–18, and Dudley Laufman, 1969–2020, who recorded *The Canterbury Country Dance Orchestra* and *Mistwold* at the Concord Academy Chapel in 1972. See Appendix D.

7. Everyone is entitled to their own opinion, but I hope to have made the case that there are a lot of ways of looking at music in general, and at this Newport Folk Festival in particular. Three months prior to the events in Newport, Ed Freeman wrote of the "electric" *Bringing It All Back Home* album, "I would venture to say that in this record, Dylan as an individual has found his natural medium. And folk music as a whole has found another step forward that can be taken." "Notes from a Variant Stanza Collector," in *Broadside* 4, no. 4 (April 14, 1965): 4.

8. Writing specifically about one of the three original academic departments of

folklore in the country, Rosina S. Miller states directly, "The folksong revival helped establish the folklore program at the University of Pennsylvania, with numerous students entering graduate school because of interests that developed out of participation in the revival"; "Of Politics, Disciplines, and Scholars: MacEdward Leach and the Founding of the Folklore Program at the University of Pennsylvania," *Folklore Historian* 21 (2003): 25.

9. Author's conversations with Nancy Sweezy, 2001–3; Kathy Neustadt, 2000–2020; Betsy Siggins, 2016–20; and Helen von Schmidt, 2017–20.

10. Author's conversations with Helen von Schmidt, 2017–20; Betsy Siggins, 2016–20; Bonnie Dobson, 2016–18; Dayle Stanley, 2017–20; and Sylvia Miskoe, 2017–18.

11. Jack Landrón, conversations with author, 2016–18.

CHAPTER ELEVEN: STAYED AROUND THIS OLD TOWN TOO LONG

1. See, for example, *The Whole Earth Catalog* (Menlo Park, CA: Portola Institute, 1968).

2. During the years 1969–70, while living on a communal farm in Belmont, New Hampshire, I had my Volkswagen maintained at Dick's Foreign Car Service in Laconia. While there, I occasionally encountered Baba Ram Dass, who lived in nearby Franklin on Webster Lake and who drove a gray Mercedes. Once, while we waited for work on our vehicles to be completed, Ram Dass quizzed me about the underlying philosophy of the back-to-the-land movement. Eventually, he made the observation that the return to rural roots was likely part of an inevitable societal reaction to the excesses of the Industrial Revolution. At which point a grease-covered mechanic working underneath the Mercedes slid himself into our view on his creeper and proclaimed, "Mistah! We *lost* the fucking Industrial Revolution!" before sliding back, forcefully, under the car.

3. Jim Rooney and Eric von Schmidt, *Baby, Let Me Follow You Down* (Amherst: University of Massachusetts Press, 1979), 304–5.

4. Larry A. Estridge, "The Flying Eye View," *Harvard Crimson,* August 9, 1968, n.p.; and author's personal observance, July 27, 1968, Newport Folk Festival, Newport, RI.

5. Ed Ward, quoted on the website of "Folk Radio UK," www.folkradio.co.uk, October 27, 2017: "The most important bands of the early '60s? Glad you asked: the Beatles, the Rolling Stones, the Byrds, and the Jim Kweskin Jug Band. I'm perfectly serious."

6. The Blue Velvet Band, *Sweet Moments with the Blue Velvet Band* (Warner Brothers WS 1802).

7. Colin Escott, *Good Rockin' Tonight* (New York: St. Martin's Press, 1991), 192.

8. Taj Mahal cited by Tony Montague in "Deep African Roots Help Shape Taj Mahal's Blues," *Georgia Straight: Vancouver's News and Entertainment Weekly,* April 13, 2006, https://www.straight.com/article/deep-african-roots-help-shape-taj-mahals-blues.

9. Dayle Stanley, conversation with author, 2019.
10. The making of the CD also resulted in a documentary film *Welcome Here Again: A Recording Session with the Canterbury Country Dance Orchestra*, produced by John Gfroerer of Accompany Video Production (which sells the DVD on its website); a clip of the Orchestra playing "Blackberry Quadrille," posted November 28, 2016, can be seen on YouTube at https://www.youtube.com/watch?v=8RzWgTUesCk.

CHAPTER TWELVE: WHERE DID YOU COME FROM, WHERE DO YOU GO?
1. Archibald MacLeish, *Poetry and Experience* (Cambridge: Riverside Press, 1960), 66.
2. Henry David Thoreau, *Walden* (Norwalk: Easton Press, 1981), 60.
3. Archibald MacLeish, *Scratch* (Boston: Houghton Mifflin 1971), viii.
4. Richard Todd, *The Thing Itself* (New York: Riverhead Books, 2008), 158.
5. Alice Parker, *Melodious Accord* (Chicago: GIA Publications, 2013), 103.

INDEX

Page references in italics indicate figures.

Flanders, Helen Hartness, 42–43, 78, 110
Flatt, Lester, 125. *See also* Flatt & Scruggs
Flatt & Scruggs (Lester Flatt and Earl Scruggs), 85, 99, 108, 136
Folk City USA (WCRB radio program, with Lurtsema), 3, 109, 210n15
Folk Dancer (label), 43
folk festivals
    Boston Freedom, 101
    Brandeis, 104, 133
    Indian Neck (CT), 104
    New England, 73
    Newport. *See* Newport Folk Festival
    Philadelphia, 86, 114, 140
    White Top, 65, 137
Folk Legacy Records, 150
Folklore Center (Denver) and Folklore Center (New York City). *See under* performance centers
Folklore Center (music shop, Cambridge), 145
Folklore Concerts Series, 75, 119, 129
Folklore Productions, 8, 75, 87, 94
Folk Music USA (WGBH TV program, with Rhodes), *xiv*, 3, 106, 109, 210n15
Folk New England (archive), 2–3, 8, 43, 98, 109, 137; founding, 199–200
Folksinger's Guitar Guide, 145
Folk Song Society of Greater Boston, 75
Folk Songs of Old New England (Linscott), 42
Folkways Records, 90, 126–28, 136, 144, 154. *See also* Oak Publications
Foster, Stephen, 50–51
Freedom Singers, 140–41
Freeman, Ed, 7–8, 99, 102, 110, 116, 134, 145, 152; photography, 139, 156, 172
Fuller, Blind Boy, 127
Fuller, Jesse, 105, 121

Garcia, Jerry, 96, 118, 166
Gennett Records, 64
Geremia, Paul, 169

Gibson, Bob, 94, 140, 149
Gill, Geula, 75
Gillette, Mary, 73
Ginsburg, Arnie, 102
Golden Ring (George and Gerry Armstrong, Ruth Meyer, Howie Mitchell, Herb Nudelman, Shannon Smith, Win Strake, Ed Trickett, and Steve White), 135, 150
Goldstein, Kenneth, 89, 114
Gooding, Cynthia, 140
gospel music, 33–34, 56, 122; Fiske Jubilee Singers, 56–57; shout tunes, 56; Silver Leaf, 122, 138
Grand Ole Opry, 122–23, 167
Grateful Dead, 166. *See also* Garcia, Jerry; jug bands: Mother McCree's; Weir, Bob
Green, Debbie, 82–83, 94, 99, 134, 165
Greenhill, Manny, 8, 74–75, 85–89, 94, 119, 129–30, 136
Greenhill, Matthew, 8
Greenhill, Mitch, 8, 89, 92, 105, 128, 134, 155; with Landrón, 99, 127
Griffith, Nanci, 8, 168
Grossman, Albert, 94, 104, 140, 166
Gude, David, 84
Guitar Nubbit (Alvin Hankerson), 88–89, 138
Guralnick, Peter, 121
Gutcheon, Jeff, 8, 126–28, 134, 154–55
Guthrie, Woody, 65, 76, 114, 128, 144, 155–57

Haggard, Merle, 163
Hall, Jonathan and Widdie, 169
Handy, W. C. (William Christopher), 58, 80
Hankerson, Alvin. *See* Guitar Nubbit
Hardin, Tim, 8, 96–99, 145
Harvey, William, 149
Hawkes, Allerton (Al), 124–25; Cumberland Ridge Runners, 124
Hayloft Jamboree (WCOP radio program, with Bragg), 85, 123–24, 167
Henderson, Jill, 102
Hester, Carolyn, 104